AUSTRALIA'S
MANDARINS

PATRICK WELLER

AUSTRALIA'S MANDARINS

the frank & the fearless?

ALLEN & UNWIN

Allen & Unwin
83 Alexander Street
Crows Nest NSW 2065
Australia
Phone: (61 2) 8425 0100
Fax: (61 2) 9906 2218
Email: frontdesk@allen-unwin.com.au
Web: http://www.allenandunwin.com

National Library of Australia
Cataloguing-in-Publication entry:

Weller, Patrick, 1944– .
  Australia's mandarins: the frank and the fearless.

  Bibliography.
  Includes index.
  ISBN 1 86508 340 2.

  1. Government executives—Australia. 2. Civil service—Australia. 3. Australia—Officials and employees. I. Title.

352.630944

Printed by CMO Image Printing Enterprise, Singapore

10 9 8 7 6 5 4 3 2 1

Contents

Acknowledgements

First and foremost I must thank those departmental secretaries who, over the past twenty years, have taken the time to explain the intricacies of their jobs and the pressures under which they work. Over that time I have talked to about 100 secretaries; they are an interesting group, some more complex than others but almost all belie the image of the colourless bureaucrat of legend. I have found the discussions challenging, sometimes entertaining, often penetrating. In particular I would like to thank the 43 I interviewed specifically for this project for their patience, and for their agreement to allow me to attribute comments to them. Their co-operation made the book fun to write; there is little more that an academic can ask for.

Several people helped in the development of the project. Liz Young was a postdoctoral fellow for a time before the attractions of a bureaucratic life took her elsewhere. Terry Wood developed the data set on which the tables in chapter 3 are based. Georgina Robinson compiled the table in Chapter 4. Anne Tiernan assisted in sifting the interviews and arranging the interview material for clearance and in the proof reading and indexing of the text. Ashley Lavelle hunted the shelves for references. Sue Jarvis edited the text and Olwen Schubert set the pages with great patience. To them all my thanks.

Some sections have appeared in a different and earlier form in journals. I would like to thank my co-authors there, John Wanna, Terry Wood and Bronwyn Stevens for letting me build on those early works and the editors of *Public Administration* and the *Australian Journal of Public Administration* for permission to rework the material first published in their journals.

This book was written with the assistance of a grant from the Australian Research Council; it could not have been completed without that support.

John Wanna and Micheal Keating gave me detailed comments on the text. Rod Rhodes and Jenny Fleming have debated many of the ideas. They told me where I was wrong; but I have not always agreed to their proposed changes. So if I am still wrong, I contend that they should have argued harder!! For the rest of the book I must take responsibility.

P.W.
October 2000

(Granatstein 1998). In Britain, Edward Bridges and Norman Brook, the dominant figures of the 1940s and 1950s, still resonate as the archetype of civil service mandarins. The Australian experience is not, therefore, unusual. The 1940s and the 1950s were seen as the era of mandarins. What has changed in the intervening 50 years? And does it matter for the good governance of our country?

We need to be careful that we do not overstate their position. Those mandarins were still advisers, even if at times to ministers who had few ideas of their own and who relied entirely on their assistance. And, as Paul Hasluck's (1998) acerbic pen portraits of his colleagues in that era suggest, there were plenty of ministers like that. Consequently, a changing degree of influence is not necessarily any reflection on the ability of those who hold the position of secretary. It can be a sign that better educated or more interested ministers want to reassert their right — indeed, that is in part the case. In addition, as the depth of talent in the APS grows, and as tertiary and postgraduate education becomes more common, the gap between leaders and the rest of the service may be less. The modern departmental secretary may be just as talented, just not so unusual.

But consider what else has changed too. In 1950 only the Treasury had the information required to forecast the Australian economy; by 1999 a dozen banks, firms and academics could appear before parliament to forecast the likely impact of the GST on the economy, each with their own models. In 1950, ministers in Canberra saw few people outside their official advisers; by the dawn of the twenty-first century, they are subjected to streams of delegations, and improved technology allows even more to send proposals or seek assistance. In 1950 officials were almost the only source of advice. Public servants could best advise because they, and they alone, had information of sufficient accuracy to make the decisions. By the beginning of the twenty-first century, this monopoly had been partly removed. Each minister has an office staff that includes policy advisers, political fixers and appointment secretaries; these support staff may be career public servants, but often they come from the parties with a different perspective and motives from the departmental secretaries. In 1950, the world was slower, more enclosed, less driven by the immediate demands of the media. For most people there was less emphasis on new policy ideas, for both political and intellectual reasons; government was about routine delivery of services. The post office made up a substantial part of the APS, and recruitment was still dominated by returned servicemen, rather than graduates. Information was less readily available; secrecy, or (to put it less pejoratively) necessary confidentiality, reigned. By 1999, reporting was immediate, demands for reactions incessant and the minister's views could be broadcast direct to every household; departmental secretaries had to serve this new media monster. In the 1950s, the position of a departmental secretary was strong. They had tenure in their position and could only be moved with their consent, unless the department was abolished from under them. They could expect to stay until a retiring age of 60 or more. By 2000, the departmental secretary was on an appointment of up to five years, liable to be terminated without notice, and anyway expecting to be rotated every five years into a new job. Their term as departmental secretary was likely to be shorter.

The impact of these changes has been acknowledged. Changes in social conditions and expectations provide the background and conditions within which the role of the departmental secretary must be understood. For instance, Allan Hawke, then secretary of the Department of Transport and Regional Development, has expressed the widely held perception that:

> The role of secretaries is shaped to a substantial degree by many intangible factors that change over time, such as the political character and style of the governments they serve, their personalities and those of their ministers, and the types of policy issues with which they must deal. No set rules or procedures, no matter how elaborate, can cover all the possibilities implicit in a secretary's role under parliamentary systems. It will always demand the exercise of a great deal of judgment on questions allowing room for argument (Hawke 1997:151).

Hawke points to a recurring theme throughout this book: the extent to which the role of secretaries is affected by changing external forces. He identifies a number of possible variables: a particular government; the personality of ministers; and the specific issues they must deal with. To this we might also add changing expectations about the way the public service functions, and its role in a modern society.

This book seeks to identify and explain these changes, and to determine what implications they have for the governance of Australia. The changes to the position of departmental secretary are important because they reflect, in microcosm, the debates about the role of the Australian Public Service (APS). The APS is fundamental to the health and smooth operations of the Australian state. If the public face of government can be found among the elected representatives, the public servants provide the sinews and muscle that make the body politic work. The public service brings expertise to the consideration of issues. It has — or at least should have — a collective memory that can draw on the experience of earlier events. It can shape the often vague aspirations of ministers into practical propositions that are economically and administratively feasible. It will implement those policies, whether through the regulation of other bodies or through the direct delivery of services. Traditionally, the APS has had a reputation for integrity and professionalism. Government without a supporting bureaucracy is not possible.

How the APS is organised is a matter of significance for any government. Institutions matter. The shape of government and the distribution between agencies will change the way that policies are considered and implemented. It is therefore a matter of concern for governments that they get the organisation of the APS right. Like any other institution, it has its traditions and established practices. In the 1950s and 1960s, these seemed uncontested. The APS's greatest claim was the professionalism that allowed it to serve any elected government regardless of its political hue. It was politically neutral — not between government and opposition, because it served the government of the day, but between governments of different parties. Every elected government was supposed to receive the same dedicated service. Tenure was regarded as an essential right to preserve the independence of the service from political interference; governments could create and abolish departments, found statutory bodies, introduce policies; but, on the whole, the APS was expected to move seamlessly from one government to another, with its personnel intact. Anonymity required that the minister took the credit, and sometimes reluctantly the blame, for the government's policy successes and failures. The APS was a career; the ambitious joined young and gradually worked their way to the top.

Or at least so the rhetoric ran. But from the beginning of the 1970s these comfortable beliefs were constantly under challenge. Ministers were not all convinced that the community received the full benefits that this model implied or that the APS had the flexibility and drive to meet the challenges of a changing society. They did not dispute that they needed a bureaucracy, but were prepared to challenge its form and operations and some of the traditions that underlay its operations. The question then was not whether it should be retained but how it should be organised.

Within the traditional framework, the departmental secretaries played a pivotal role. Whether they still do is a matter for investigation. Institutionally the departmental secretaries retain a highly strategic position. They are the link between the elected and the appointed. They have extensive managerial and accounting responsibilities as they often control large organisations. They have constant and direct dealings with their ministers: advising, warning and receiving instructions. When they themselves do not deal directly with the ministers, they can determine who within the department will and how that access will be organised. In a real sense, then, the role of the departmental secretaries, their standing and their history can be taken as a proxy for the health and position of the APS as a whole. Certainly they are the most successful members, the ones who have risen to the top in an often very competitive field. The group sets the tone for the operations of the public service, and deals directly most often with the ministers, the parliament and increasingly on broad issues with the public. Their fears and hopes may reflect starkly some of the broader debates that are concerning the APS as a whole and their treatment may be a foretaste of what will later affect the other public servants. Consequently, at the end of this book, we will return to the question of what broader conclusions can be drawn from the discussion for the future of the APS.

That some tension existed between the elected and the servants should not be a surprise. Even if the links between the two are meant to be a partnership, in the competitive world of high politics there is a constant concern that departmental secretaries are trying it on. Fiction has influenced fact. Every politician has watched *Yes Minister*, that British comedy where the manipulative Sir Humphrey uses all the bureaucratic wiles to bend a sometimes bumbling minister to his own wishes. Never mind that, like all good satire, the images are exaggerated; they had enough truth, and were based often enough on real events, that they convinced every minister that at some time their departmental secretary was trying to manipulate them, and made them determined not to be manipulated. In every parliamentary system, ministers watched and often drew the wrong lessons. Words like 'courageous' took on new meanings in the political lexicon. If there was concern before, now ministers could identify the techniques, the tricks, the verbal games and the euphemisms, or at least they thought they could. The programs become funnier, more biting, the more the observer knows about politics. *Yes Minister* has also been corrosive in the relationship between minister and departmental secretary, often making explicit what had earlier been an indefinite feeling of helplessness among weaker ministers.

Yes Minister may have made the tensions more public, but they already existed. There were in essence five debates that affected the position of the departmental secretaries:

- their responsiveness to ministerial direction and/or the increased level of political control;
- their professionalism as managers (particularly by contrast to the reputed expertise of managers in the private sector);
- their capacity to act as effective policy advisers to governments;

- their position as part of a career service; and
- the degree to which the appointment to the rank of departmental secretary has become politicised.

These debates will provide continuing themes in the discussions about the roles and position of departmental secretaries throughout this book.

Responsiveness to government directions and/or increased political control

The traditional model of the relationship between the departmental secretaries and their ministers emphasises the superiority of the minister. Whether policy is made by ministers (a usual interpretation of the Westminster system) or determined through a partnership between the departmental secretary and the minister, with the minister having the final say in a case of dispute (a more reasonable interpretation), the superiority of the minister is taken for granted. But, in the same breath, there is an acknowledgment that the formal process can only capture a small part of the real relationship. Ministers are essentially amateurs, often rotated through positions, with the junior ministers averaging only two years in a post; they bring political skills to the partnership, assessing policies through that lens and then taking the responsibility for the presentation, selling and defence of the policy. How much influence they have on particular policies will differ from minister to minister.

The institutional arrangements of the 'Westminster system' therefore create a potential mismatch between the allocation of formal authority and the actual capacity for it. It need not mean that the two will live at loggerheads — much of the time they will cooperate effectively because they realise the joint benefits. But there is scope for suspicion and tension built into the core of the system if ministers feel that they are not getting adequate support in both policy and administrative matters.

In Australia, there was an additional legacy, drawn particularly from the experiences of the Whitlam government in which ministers felt they had been undermined by a public service that did not like what they sought to do or the way they were seeking to do it (see, for example, Hawker's evocatively titled 1981 book, *Who's Master, Who's Servant?*). Even the coalition ministers of the Fraser government were not satisfied with the service they often received, as the decision to split the Treasury in 1976 and the later establishment of an inquiry into the APS in 1982 illustrated. Consequently when Labor returned to power, the ministers sought to reassert, as they saw it, their constitutional supremacy over the public service. These wishes were implicit in the White Paper *Reforming the Australian Public Service* and in the changes made to the *Public Service Act* in 1984. As prime minister, Keating too asserted that, under the Labor government, the system had been returned to its proper balance, with ministers making policy and the departmental secretaries carrying it out. He reiterated an earlier comment he had made:

> Only politicians can make major changes to the way a country conducts its business ... Change cannot come from the bureaucracy no matter how well motivated, or gifted, because the bureaucracy has no authority to rank priorities or make decisions ... In the end, politicians have to have the foresight to see the need for change and the courage and strength to carry it through (Keating 1993).

Both sides of politics would at least agree on that sentiment.

But not all observers seemed to agree it had been achieved. They attributed considerable power to the public service in general and — implicitly at least — to the departmental secretaries in particular. Michael Pusey, for instance, surveyed the senior public service in the mid-1980s and concluded that the changes in training, with an increase in the significance of economics degrees, and in attitudes to public policy, had led to a dramatic change in policy directions. His sub-title was *A Nation State Changes its Mind*, although he did not prove empirically that it had been different before or had changed recently. His argument was that, in the mid-1980s, a group of public servants, whom he described as economic rationalists, changed the way that policy was developed and in effect hijacked the national agenda. Implicit in his argument is the view that it was these public servants, not ministers, who drove the agenda, even in the 1980s when the new Labor government believed that its ministers exerted more control than in earlier regimes. Thus ministers were captive to a doctrine held by the crucial departmental secretaries. Pusey clearly disapproves of the new directions. But it is not clear precisely what he disapproves of. Does he object to the idea that the departmental secretaries were able to call the tune when for democratic reasons the power should be in the hands of the elected, and therefore he wanted to reassert ministerial direction? This is unlikely, as he pays little attention to ministers. Or did he believe it was reasonable for the senior officials to wield power, as perhaps they did in the 1960s, when their aspirations for 'nation-building' were sympathetic to the views that Pusey espouses? Whichever the case might be, the debate added to the concern among politicians that the APS was not adequately responsive to the wishes of the elected government and they continued with changes to make them more responsive.

Several methods were adopted to ensure the dominance of ministers and the responsiveness of officials. They included the placing of departmental secretaries on contracts, rotation of departmental secretaries to acknowledge the need for generalist management skills, discussions of performance appraisal and other managerial innovations; each was seen to have particular benefits. Some innovations were driven by officials seeking to provide a more effective public service; others were ministerial in origin. In total, they were consistent with the view that the ministers wanted to assert greater control. They will be considered in detail in later chapters. But the general debate does lead to some significant questions. Accepting the principle of the superiority of the elected minister, how responsive ought a departmental secretary be to the demands of the minister? Indeed, can they be too responsive, too prepared to do the minister's bidding? To what extent can or should they argue with the minister if the government seeks to introduce a policy that is likely to fail or have substantial problems? Does the APS have responsibilities that go beyond those of the elected government to some notion of a national or common interest, or to tenets of continuity and policy efficiency (Keating 1995a)?

Is public management different?

The traditional image of the APS is of a body that is committed to procedure at the expense of effective outcomes. Due process was the god. Controls from the centre, whether the Treasury monitoring the expenditure, or the Public Service Board giving approval for the changes in employment and classification, ensured consistency between departments and — at least in theory — prevented any irresponsible misuse of public funds. Moneys were appropriated annually and for items of expenditure, not for programs, and they had to be spent within the headings listed. Under-expenditure was seen by parliamentary committees as a sign of inefficiency or even incompetence. Departments saw themselves, at least rhetorically, as an extension of the minister.

But then there were demands for reform, often based on the view that the public sector should be organised more like the private sector. Much of the language of the private sector was imported. Corporate management, mission statements and strategic plans were adopted, not only for statutory bodies that had clear products to sell, but also for those departments that had no bottom line and no balance sheet. New accrual accounting methods sought equivalences with the private sector. Funding was organised first by programs and portfolios and then by 'material agencies' responsible for their own operating statement and balance sheet. In some states, heads of departments were called CEOs (leaving uncertain what role the minister might play). Talk of risk management became frequent. Suddenly officials were required to give a service to the community, rather than provide entitlements to those fitting the criteria determined by legislation. Entrepreneurial managers were in demand. At the same time, parliamentary committees became more demanding and inquisitive, making the risk of mistakes becoming public more real.

So there are some fundamental questions for the departmental secretary. In what ways and at what times is the public sector the same as the private sector? Are the demands on managers now greater than in the past? Do the demands for accountability (from the parliament and the minister, to the auditor and the citizens) make the job so different that it does not really make sense to talk in terms of managing in the same way? Is public management therefore a unique skill, whose ramifications have not been understood, even while the managerial pressures on the departmental secretaries have increased?

Are departmental secretaries still the ministers' principal policy advisers?

The image of the 1950s is of the official adviser, buoyed with expertise and knowledge, bolstered by a monopoly of access, dominating many of the ministers. At times they were credited with the wisdom that allowed them to determine a national interest over and above that decided by the cabinet and the elected representatives. Even if they would all accept the Westminster system that declared that the ministers made policy and the public servants implemented it, their influence was accepted as massive. In addition, they all accepted that policy advice was the main game, that their reputation depended on their ability to give good advice and to support, and sometimes protect, their minister.

Has that changed dramatically? Are departmental secretaries still principally policy advisers and do they still control the process? Several factors have emerged in the last decades that might alter the balance of responsibilities. Additional sources of information have entered the fray, so that ministers have more choices, from staff to consultants and think tanks. Access to the minister has become more open to different levels of most departments. The expertise and authority of the APS is questioned more readily. The departmental secretaries now have more direct management responsibility, as powers of decision once exercised by the Public Service Board and the Department of Finance have been devolved. So there are far more responsibilities than just policy advising on their agenda.

Yet, to ministers, nothing except the advice is really seen as significant. They have never been concerned with the management of the department or even the management of policy advice. They do not appreciate many of the dimensions of the departmental secretary's job. That creates a tension. The departmental secretaries must deliver across the board, but their credibility with ministers is largely based on their policy advice. At the same time, they have to compete harder to be heard above the continuing babble of ideas that make up the background of current politics.

Given these changes, maintaining the relationship between policy adviser, ministers and policy outcomes becomes an essential but potentially more fraught. Has it changed and with what effect?

Is there still a career service?

In traditional terms, promotion to the position of departmental secretary was part of a career. Every member of the APS was, in embryo, a potential secretary, as the legend of the telegram boy to departmental secretary retained its piquancy. It was not mere myth either; Bob Lansdown started as a telegram boy at Strathfield post office in the mid-1930s; by 1949 he was setting up the prime ministerial office for Robert Menzies; in 1972 he became secretary of the new Department of Urban and Regional Development. Bill Cole, too, started as a telegram boy and rose to be chairman of the Public Service Board and departmental secretary of Finance and Defence. Opposition to lateral recruits — people brought in above the base grade — had always been ingrained. There was extensive grumbling when Roland Wilson was brought into the Bureau of Statistics as heir apparent to the top job in the 1930s. It was easy to alter the idea that every base grade recruit should be able to rise to the level of departmental secretary into a doctrine that every departmental secretary should have joined at the base grade.

The principle was based on the notion of a *career* service. Tenure lay at its core. It was a safe profession, with secure employment and, if desired, good prospects. Both an inclination for security and a favourable superannuation policy led to the assumption that people would stay — sometimes even in the same department — throughout that career. The retirement age was set at a minimum of 55, more often taken at 60. If bright and efficient public servants reached the top at a young age, and some did in those early days, they had the opportunity of serving as a departmental secretary for many years, and leaving at a time of their own choosing. They often were then able to find alternative employment in the diplomatic corps or in some other lucrative agency.

There were some severe limitations in that system too. Women had to resign when they got married. They could thereafter hold only temporary positions (some did for years), but could not compete for the permanent ones that led to promotion. It was a male service until that marriage bar was removed in 1965. If for a time it was possible to defend the lack of women at departmental secretary level because it needed time for them to work through the ranks, that excuse is no longer valid, as most departmental secretaries joined the APS well after that date. The fact that in 2000 only one woman has risen to departmental secretary level still deserves comment and perhaps requires explanation.

There were in the 1950s, and still are today, good reasons for the development of a career service. It was possible to attract talent, particularly once the graduate programs began in the late 1950s to recruit from among the products of an expanding tertiary education sector. Security and good superannuation could be balanced as compensation for the comparatively poor pay. For senior officers, an interesting job and the possible ability to have an influence on public policy were the attractions of a career in public service.

But has that now all changed? Departmental secretaries are now on fixed-term appointments up to a maximum of five years. If their employment is terminated, as it can be by a phone call and without any detailed reasons, then they no longer have a job in the public sector. Certainly the disparity in pay between the public and private sectors has been partly reduced by an increase in remuneration in early 1999, but it is still significant. The secretaries no longer have the comfort of guaranteed employment that went with the position some years ago. They are in some ways a group apart from the service from which most of them have risen.

So what are the implications of this change? Does it make employment in the public sector less attractive for the bright graduates? Does it make promotion to departmental secretary less desirable to those who, on the rungs below, wonder if they want to give up their security for the additional responsibility and increased insecurity that goes with a top job these days? Does it make the departmental secretaries themselves more concerned about their position to the extent that, one way or another, it affects their performance, reducing their willingness to give fearless policy advice, their commitment to the public sector, or in other ways?

There is a broader question: to what extent does an incumbent government have the right to shape the APS entirely in the form it wants? This proposition can be put another way: does the government have a responsibility to hand on to its successor (whenever the government loses power, as one day it surely will) a public service that has the ability to provide proper support to that new government? Another, more evocative, way of asking the same question is to query whether the government holds the APS in freehold or leasehold. Does it own it, or is it holding it in trust for some broader entity?

Politicisation or personalisation?

The most common debate about the role of the departmental secretaries concerns the question of whether they have been politicised in the last decades. The debate is essentially muddled. The argument, usually propagated by the opposition, is that a government is selecting as departmental secretaries people who are sympathetic to it and therefore too close to the ministers to give the fearless advice that is required. As a consequence, they will be unable to give a proper service to the minister if the government changes, as they are too ideologically committed. This criticism has been launched at just about all governments.

It is difficult to define just how wide the criteria for a political appointment should be spread. A decade ago I argued that it occurs when appointments and promotions are motivated by party politics instead of based on the merit principle, and when the public service is used for party purposes, as distinct from government objectives (Weller 1989a). Mulgan (1998), by way of contrast, has sought to broaden the meaning of politicisation. In addition to my definition, Mulgan identifies two other forms of politicisation. First, there is policy-related politicisation where people are appointed because of their association with a particular policy position. And second, there is managerial politicisation, where incumbent public servants are replaced simply because a new government wishes to stamp its authority on the public service by putting in place personnel it has appointed (Mulgan 1998:7). What these cases have in common — and this is Mulgan's justification for placing them under the politicisation banner — is that they undermine a secretary's capacity to serve alternative governments, and sometimes even an alternative minister from the same party.

Defining this behaviour as politicisation, however, does little to clarify its consequences. While politicisation remains a term limited to party-political interference in the public service, it has a specific meaning that draws attention to a relatively straightforward question: is party interference in the public service occurring and is such interference acceptable? When the term is broadened, it only serves to muddy the waters by collapsing a number of important distinctions. The ability of a secretary to be employed by alternate governments, for instance, should not be confused with the issue of whether a secretary has been employed for partisan reasons or if she or he is working on behalf of the government. It is this sort of differentiation that Mulgan's classification blurs, yet it lies at the very heart of the politicisation label.

Politicisation might be difficult to define but, as Michael Keating notes, it is even harder to provide evidence of it occurring (Keating 1999:45). One reason is that such behaviour is not viewed as legitimate within the Australian context. As a result, governments are hardly going to advertise the fact that a decision relating to the appointment or termination of a secretary was made on partisan grounds, with other more legitimate explanations found to justify the decision. Nonetheless, there is a need to ask whether it has occurred and to what degree.

There may be better ways of expressing the apparent desire of ministers to select departmental secretaries with whom they now can feel comfortable. A better term for this practice may be the *personalisation* of the position of departmental secretary: the selection of a departmental secretary for the style and approach, rather than for any partisan views. It is vital to say what this concept of personalisation should not include. It does not refer to mateship, or suggest that minister and departmental secretary should be drinking buddies. It does acknowledge that there may be a chemistry that, in some way or other, works. It is more than just saying a departmental secretary is suitably responsive. After all, there have been departmental secretaries who worked effectively with a number of ministers but then fell out with another and were removed. It was not that they were no longer professional public servants or that they suddenly ceased to be responsive — that would imply that the departmental secretaries were always responsible for the problems and that is not a defensible position. There may have been no particular mistake or decision that created the rift. Rather, the minister did not like a person with that style or that personality. While the minister and departmental secretary work well together there is no problem. When there is a rift, for whatever reason, many ministers — and, indeed, most departmental secretaries — believe it is the departmental secretary who must go. This may create problems. If it is too easy to make a change, there can be little incentive to make the relationship work. Decisions to remove a departmental secretary will finally be taken by the prime minister. They may not be concerned with the political views of departmental secretaries, but with their ability to keep each minister satisfied with the service that is being provided. Personal characteristics become a key factor, hence the concept of personalisation, rather than politicisation.

That personalisation can be extended to the requirements deemed necessary for appointment or rotation too. There are times when a department needs a different style of management, regardless of who is minister or which party is in government. Some departments may require a shake-up; others will need consolidation. Each case will demand different styles and skills. Choosing the right people for their approach makes sense, as does changing them when the circumstances (not necessarily political) change.

Whatever the situation, we might also ask to what extent it matters. The concerns about politicisation are common in systems derived from the British experience, where senior public servants usually ensure that any personal political views are kept to themselves. It is not so common in other European systems where the political affiliation of senior officials is known and accepted. Rotation there after a change of government is part of normal practice; it is not controversial. So it is not necessarily a prerequisite for an efficient public service that it has no political alignment.

These five debates provide a framework within which the position of departmental secretaries can be reviewed. Their competence is seen as essential for good government. Indeed, it is under constant debate and review. It is difficult to refrain from an additional observation, an anomaly amidst all the formal reviews and legislation: governments rarely ask anyone else about, or seek to formally review, the performance of ministers! That remains part of a continuing but informal process for the prime minister and his close colleagues

Levels of analysis

In this book, the influences on the position of departmental secretaries are explored at three different levels. At the systemic level are the changes in economic structure, the opening of the economy to international competition, the technological advances for the organisation of information, speedier media coverage and hence the more immediate demands on ministers, the growth of think tanks and policy-wise advisory bodies, the changes in intellectual trends about the role of the state, and the different attitudes to work and careers. There have also been changes in society, with less trust of politicians, less respect for authority and less belief in the persuasiveness of expertise. These changes have altered the very environment within which the departmental secretaries must work; they were not within their control — indeed, they have affected everyone.

At an intermediate level, stand the legislation and the rules that define the conditions of employment of the departmental secretaries, and the conventions of behaviour that define their role. There have been some substantial changes. In part, they reflect the ideas of a series of governments on what the departmental secretaries should do; in part they illustrate how the reality has changed as the conventions and understandings of roles are examined and codified, directly or indirectly, in legislation. Legislation may not always reflect practice, but it may reflect either what is desired or what the drafters hope that people will believe to be their policy. The method of selection and the terms of employment, because they are related to all secretaries, come under this category. These intermediate changes are outlined in the next chapter.

At the most intimate level is the individual relationship between the secretary and the minister. It may be a harmonious relationship; it may be tense; it may drift between those two. Because the discussion is inevitably about the chemistry of two individuals, it must vary, from time to time and between pairs of people. Some ministers would have been dominant in the 1950s; some secretaries in the 1990s. In this area we can best analyse patterns in terms of the atmosphere and flavour of the relationship, to see if there is a broad feeling that the nature of the relationship has usually changed and what may be the cause of it.

I need to emphasise that I am concerned to explore the position of departmental secretaries across these different levels of analysis for two reasons. First, I am interested in what has changed. The book is not intended to provide a snapshot of the situation in 1999/2000, but to look at 50 years of development, at the causes of the changes and the likely consequences. Second, it allows us to escape the narrower confines of debates that concentrate too much on the individual and the ephemeral. The debate on politicisation, for instance, has looked at the decision of the Howard government to terminate the employment of six secretaries on coming to office in 1996. It was significant, but in the longer context perhaps not surprising, and we need to interpret the concept of politicisation in that broader context.

Sources and evidence

This study uses all the traditional sources available to political scientists: legislation, parliamentary debates, newspapers and the secondary literature written by and about departmental secretaries. We are fortunate that, over the years, senior public servants have regarded it as worthwhile to explain and defend their profession and practices. Sir John Crawford was the first (1954, 1960) to write explicitly about the role of the departmental secretary. Alan Cooley

(1974), Sir Geoffrey Yeend (1979), Mike Codd (1990, 1991) and Michael Keating (1989, 1990, 1995a, 1995b, 1996, 1999) have followed his lead. John Bunting (1988) and John Menadue are two secretaries of the Department of Prime Minister and Cabinet who have reflected on their experiences. Several former departmental secretaries have used Garran Orations for this purpose (Wheeler 1980; Tange 1982; and Ayers 1996; see also Cole 1979, 1980). We therefore know more about the ideals and assumptions of the departmental secretaries in Australia than in many other countries.

In addition, this book uses a series of interviews with departmental secretaries held since 1978. In 1978 I interviewed 29 departmental secretaries for the book I jointly wrote with Michelle Grattan: *Can Ministers Cope? Australian Ministers at Work* (Hutchinson 1981). We took notes of the discussions that concentrated on the relationship between ministers and departmental secretaries and covered in particular the Whitlam and Fraser governments. In 1985–87, in writing my study of a prime minister in action, *Malcolm Fraser PM* (Penguin 1989b), I talked to a further fifteen senior officials about the role of the prime minister (PM), the relations of the PM with senior officials and the links between ministers, departmental secretaries and the PM. In 1996, I wrote a report for the IPAA (ACT Division) with John Wanna on the conditions of appointment and termination of departmental secretaries (Weller and Wanna 1997). We interviewed 21 departmental secretaries, past and current. For this project, 43 departmental secretaries have been interviewed. I tried to get into contact with as many as possible in the available time, with a bias to those who had served longer rather than shorter times. There was no way that any representative sample could have been drawn; departmental secretaries are all too different for that. (For the list, see the Appendix).

I therefore have the records of a series of interviews over 20 years. In strict terms, they may not be comparable; the focus in each case was slightly different: in 1978 on the performance of ministers; in 1986 on the role of the prime minister; in 1996 on the conditions of appointment and termination; in 1998 and 1999 on the role of departmental secretaries themselves. Nevertheless, they did all concern the relations between minister and official and traverse similar debates. In some cases, the same person has been interviewed more than once, in one case as a participant in every panel. Consequently it is possible to use the interviews to identify changes in attitudes towards the job and in perceptions about how those crucial relationships may have changed.

Some people had obviously given thought to the topic; others fitted me into a busy schedule and reacted as I asked the questions.

Some sloppy expression, the occasional rewriting of history, sometimes even selective forgetfulness may have occurred. We all tend to tell history from our own experience, both of what happened and what we would like to have happened. That is natural. Every interview was not equally valuable, but most served to provide some insights. In each case, the understanding was the same: nothing in the interviews would be attributed to the individual departmental secretary unless it was specifically cleared with that person first. Such a condition is necessary to allow the participants to talk freely about their job. When the comments are attributed, the name appears at the end of the quotation. Where they have chosen that direct quotations should not be attributed, I have only provided the decade (1965–75, 1970–80, 1975–85 and so on) in which they served the majority of their term as departmental secretary to provide some indication of the perspective that they bring to the issue.

Extensive interviews with people who have served as departmental secretary provide extensive data, but not of the type that can be coded and subjected to analysis. The interest is in the nuances, the slight differences, in attitude or approach. I have selected quotations where they best make the case or illustrate the point at issue. A neat turn of phrase catches attention and acts as surrogate for others. In almost all cases, I could provide several additional but similar comments that might consolidate or reinforce the points but would also be tedious and repetitive. A few must stand for the many.

Interviewing departmental secretaries is interviewing winners. Even if they later lost their jobs, they did reach those heights. Given the number of aspirants, that is no small achievement. Their views will reflect that success. Those who did badly under the changes and did not rise to the top are not represented here. There is therefore a need for caution in assessing the evidence, to take account of the self-justifications and biases. For instance, every departmental secretary declared that the new contract conditions made no difference to the fearlessness of *their* policy advice, but several noted that some of their colleagues were more cowed. It is not possible for both to be true, unless the departmental secretaries who grumble about their ministers to their colleagues do in fact behave differently when they are giving advice to those ministers. But the example does provide an illustration for the need for some care in the treatment of the evidence. One instance by itself may not be persuasive, but as more and more say roughly the same thing, there is reason to give weight to the case that is being made. That is largely the strategy used here: to build up a number of instances and views to give cross-checking corroboration to a case and then to consider the evidence critically.

Departmental secretaries can provide some perspective of change too. They worked for their seniors for many years before they reached the rank themselves. By contrast, ministers mostly learn about the APS only when they are sworn into office. They do not have the same horizons, as few survive beyond the term of one government.

Interviewing over 100 former or present departmental secretaries does give some picture of them as a group. There certainly is no identikit departmental secretary, either in the past or now, except that they are over 99 per cent male and white. Some are driven, determined, steely eyed; others appear relaxed and cooperative. Some are bemused by their fortune in rising so far; others see it as a natural and deserved progression to the top. Some are gently spoken, inclusive in style, sometimes almost diffident; others are far more emphatic, sure of their opinions, certain in their judgments. Some are cerebral in reflecting on the job they do; others are instinctive in their reactions, doers not thinkers. Some were feared, others revered, a few were both feared and revered. Some genuinely liked the ministers for whom they worked; others regarded almost all ministers with disdain. The tough, the cerebral, the social and the inclusive all had subordinates who thought they were good as bosses. It takes all types to make an APS. Yet almost all are interesting to talk to, as they think back on their experiences and reflect on the job. It may seem easy to guess what they might be like to work for, but it is not always so. An interviewer is in a unique position: as chronicler of their past and as a person who can explain their life and job, their visions and fears, to a wider public. Few of them see that function as their job: the tradition for partial anonymity remains. In part this book thus serves as a collective biography of a group which has had a distinct influence on Australian administration and politics.

The next chapter provides the framework for their job, noting the principal mileposts that have marked the changes of the last 50 years. The third chapter gives a picture of the changes of careers by analysing the data collected on the careers of the 183 departmental secretaries who served between 1950 and 1999. Not all the biographical data was complete, but the analysis does illustrate some distinct trends in the evidence.

Chapters 4 to 7 look more closely at the careers and attitudes of the departmental secretaries. The recruitment, careers and appointment of the departmental secretaries are considered, then the relations between departmental secretaries and their ministers, the role as department manager, the implications for demands for accountability and appraisal, and finally the possible consequences of the new methods of termination. These chapters both describe what happens and explore the degree of change over the past decades.

In Chapter 8 the lens is shifted. Instead of looking at the

departmental secretaries as a group, it takes the careers of a few individuals and asks how they look back on their careers and whether they perceive that the position of departmental secretary has changed dramatically. These accounts do not pretend to be critical biography. They seek to discover how some of the principal actors interpret the changes; they provide an inside-out look at the departmental secretary's role.

Chapter 9 takes a case study: the spectacular sacking of Paul Barratt from his position as Secretary of Defence in 1999 and the subsequent court case. Here was an incident when all the pressures that had been building up over the position of the departmental secretary broke into public view. The case study brings together all the themes that have been debated in the earlier chapters.

Finally, the Conclusion brings the debate back to the crucial question: how and why do these issues matter. It is necessary to determine what these changes mean, for the running of the APS, for the service provided to the government, for the management of services to the community and, most broadly, for the good governance of Australia.

2

The changing environment and framework

Governments reflect society. They change as the demands on them respond to the economic and social imperatives change. So too must the public service change. As it serves the government, so it must reflect its interests. As its members are part of a national workforce, their conditions of employment and working conditions will be amended to take account of that wider world. Naturally the position of the departmental secretary will have changed since 1950; indeed, it would be a matter of concern if it had not. This chapter will suggest some of the broad conditions that have changed the position of departmental secretary: the roles that governments play; the openness of governments to competition and review; technological changes; and the improvement in the educational standards of the APS and the Australian electorate. Then it will chart more precisely the changing conditions under which the departmental secretaries were required to work between 1950 and 2000.

A changing environment

The role of government has changed its emphasis several times in the last 50 years. In the postwar era it expanded the services it delivered and its involvement into the economy because Keynesian theory gave a substantial role to government initiatives in managing that economy. Governments delivered most of the programs too, with the post office the largest of government departments and an extensive bureaucracy seen as the best way to provide a fair and efficient service to the citizens. It was a period of optimism in which government intervention was a route to the alleviation of society's woes. Experts would know the answers. But that changed in the 1970s. Promise of great changes was lost in the inflationary world that followed the oil shock. Vietnam undermined faith in government. Unemployment rose and poverty continued.

By the 1990s there was a different attitude to government. Trust was declining fast. Big government was suspect, seen to be as much part of the problem as a solution. Governments were still heavily intertwined with society, but in different ways. They did not always deliver the services themselves; some had been outsourced, others privatised. What had once been government monopolies were now open to competition, even the delivery of job placements for the unemployed. Contract management, as much as service delivery, was the principal responsibility of the leaders of the APS. Instead of managing a large hierarchy, the departmental secretary might be facilitating a network of advice, contracts and private delivery agents.

The environment was far more open, as much a matter of necessity as a choice. More people had access to data and were able to form well-founded opinions in policy issues. Internally, administrative law forced the APS to justify and explain its decisions to its citizens. Externally, Australia had become more outward looking, seeking to relate to its region and to trade more aggressively with its rivals. International agreements required it to pay attention to the opinions and views of world bodies. Travel broadened the outlooks of the citizen, who knew what was done elsewhere. Globalisation is sometimes seen as a threat, sometimes as an opportunity; however it is interpreted, Australia was inextricably part of the world trade and cultural network.

Australians were more educated too. The expansion of universities had produced more graduates, many of whom flocked to join the APS. Departmental secretaries with degrees became the norm, and more of their subordinates were well qualified too. But the impact went much wider. Many of the ministers were better educated, better able to ask the probing questions. Commentators, journalists, bankers and academics could comment authoritatively on government decisions and question policies. Ideas were imported from overseas. The OECD and the World Bank were conduits for the latest economic or managerial fashion. Comparative examples were sought. Travel was fast; geographical isolation became insignificant. No longer did the departmental secretaries have the benefit that unchallenged expertise had once brought arguments to an end. Others had the skills and the knowledge too. The worlds of policy and governmental ideas shifted from a near monopoly to a highly contested environment.

The society questioned more and accepted less. Authority was challenged, whether from the family or the government, and the decline in trust was continuous. A belief in expertise was one victim of the growing scepticism. No longer were the experts seen as infallible, properly so as their solutions had often failed to solve problems. As new movements arose, espousing the cause of women, Aboriginal people and the environment, the old solutions no longer seemed adequate or appropriate. The decline in certainty affected the position and influence of senior officials as much as society.

Technology hastened the process. The media required fast responses to the crises as they emerged. Television became a constant companion for decision-makers, providing opportunities to deliver a message direct to the people, but also capable of stripping away the defences of a policy that was ill-devised. There was no capacity to stall for long. Computers provided information and immediate communications; they made possible a number of managerial changes but at the same time changed the way that work was done. Productivity increased; electronic transfers were far faster than writing and posting cheques.

The public sector can never be isolated from the world outside. Even if there were distinct differences between it and the private sector, there were also seen to be managerial similarities. Sometimes the benefits of adopting private sector techniques may be illusory, based more on an ideological belief in the efficiency of the latter than any strong empirical evidence. But the two watched each other, learnt sometimes, copied at others. The distinctions were seen as less significant. Competition, contract and client became the watchwords for public sector reform across the 1980s and 1990s. (See Keating 2000 for a lengthier debate on the pressures for change.)

This catalogue of change could be extended much further. But the message is clear. The APS could no longer just examine itself and seek change. It had to compete for talent and ideas. The people still wanted services, even if they did not want to pay any increased taxation. Expectations were higher than government income, so the departmental secretaries had to do more from the scarce sources available. The changes in the position of departmental secretary must be understood in the context of this ever-changing environment. Government in the twenty-first century is very different form the more leisured pace of the 1950s. So too is the world of the departmental secretary. It reflects both its history and its environment. There is no other way it could be. The lens that explores their world needs to be both broad and focused at the same time.

The 1950s and 1960s

Looking back over the history of the APS, the 1950s and 1960s seem to provide an apparent oasis of stability. There was no change of government, few changes to the substantive way government did business and a core of senior officials who had been appointed at an early age and were to dominate much of that era. It has been described as the heyday of the mandarin.

That stability can be exaggerated. It was preceded by some turmoil. The Chifley Labor government had made some appointments that were considered radical; John Burton, head of foreign affairs at the age of 32, was the most obvious. There were claims of politicisation during the 1949 election and a few permanent secretaries found themselves without a department after the machinery of government changes. Burton was made high commissioner in Colombo. When Menzies was elected, his:

> respect for the British tradition of government guaranteed that he would have firm expectations of the impartiality of the civil service: that its members would simply take it for granted that, whatever their personal political views, they would as administrators serve successive governments equally (Martin 1999:136).

He resisted demands from Country Party ministers to replace leading figures such as Coombs and was prepared to give people the chance to perform. One interviewee, who as a young man was a member of the Labor Party, had thought Menzies the symbol of all that was evil in Australian politics:

> Menzies summoned him and told him that his political opinions would have nothing to do with their relations as long as he did his job. This witness then used the same metaphor as Hasluck. Menzies, he said had a fence round himself and if you were inside you were one of a special group. 'You know, within six months, I loved the bastard' (Martin 1999:138).

There were many bitter struggles within the APS, sometimes reflecting the differing interests of the ministers, sometimes based on the personalities of the permanent heads. The battles between the trade department, under the direction of the deputy prime minister, John McEwan, and assisted by the effective secretaries, Sir John Crawford and Sir Alan Westerman, and the Treasury, headed by Roland Wilson and Richard Randall, were the stuff of Canberra legend. So was the antipathy between Sir Frederick Wheeler and Sir Lennox Hewitt. One of Wheeler's personal assistants recalls:

> We had a major postal dispute that Gorton wanted us to settle. Fred thought that would be a bad precedent for wages and all that and wasn't too interested in this Prime Ministerial interference in the Board's matters. Hewitt had [a FAS] phone up to find out what was going on with the negotiations. And the FAS told me that I was to go and ask Sir Frederick because there was a break in the negotiations. It was about six. I went in and [the FAS] said he had been told by Lennox Hewitt: stay on the phone until he got an answer. So I went in and saw Fred: 'the FAS's on the phone to ask about progress on the negotiations'. 'Have a scotch, Mr Beale'. 'But Sir Frederick, he's waiting'. 'Just have a scotch'. 'Sir Frederick,

he's actually on the phone': 'He is a Second Division officer. Second division officers are paid a lot of money because they are very good when frustrated. Have a scotch' (Beale).

It may have looked smooth on the surface, one participant recalled, but 'like a duck I was paddling like hell below the surface'. Battles about content, structure and process were constant. Yet the position of permanent heads remained largely untouched. They were appointed to head a specified department of state and could not be removed without their approval. It was possible to appoint an outsider to a permanent head position; Hugh Ennor, deputy vice chancellor at the ANU, was made the first head of the new Department of Education and Science in 1967. But such a choice was rare. Most heads of department came from within the APS and were tenured in their position.

Perhaps the flavour can be best given by the comment of the former departmental secretary of External Affairs who commented that 'any private citizen who is sufficiently confident of his own opinions to tell a government precisely what it should do from day to day demonstrates not only his courage but also his rashness and perhaps his vanity' (cited in Gyngell and Wesley 2000:223). Sir Roland Wilson delivered a similar message to his part-time critics; they needed to be involved full time to understand the problems and give advice (see Chapter 8). In each case, the message was the same. Leave it to those experts; the full-time advisers know best. They probably did, but there was an exclusiveness about the message that was not to survive for long.

Gradually it changed. This next section seeks to note the main signposts over the last 30 years as a means of providing a framework for the discussion in later chapters where the developments within the framework, and the implications of these changes, will be discussed at greater length.

The changing framework

The first step can be identified as a decision in 1968 by the newly elected prime minister, John Gorton, to rearrange the machinery of government so that he could put his preferred adviser into a key position. He wanted to install Sir Lennox Hewitt as his head of department. He therefore divided the department into two. The Cabinet Office was to be headed by Sir John Bunting, the former head of the department, and his two deputies were also placed there. Hewitt was made head of the new Department of the Prime Minister. The reason for the change was simply the preference of the prime minister for a particular adviser. Bunting had little choice but to accede. It was an illustration that the machinery of government could be manipulated to provide the prime minister with the adviser he sought.

When the Whitlam government was elected in 1972, problems associated with the tenure of departmental secretaries came to the fore. At this time, conditions of secretaries' appointments and terminations were established in the *Public Service Act (PSA) 1922*, which stated that a secretary had to give his or her consent to being moved from the position. While there were some exceptions to this (including ill-health, behaviour demanding disciplinary action or an extremely high level of inefficiency (Spann 1976:116)), they were rarely used. The only way that the government could force a person out of the nominated position was by abolishing a department from under the secretary, either reconstituting it under a different name or spreading its functions to other agencies. In this event, the departmental secretaries retained their salary and were usually given a position that was allegedly of equivalent status (but which, almost by definition, seldom was). It was both a ponderous and onerous system and before 1972 it was rarely used.

The election of the Whitlam government altered this situation. Labor had been in opposition for 23 years and was suspicious of a service that had served the same government for 23 years. Several departments were abolished, leaving their heads without a position and thus unattached. In one case, a departmental secretary was persuaded to take an overseas appointment in order to allow a minister's choice to head a department. All those displaced were found positions, even if at one stage four were ambassadors to different international bodies in Geneva or Paris. The precedent was set. Even if there was no distinct reason for the change, a new government could be expected to change the personnel if it so desired. Gradually, over the three years of the government, the majority of departmental secretaries were shifted.

In 1974, the Labor government established the Royal Commission on Australian Government Administration (RCAGA). It in its turn commissioned Professor R.N. Spann to write a report on permanent heads. Spann saw no reason to change the terms and conditions, although he thought it might be useful to formalise the processes of appointment. He was more concerned about the procedure that allowed the government to abolish a department from under a permanent head, potentially leaving a core of secretaries floating. He commented in a report to RCAGA that 'it is doubtful whether most Permanent Heads could resist long-continued pressure for their replacement, especially if they knew that the Prime Minister as well as their own minister was against them'. But he concluded that the 'system as it has operated since 1972 has little to recommend it'. He cited the comment of one permanent head of the day: 'nothing could be worse than the hybrid system that seemed to be developing ... it would be better to make a much more rapid shift to the American system, or make much better provision for early retirement on a reasonable financial basis'. This in 1974! Spann thought that ministers should not be allowed to change their departmental heads without a reasonable trial to judge their competence. He also touted other important initiatives such as the concept that secretaries should be moved between departments as a matter of routine to improve the flexibility and responsiveness of the public service. His report recommended that the process of appointment be formalised. Aside from section 36 of the *PSA*, there were few legislative arrangements to prescribe how this process should operate. While subsection 54(1) of the Act provided a role for the PSB in advising the governor-general over appointments, subsection 54(2) established that there was no compulsion to do so. As a result, this process relied on convention, one which Spann noted had broken down with the election of the Whitlam government. He proposed that, when a vacancy arose, it should be advertised within and outside the public service (Spann 1976:105–6). Applicants should be considered by an Advisory Appointments Committee made up of the chair of the PSB, heads of Treasury and PM&C, two other permanent heads (peer elected) and two outside appointees nominated by the prime minister (1976:110). While the final decision remained with the government, Spann believed the formalised procedure would allow a proper consideration of the appropriate personnel to fill the post.

But governments do not wait for the results of commissions. Political imperatives have a habit of writing their own rules. In early 1975, Whitlam appointed John Menadue as head of the Department of PM&C. Unlike Hewitt, Menadue was not a public servant, but an executive of News Corporation. He had been Whitlam's principal private secretary for several years while Whitlam was in opposition, and before that he was for a short time a junior public servant. Menadue was to work effectively within the accepted bounds of the APS. When Whitlam was sacked on 11 October 1975, Menadue properly excused himself from the Lodge to go to work for Fraser as the official prime minister (he left with an abruptness that he later regretted and for which Labor never really forgave him) (Menadue 1999). He was to have a distinguished record of public service over the next decade. Nevertheless, the appointment of a former staff member, followed later that year by the appointment of two other former staff members, Peter Wilenski and Jim Spiegelman, as permanent heads, showed a preparedness to choose people, talented as they certainly were, from unconventional — indeed, directly political — quarters when it suited the prime minister.

The royal commission eventually reported to the Fraser government. The report of RCAGA recommended that the process of appointment be formalised with a committee of senior officials developing a shortlist of nominees for the prime minister and the relevant line minister. It noted the belief of senior officials that departmental secretaries should not be removable at pleasure, but disagreed that they should either be immovable or entirely vulnerable. The report concluded that 'any advantages accruing from a system of fixed term appointments are outweighed by the disadvantages', and that the rotation of departmental heads could be achieved more satisfactorily without such a system. It saw the need to reconcile the government's desire for flexible and responsive administration with the necessity to make best use of those who worked for it. The report supported the idea of rotation. If a minister wanted a change of head and the secretary was not willing to accept a transfer, the report recommended that the case be referred to the selection panel to seek mediation. The report saw no need for automatic changes when there was a change of government and commented that:

> The unquestionable need for departmental heads to serve faithfully the government's aims does not mean that a person's capacity to give such service can be judged on the simple basis of whether he owed his initial position to a government of the same or a different political persuasion. Extensive changes in the headships of departments during the 'settling in' phase of a new government could prove disruptive and could deprive the new government of knowledge and experience on which it should rely heavily during its early days in office (*Report*:101–2).

The Fraser government put many of the processes recommended by the RCAGA report into legislation. It formalised the appointment process and made a distinction between those appointed from the list presented to the prime minister by the panel, who were to be tenured and known as 'established candidates', and those who were appointed after being added to the list by a minister or cabinet and who were to be known as 'non-established'. The tenure of the latter would be for the term of a contract or for the duration of the government. (Some observers thought the real distinction was between establishment and non-establishment candidates. None in the latter category was ever in fact selected; the distinction between the two types of appointee was later removed by the Hawke government.) Fraser was traditional and proper in his treatment of senior officials. He was prepared to accept public servants on the basis of their perceived competence, rather than worry about

connections with the previous government. He kept Menadue as
secretary for nine months before appointing him ambassador to
Japan. When appointments to his department were made, and senior
officers were concerned he might object because of the background
of the candidates, he asked only whether they were any good.

But problems with the APS continued. They included failures
in tax and quarantine administration and even a colourful scandal
where a staff member was running a callgirl racket from the solicitor
general's office in Perth. So Fraser established *The Review of
Commonwealth Administration*, chaired by John Reid, in 1982. It
largely endorsed the views of RCAGA. It had been appointed by
Fraser in the aftermath of the scandals over the bottom-of-the-harbour
schemes in 1982, but it eventually reported a week before the election.
The Hawke government therefore had to consider its findings. The
report defended the idea of tenure to provide a target for aspiring
young, to provide freedom from concern and, above all, for the
'preservation of intellectual integrity. Completely honest policy
advice from a person whose training and experience have fitted him
to give it, is an essential part of our machinery of government'. It
regretted that at times ministers and departmental heads had barely
tried to work out their compatibility before changes were forced on
them. The RCA supported the concept of mobility after a secretary
had been in a position for five years, but disagreed with a proposal
from the Public Accounts Committee that appointments should be
for five-year terms, with tenure held at the deputy secretary level. It
saw difficulties in such a proposal, particularly in determining when
and by whom the evaluation of performance would be done. It
endorsed the views of RCAGA that the advantages of fixed terms
were outweighed by the potential problems.

The Hawke government had its own ideas for the changes that
were required to the APS. *Reforming the APS* was a White Paper
published in 1983 and building on the work done in opposition,
principally by Gareth Evans and Peter Wilenski. Initial ideas were
unveiled in the manifesto document, *Labor and Quality of
Government*, released before the 1983 election. The White Paper spelt
out the government's intentions that were then incorporated in its
1984 legislation. In 1984, the Labor government made some
substantial changes to the position of secretary. It symbolically retitled
them as 'departmental secretaries', rather than as 'permanent
secretaries'. They were still regarded as permanent appointments to
the APS, but the new Act stated that the departmental secretaries
could expect to be rotated after five years in any position.
Importantly, the *Public Service Act 1922* was amended to give the
governor-general, under the advice of the prime minister, the power

to terminate a secretary without providing an explanation for this termination (*PSA* 1922, s. 76E(1–3); Codd 1990: 83). Two conditions, however, were put in place to protect secretaries. First, the prime minister had to receive a written report from the secretary of PM&C before the termination could be initiated and the report had to summarise the reasons for removing the departmental secretary. Second, the government (in effect the chair of the Public Service Board) had some responsibility to find them an alternative position if it could not use their services as the secretary of a department. Fairly quickly, a cash offer for compensation sometimes replaced the offer of alternative employment; there were no guidelines and considerable discretion for the chair of the PSB.

The 1984 legislation required that the minister be consulted in the appointment of secretaries, although there is a general clause that allows appointments to be made legally without all the official steps being followed. The level of input contributed by the minister in making this decision depended on the timing of the change, the influence of the minister, and their relationship with the prime minister, who makes — or at the very least confirms — the final choice. At one extreme the minister might become involved in the process to the extent of interviewing prospective secretaries. An inexperienced minister, by way of contrast, might have very little influence over the decision.

The legislation added the words 'under the minister' to the paragraph that gave responsibility for the general management of the department to the departmental secretary. Some years later, Paul Keating (1993) summarised his view of the changes:

> you will recall the small change at the time which marked the direction of all the changes, the amendment of section 25 of the Public Service Act. We added three words to the description of the responsibilities of heads of departments: 'under the Minister'. Three simple words which say it all. And we stopped using the description 'Permanent head.'

Both in tone and detail, Keating's understanding of the new clause is unmistakable: ministers wanted to call the tune.

The legislation began a process that was to have a more fundamental shift to the management responsibilities of the departmental secretaries. Gradually, the central agencies tried to change their controls, to relax the details and to provide the departmental secretaries with the abilities to manage their own funds and personnel. The Public Service Board was abolished in 1987, some years after the financial controls over staffing had been moved to Finance and its central role in wage determination to Employment and Industrial Relations. The greater freedom over resources was designed to give the departmental secretaries an ability to shift funds, plan on programs rather than inputs, and develop corporate plans, mission statements and portfolio budgets. How well it worked is a matter of dispute. But it clearly changed the management function of all departmental secretaries and made them more directly accountable for the use of resources.

In 1987, in addition to the abolition of the PSB, there was a substantial change to the machinery of government. Whereas legal interpretation previously has required that each minister had a separate department, in 1987 it was argued that more than one minister could be appointed to 'administer' each department, as long as they were not officially made assistant ministers. In fact, of course, that is just what the junior ministers were. One consequence was that it was possible to reduce the number of departments from 30 to around sixteen. That naturally meant that the number of departmental secretaries required fell too. In the reorganisation, a number of incumbents were inevitably left without departments. Several were made associate secretaries; they kept their levels of pay and conditions but were now one rung down. Over the next few years, some left the APS; a few were given other appointments; others waited their turn and were later reappointed to departmental secretary rank.

Hawke explained that the changes would:
• substantially reduce the number of government departments to achieve administrative efficiencies and savings, better policy coordination and improved budget processes; and
• enhance ministerial control of departments by moving to a two-level ministerial structure.

He reiterated in his speech to parliament that the government had been concerned with two basic objectives: to enhance ministerial control over the public service and to give to department managers more responsibility for day-to-day management. 'By establishing mechanisms for greater ministerial control, we have been intent upon increasing the responsiveness of the bureaucracy to the Government's wishes and upon increasing democratic accountability, through Ministers, to Parliament and the community' (*Hansard*, 17 September 1987). Indeed, for the remaining secretaries, the management function often grew, as they had to integrate several diverse sections into a single unit. It was not always successful; indeed, fifteen years later, only the amalgamated Foreign Affairs and Trade has remained united. Some departments, such as Transport and Communications, were later redivided; others have had functions redistributed. In most cases, the task of management has grown. At the same time, departmental secretaries often are required to relate to more than one minister.

Although the portfolio minister is clearly the senior, there have been occasions (as in Foreign Affairs and Trade) when more than one has been in cabinet and both have been senior.

In 1994, legislation shifted the position of secretary from tenure to limited term appointments. The initiative came largely from within the APS. The incumbents were offered the choice of a 20 per cent rise in their pay in exchange for giving up their tenure and signing a limited term agreement with the government. The figure of 20 per cent was recommended by a committee of secretaries and confirmed by the Remuneration Tribunal. Several studies had been undertaken on relativities by the Department of Finance, but the final figure of 20 per cent was based as much on what was regarded as feasible by a small group of key secretaries under existing wage guidelines as it was on any really clear calculation of comparative worth with the private sector or with other public sectors.

Many secretaries thought in retrospect that the sum was an inadequate tradeoff for the loss of tenure (even if they did not say so loudly at the time), a point with which the Remuneration Tribunal might have agreed had it been asked to set the figure. Those over 50 were told that, given the benefits of superannuation, they had nothing to lose. Several of those under 50 had concerns, but felt they would be regarded as weak if they did not accept. When put to the test, all but two secretaries agreed to sign, in part because it was the only way to have any reasonable increase in pay, in part because at least it was superannuable, in part because they really felt that to accept the limited-term contracts was something that was expected of them. There was a further pragmatic reason: most felt that tenure that already been lost in practice as there was a line of departmental secretaries over the past few years who had been pushed aside. The benefit of the new scheme was that the compensation was now transparent and predictable.

One of those who declined to accept did so as a matter of principle, as he believed that existing arrangements were of profound importance to the professionalism of the public service. The second, Helen Williams, commented:

> I didn't take a contract at that time, despite the higher salaries available, for both principle and pragmatic reasons. In principle, I was concerned that contracts could undermine the close working relationship between Minister and Secretary and could lessen frank and fearless advice — both of which are very real competitive advantages for government. On purely pragmatic grounds, I doubted that Tourism, while important for the country, had a future as a separate department and I had to face the fact that disappearing departments often took their secrearies with them.

Later appointees did not get the choice; they were required to accept the limited-term agreement as a condition of appointment.

Under the terms of the agreements, appointments are for the term specified. Initially they were all for five years; more recently some have been for shorter terms. The occupant is eligible for reappointment. The appointment can be terminated at any time by the governor-general. If the departmental secretaries are not given another job, they cease being a member of the APS as soon as they leave the position of secretary. That was a substantial change. As the prime minister, Paul Keating, noted in 1993 when introducing changes:

> all secretaries, whether from inside or outside the service, have been appointed on the basis that, while they do not have tenure in the particular position of secretary to which they have been appointed, they do have continuing tenure in the public service.

No longer. They can be compensated for loss of office by payment at a rate of one-third of the remaining contract, up to a maximum of 12 months' salary. Secretaries do not have to be given reasons when terminated and these decisions were excluded from appeal under administrative law. In his notes sent to ministers after the election of the new government in 1996, the prime minister noted:

> Secretaries are appointed for fixed terms, usually five years. In general, it is expected that a secretary will not remain in a particular post for more than five years but would be rotated into another secretary position after that time. Appointment to another office after the expiration of the term is entirely at the discretion of the government. The government is able to terminate a secretary's appointment before the expiry of the term if performance is unsatisfactory but this would not be undertaken lightly, involving as it would formal action by the Prime Minister under the *Public Service Act* and the payment of compensation.

The changes contained in the 1994 legislation were significant. Before 1994, the government had to make a decision after five years whether it wanted to rotate a secretary or maintain the existing arrangements; if rotation was chosen, it had to find a vacancy and then fill any subsequent holes. The incumbent remained unless a positive decision was made to change the personnel. There was an expectation, not always fulfilled, to find suitable places — or at least acceptable ones — for displaced secretaries. By 1994 that expectation had declined as several displaced departmental secretary left the APS. After 1994, the balance shifted further. When a contract expired, there was a vacancy to fill and no incumbent holding rights to the position. The government was in a much freer position to reappoint, shuffle or replace without any need to consider or provide further employment for the person whose contract had expired. Normally, action will have been taken before that occurs; arrangements will be made to extend contracts or find alternatives for good departmental secretaries. That would just be part of good management and a way to keep talent in the APS. But there was a difference. The old presumption was the secretary stays within the APS, while the new presumption is less certain.

What happens is likely to vary. Some — indeed, the majority — may have their contracts renewed or another position found for them when the term of the contract is up. That has occurred at times in the past and there is certainly too little talent to dispose of all departmental secretaries when the contracts expire. Before 1993, departmental secretaries could expect to be rotated after five years in one position. Not all were rotated; when their services were appreciated by their minister, they could easily be extended (as Codd and Keating were in 1990). The position was never secure — note the number who were shifted in the three years of the Whitlam government. But the law seems now to have caught up with the practice.

The degree to which the existing circumstances could cause problems was illustrated in 1996. After the election, six departmental secretaries had their contracts terminated by the prime minister before the government was sworn in; thus a third of the departmental secretaries had no opportunity to test their skills in the service of the new government. After the 1998 election, stories emerged that a meeting of departmental secretaries had been told that the prime minister was only satisfied with the performance of a few of the departmental secretaries (although there are several different accounts of what precisely was said and even more about what was intended). A few satisfactory performers were noted; when the recently appointed were added to that list, those remaining had some concerns about their future. It set off what the press described as the 'lemon' hunt. (One departmental secretary later said he was described not as a mandarin or a lemon but as a cumquat — small and bitter!!) Insecurity was rife. Six months later, they were told no changes would be made and salary raises, with an additional component after performance appraisal, were granted.

Under the Howard government, the impetus for reform to the APS, including the conditions of secretaries, has been continued. As Minister Assisting the Prime Minister for the Public Service, Peter Reith issued a discussion paper entitled *towards a best practice australian public service* (TBP), where a number of ideas were floated regarding the role of secretaries. The first was a proposal to reclassify agency heads/secretaries as chief executive officer (TBP 1997:11). The argument was put that this would 'acknowledge ... the important strategic leadership role of Agency Heads' and secretaries' responsibility 'to the Minister for their agency's performance ... [would] be explicitly recognised' (TBP 1997:11). A second proposal was to introduce performance agreements to hold secretaries publicly accountable for their performance (TBP 1997:11).

Towards a Best Practice Australian Public Service was written as a discussion paper in the lead-up to the government's plan to rewrite the Public Service Act. Neither of these two proposals was explicitly picked up in the new Act. The term 'secretary' was retained and there was no mention of performance agreements, although the government remains firmly committed to developing the latter of these proposals.

Sections 58 and 59 of the *Public Service Act 1999*, regarding appointments and terminations of secretaries, replicated much of sections 36 and 76E of the old Act with a number of notable points of departure. In the previous Act, it was the governor-general who appointed and terminated the appointment of secretaries, albeit under the advice of the prime minister. The new Act strips the governor-general of this role and gives it to the prime minister. One minor constraint to the prime minister's power exists in this respect. Before making the appointment, the prime minister must receive a report from the Secretary of Prime Minister and Cabinet (and, in the case of it being the secretary of Prime Minister and Cabinet being appointed, the Public Service Commissioner). The relevant minister must still be consulted in making this report. When it comes to terminations, however, the new Act — unlike the old — does not require the minister's input. Hence the power to terminate a secretary is concentrated in the hands of the prime minister. A final difference between the two acts is the specification that a secretary's appointment is limited to a contract of up to five years; what was common practice is now to be law.

In June 1999, the departmental secretary of Defence had his contract terminated because the minister decided that he could not work with him. Technically it was argued that the departmental secretary had lost the confidence of the minister. Paul Barratt had been brought back to the APS by the Howard government in 1996 and, 18 months earlier, had been made secretary of Defence. A new minister was appointed after the 1997 election. Relations quickly broke down. Warned of the impending dismissal, Barratt took the government to court. For the first time, the relationship between departmental secretary and minister was tested legally. The court upheld the decision, but required that Barratt be given procedural fairness. (See Chapter 10 for the detailed discussion of the case.) It did not prevent the termination of his position. Departmental secretaries were now seen as more vulnerable than ever, with the court agreeing that all that was legally needed for the contract to be ended was for a minister, with or without a justifiable reason, to declare a lack of trust in their departmental secretary.

The implications

These descriptions of the changing framework over the last 30 years demonstrate three points. First, the APS must not be seen in isolation; it changed as society changed, as demands on it were transformed and as new challenges emerged. New expectations, greater resource pressures, wider dispersion of information, a better informed citizenry and political class, new theories of government, greater entanglement with the world outside and more competition to be heard have all had an impact on what the departmental secretary might do; they are, besides, factors over which the departmental secretaries have no controls. They must ride the wind.

Second, there is a danger in proposing that the comparative stability of the 1960s was in some way an ideal time from which future shifts are unfortunate aberrations. That stability was caused as much by the continuing tenure of a government that was not much interested in changing the shape of the public service as by any inherent superiority of the existing practices. Indeed, the Labor government of 1972 and its successors made changes precisely because they were unconvinced of the effectiveness of the model they inherited in serving a government. Thereafter a number of steps were taken — some initiated by ministers, some by officials — to make the system work better. Whether they succeeded may be a matter of judgment, but in much of the public debate there are constant comparisons made — sometimes explicitly, more often implicitly — between the existing methods and those that were dominant in the 1960s. The line 'it would not have happened in Sir Arthur [Tange]'s day' may be a tribute to that mandarin's reputation, but does little to recognise what has changed. Such a debate is likely to be useful only if the strengths and weaknesses of both arrangements are considered.

Third, there should be no assumption that the situation of the departmental secretaries is now fixed. Comments that they are in a state of transition imply that there is a shift from one fixed point to another. Such comments have been around for 30 years; there is no evidence that it has reached a state of stability. It is not possible to suggest, for instance, that there is a shift from a British to an American model as though that has a degree of inevitably. It does not. The job has been affected by more fundamental factors; the adjusted conventions and the amendments to the legislation are attempts to absorb the new requirements and the changed conditions.

Rather, it is useful to explore how the job has been changed by the altered expectations and whether the resulting framework is now appropriate or dysfunctional, and to ask whether these circumstances as they have now developed are best suited for the departmental secretaries to provide the service to governments, and through them the country, that both require for good governance.

3

The mandarins: A collective portrait

Who are the Australian departmental secretaries? This chapter seeks to provide an overview of their careers and qualifications in order to seek trends about those careers that might be used to support the interview data collected over the years. It provides an analysis of the career patterns of secretaries as a group over time to determine whether those patterns have changed, in what direction and what the implications might be.

The career data

Career information was collected on all departmental secretaries in office between 1950 to 1998. Lists of departmental secretaries are available (PSB 1973), but the Public Service Commission has no consolidated listing of secretaries. The data had to be found from a wide range of sources.[1] Consequently, not all the information is available on the same basis for every secretary. Missing numbers are noted in each table. Exact dates, in terms of month of appointment or taking up duty, were not always found. Consequently some calculations — of time served, of age when appointed — cannot always be precise, although they are likely to be correct to within a year. Given these problems with the data, the findings are about as close as can be achieved; however, the purpose is seek trends, rather than absolute precision.

The initial question was precisely who should be included. At different times, departments have been headed by permanent secretaries, comptroller-generals and director-generals. Now the term 'secretary' is specified in the *Public Service Act*. In the past, many officers have been given the powers of the permanent head, to provide authority to their statutory position. But for the purposes of these calculations, only the heads of the core government departments have been included. Only periods as a departmental secretary (but not periods as acting, interim or associate secretary) were considered in calculations. Other senior positions were not included in terms of service. While distinguished departmental secretaries have at times served as Commonwealth Statistician (Sir Roland Wilson, Sir William Cole and Ian Castles) or as chair of the Industries Assistance Commission (Mike Codd), determining which other positions might be considered as equivalents of departmental secretaries would lead to constant dispute, particularly as these positions sometimes had permanent secretary powers and at other times did not. The one addition was that a period of chair of the Public Service Board or Commission was included for a person who also served as the secretary of a department.

The departmental secretaries were then divided into six categories according to their date of *first* appointment: those incumbent in 1950 (17), and those appointed by the Liberal governments of 1950–72 (64), by the Whitlam government (20), the Fraser government (28), the Hawke/Keating governments (45) and the Howard government up to April 1999 (10). Putting secretaries in the category of their first appointment, even if they later served in a department in a different category, may create some apparent anomalies. Mike Codd and Michael Keating, for instance, were both initially appointed to the Department of Employment and Industrial Relations, even though their reputations are likely to be made more by their service in the Department of Prime Minister and Cabinet.

Inevitably anomalies occur too where departmental secretaries have broken careers, either because they served elsewhere because they were out of favour with a government, or because they served in a statutory or diplomatic position before being reinstated as secretary. Those interim periods have not been included in the data; consequently a period of 10 years' service may, in a very few cases, be spread over fifteen years. These problems can only be solved by an exercise of judgment.

As a second way of analysing the data, we divided the departments into five broad functional categories (central agencies, economic/ trade, infrastructure, social, defence) to see if career patterns changed depending on the type of governmental activity.[2] Again, the allocation of departments to categories presents in places a need for judgment.

Despite the shortcomings in the material that was collected, the data tell a story of considerable change. Such dramatic patterns invite explanation.

Age and length of service

Table 3.1 provides basic information about the average age of appointment and termination of secretaries, their mobility and their length of service. Table 3.2 puts some more detail on those broad figures in relation to age. Table 3.3 disaggregates information about the length of service. Combined, they illustrate distinct trends.

Table 3.1: Average ages, number of departments, length of service by first appointment

When appointed	*N*	*Av age at app'tment*	*Av age at departure*[a]	*Av no departments*	*Av length of service*
Pre-1950[b]	17	50.6	62.8	1.2	12.5
Menzies to McMahon	64	50.1	59.6	1.4	9.5
Whitlam	20	48.2	55.3	1.8	6.1
Fraser	28	49.4	55.8	1.6	6.9
Hawke to Keating	45	47.1	51.8	1.6	5.0[c]
Howard	10	50.9	-	1.1	1.7[c]
Total	184	49.1	57.1	1.5	7.5

a 19 absent (of whom 18 currently in office).
b Includes only those departmental secretaries in office at the time of Menzies' second prime ministership.
c As these include serving officers, they distort the result; see the text for discussion.
Note: A change in name of department or modification of departmental responsibilities counts as continuity of service, not a change of department.

Table 3.2: Age at first appointment

When appointed	*N*	*>40*		*40–44*		*45–49*		*50–54*		*55+*	
		N	*%*	*N*	*%*	*N*	*%*	*N*	*%*	*N*	*%*
Pre-1950	17	1	6	1	6	6	35	·4	24	5	29
Menzies to McMahon	64	4	6	8	13	19	30	14	22	19	30
Whitlam	20	4	20	2	10	2	10	7	35	5	25
Fraser[a]	27	-	-	4	15	9	33	10	37	4	15
Hawke to Keating	45	1	2	16	36	16	36	8	18	4	9
Howard	10	-	-	-	-	3	30	6	60	1	10
Total	183	10	6	31	17	55	30	48	26	39	21

a One missing.

Table 3.3: Length of service by first appointment

When appointed	N	>2 N	>2 %	3–5 N	3–5 %	6–9 N	6–9 %	10+ N	10+ %
Pre-1950	17	-	-	2	12	4	24	11	65
Menzies to McMahon	64	2	3	19	30	17	27	26	41
Whitlam	20	3	15	7	35	8	40	2	10
Fraser	28	3	11	14	50	6	21	5(1)	18
Hawke to Keating	45	5	11	29(6)	64	10(2)	22	1	2
Howard	10	6(6)	60	4(3)	40	-	-	-	-
Total	184	19(6)	10	75(9)	41	45(2)	25	45(1)	25

(n) = still serving
Note: <2 = less than 2 years; 3–5 = more than 2 years but less than 6; 6–9 = more than 6 years but less than 10; 10+ = more than 10 years.

Appointments are throughout the period under review generally around the age of 47 to 51, but there were twice as many appointed below the age of 45 in the Hawke/Keating period than in the Menzies/McMahon or Fraser periods.

Appointment over the age of 55 were quite common before 1975 with about a quarter of appointments reaching that rank towards the end of their career, but that group has become increasingly rare since. Fifty per cent of Fraser's and more than 70 per cent of Hawke/Keating appointees were under 50 — indeed, a third of the Hawke/Keating appointees were under 45. It is becoming a younger person's position, even if there were fewer very young appointees — that is, those under 40. Under Whitlam, all three such young appointees (Menadue, Wilenski, Spiegelman) had previous service in his personal office and did not come through the traditional public service route.

The most striking changes are the dramatic decline in the average age of departure and the average length of service. In the 1950s and 1960s, an appointee could expect to serve around ten years, leaving at the age of 60 or thereabouts. As Table 3.3 illustrates, over 70 per cent served at least five years, and 37 of the 81 pre-1972 appointments served over ten years. By contrast, only five of 28 Fraser appointments did — three of them (Ayers, Blunn, Volker) continued throughout the Labor government and two (Ayers and Blunn) into the Howard government. Only one of the 45 Hawke/Keating appointees (Michael Keating) has served 10 years. That length of time seems likely to be less common in the future. Longevity has become rare; only a quarter of the Labor government's appointees even served the five-year term that the new contracts anticipate as normal.

This decline in the length of service is reflected in the average age of departure, which has fallen from 60 in the first group to under 52 in the later cases. These figures may in one respect be misleading. Of the Hawke/Keating cohort of 45, eight were still serving. Obviously their continuation in office will increase the average length served. Of those eight, only two have so far served five years. To see if the downward trend continued, we recalculated the figure for length of service on the assumption that they *all* served the same time as the Fraser appointees: 6.9 years. The average term served then only rises to a figure of 5.3 years. Even if we assume the eight incumbents *all* served for ten years — a most unlikely eventuality — the average only rises to 5.9 years. Consequently, even if all the remaining cohort were to serve the average of the Fraser cohort or longer, the downward trend in the time served still continues. (As only two Howard appointees have left, that figure is not significant.) Departmental secretaries are now leaving, on average, in their early fifties, after serving much shorter times in office.

Departures

The fall in the average age for departure suggests that there is a distinct shift in patterns. This change is most notable when the reasons for final departure from the secretary's position are reviewed. Table 3.4 explains the reasons for departure. In this instance, we recalculated the figures by placing departmental secretaries in categories according to the government in power when they left.

There are, of course, some intermediate absences in diplomatic positions or in statutory offices that mark broken careers. In this table, we are concerned only in the final shift from the departments of state. Diplomatic posts include overseas postings to the World Bank, the OECD, the ILO and similar international organisations. 'Transferred' signifies a shift to another government position — often they were appointed to head a statutory body. 'Moved' indicates that departments have been abolished and the secretary is now holding a more subordinate position in a larger entity; these moves occurred principally when the three service departments were folded into the enlarged Department of Defence in 1973 and when several 'associate secretary' positions were created after their departments were abolished in the 1987 machinery of government changes. Some of them rose again to departmental status; those noted here did not. The difference between a resignation to take up a position outside the service and retirement may be marginal. At times, too, a

Table 3.4: Reason for departure by government at time of departure

When appointed	N	Died	Ret	Res	Dip	Trans	Movd	Term
Menzies to								
McMahon	53	3	33	2	6	9	-	-
Whitlam	17	-	5	1	4	5	2	-
Fraser	32	1	16	2	4	9	-	-
Hawke to								
Keating	51	2	10	9	6	15	5	4
Howard	15	-	2	2	2	-	1	8
Total	167	6	65	16	22	38	8	12

Note: Retired (Ret), Resigned (Res), Diplomatic Post (Dip), Transferred (Trans), Moved (Movd), Terminated (Term).

retirement may be a consequence of a not-too-subtle push and is taken as a means of maintaining dignity. But since the introduction of five-year term appointments, a secretary who is terminated may be able to gain the benefits specified in those contracts, while a person who resigns does not; hence there may be benefits in being terminated rather than resigning.

Even given all those caveats, the increase in terminations is marked. In the early period, the majority retired at the end of their career. Another group went on to other positions, particularly diplomatic ones. There was a good reason for looking after them. Under the old Public Service Act, secretaries could only be moved with their consent; the only way to force them to be unattached was to abolish the department they headed. Even then, they had officially to be found a suitable position of almost equivalent status and conditions (even if it did not always happen).

By contrast, few of the later appointments have been able to serve until retirement. Eleven have now been terminated, being paid out according to the terms of their contract. More are leaving the service at a time of their own choosing. In part, that may be a consequence of there now being fewer statutory positions into which these people can be placed; privatisation and corporatisation have reduced the scope for government patronage. But it is primarily a function of a different attitude to the careers of secretaries. First came the acceptance that secretaries could be moved from one job to another at the end of a five-year term, then it became accepted that they could be removed from the public service itself. If the Hawke/

Keating governments assumed that secretaries could expect to be rotated every five years, the later contracts implied that there was no certainty that they would necessarily be re-employed at the end of the contract. As a result, they may be more inclined to look for alternative opportunities before the contracts expire. That shows in the trends for earlier and younger departure. Indeed, the changes raise questions about whether the position of secretary still remains part of any concept of a career service.

Education: An economics profession?

An education profile is harder to develop because the details are not always available. School data in particular are not complete. Further, the educational qualifications of secretaries reflect broader social trends, particularly the expansion of tertiary education since the 1960s. It would be amazing if the increase in secretaries with degrees did not follow the national trend. So too much should not be made of the increase in qualifications. But available data emphasise the wide range of educational backgrounds from which secretaries were drawn. In particular there are a substantial number with a state school background, even when it was rare. For the Menzies/McMahon period, 33 went to state schools, eighteen to private schools and six to Catholic schools. The later figures are eight, two and three respectively for the Whitlam appointments, ten, seven and five for Fraser, and 21, six and eight for Hawke/Keating. Even though the figures do not cover all the people, it is noticeable that, in all but one of the groups, more than 50 per cent came from state school backgrounds.

But clearly the chances of reaching the top without tertiary education have, since 1972, been extremely limited. A substantial number of the early appointments were able to reach their position without the benefit of tertiary education, not perhaps surprising when there was a limit (apparently never reached as they were a very small proportion of the workforce) to the number of graduates that could be recruited each year. By contrast, since 1972 a degree has been almost a prerequisite for promotion, and in recent years a quarter have gone on to postgraduate studies (see Table 3.5).

Initially, the great majority went to Sydney or Melbourne Universities — these were, for many appointed in the 1950s and 1960s at the age of 55, often the principal places available for study. By the time of the 1980s, the spread of universities was much greater; regional universities such as the University of New England had their share of successful graduates. The educational profile suggests that there never was an equivalent of an elite 'public school'/Oxbridge route

Table 3.5: Level of tertiary education by first appointment

When appointed	N	None N	None %	Undergraduate N	Undergraduate %	Postgraduate N	Postgraduate %
Pre-1950	17	11	64	2	12	4	24
Menzies to McMahon	64	15	23	37	58	12	19
Whitlam[a]	19	1	5	11	58	7	37
Fraser[b]	26	1	4	23	89	2	8
Hawke to Keating	45	2	4	25	56	18	40
Howard	10	-	-	6	60	4	40
Total	181	30	17	104	58	47	26

a 1 missing
b 2 missing

into the administrative class and thus to the top of the public service as can be found in Britain. University education may not formally be a requirement, but it is now probably a necessity. However, it appears to matter little what school was attended beforehand, or which university granted the degree.

But what kind of education may be required? The arguments advanced by Pusey about the prevalence of economics as a dominant discipline, and the consequential regime of 'economic rationalism', mean it is worth asking what percentage of secretaries had a degree in economics. There needs to be a caveat. An initial degree in economics does not mean, 30 years later, that the secretaries would regard themselves as neo-liberal economists — indeed, far from it. Many argue that they are now managers. Nevertheless, there has been a gradual increase in each cohort of secretaries with degrees in economics, but there was no sudden increase in the late 1980s: the reputed age of economics dominance (Table 3.6). We will return later to the question of where they may be found.

There may be nothing remarkable about economics figuring prominently in the qualifications of senior public servants, as economics plays a substantial role in the decisions that a federal, rather than a state, government must play. But the question is whether this is an Australian, rather than an international, trend. To an extent, it is. Comparative figures from other studies suggest there is no equivalent upsurge in other parliamentary systems (Rhodes and Weller 2001).

Table 3.6: Economics qualifications by first appointment

When appointed	N	Economics	
		N	%
Pre-1950	17	1	6
Menzies to McMahon[a]	63	20	32
Whitlam[b]	19	7	37
Fraser[c]	26	11	42
Hawke to Keating	45	20	44
Howard	10	7	70
Total	180	66	37

a 1 missing
b 1 missing
c 2 missing

Mobility

Mobility may be found in several guises. One indicator is the number of departments a secretary has headed: how far are the skills regarded as generic, able to be applied to all public matters without attention to the subject matter or how far is particular expertise regarded as essential? A second can be seen as the reverse of that coin: how many secretaries have had a narrow and specialised career moving through the ranks and heading the department in which they entered the Senior Executive Service (SES) (or its predecessor, the Second Division). In these cases, we have assumed that experience at levels lower than the SES is only of limited value. However, since we do not have full career details, some secretaries who were promoted to the SES in the department in which they were appointed secretary may have moved to other departments while in the SES and then back as secretary. These will appear here as non-mobile and thus may inflate the figures, though not by much. A basic point to make, in addition, is that the number of departments increased in the 1960s and 1970s and there was greater instability in departmental structures (Davis *et al.* 1999), so there were more opportunities for a secretary to move from one area to another, both in a technical sense of it appearing to be a new department and in an actual way. Greater mobility might be expected.

The degree of mobility as secretaries indicated by the average number of departments headed has not changed (see Table 3.1). The majority (18 of 27 Fraser appointees, 25 of 45 for Hawke and Keating, 59 of 80 before 1972, 11 of 19 under Whitlam — a total of 113 of the 180) served in only one department. But there are a number who have shifted around: Wilenski and Tony Blunn headed five agencies, with a total service of eight and eighteen years respectively; George Warwick Smith and Tony Ayers served in four departments, for 14 and 19 years respectively. A further 11 have headed three departments. It is a trend that is developing, with many of the multiple heads appearing in the last 15 years. That is to be expected; it is government policy to rotate departmental secretaries and they now assume they will not be appointed to head only their present department or stay in one position for more than five years.

Not surprisingly, there is also a decline in the number of secretaries who have continuous service, becoming secretary in the department in which they reached the SES or its equivalent (see Tables 3.7a and 3.7b). Again, some judgment is required to determine what remains the same department, given continuous name changes. Under the early regimes, half the secretaries were promoted within departments; by the Hawke/Keating period, this was reduced to less than 20 per cent. Among departments, Foreign Affairs, Attorney-General and Treasury tend to appoint from within most commonly, between them accounting for a third of all cases, but these are traditionally departments that incorporate a narrower 'professional' career within a career service.

Two sub-sets of the data on mobility are provided. The first refers to the speed of promotion: how long did it take to move from the entrance to the SES and secretary rank (see Table 3.8)? Some secretaries are appointed direct to a position; they may be outsiders,

Table 3.7a: Continuity from SES level to head of department by first appointment

When appointed	N	Continuity	%
Pre-1950[a]	15	6	40
Menzies to McMahon[b]	60	31	52
Whitlam[c]	18	4	22
Fraser[d]	23	7	30
Hawke to Keating	45	8	18
Howard[e]	9	4	44
Total	170	60	35

a. 2 missing   b. 4 missing
c. 2 missing   d. 5 missing
e. 1 missing

Note: Those commencing in Treasury prior to 1976 but heading Finance are counted as having continuity. Defence to Air, Army, Navy or vice versa are counted as having continuity.

Table 3.7b: Continuity from SES level to head of department by department

Department	Pre-1950	Menzies to McMahon	Whitlam	Fraser	Hawke to Keating	Howard	Total	All appointments
Aboriginal Affairs	-	-	1	-	2	-	3	6
Administrative Services	-	-	-	-	1	-	1	8
Attorney-General	-	2	-	1	1	-	4	8
Defence (Army, etc)	2	3	-	-	-	-	5	21
External/Foreign Affairs (& Trade)	-	5	1	2	1	2	11	15
Employment and Industrial Relations	-	1	1	1	-	-	3	15
Health	-	-	1	1	-	-	2	12
Immigration	1	1	-	-	-	-	2	10
Postmaster General	-	4	-	-	-	-	4	8
Primary Industry (& Energy)*	-	3	-	-	1	2	6	12
Prime Minister (& Cabinet)	-	1	-	1	-	-	2	9
Shipping & Transport	-	1	-	-	-	-	1	3
Supply (& Development)	1	3	-	-	-	-	4	7
Trade and Customs (& Excise)	1	3	-	-	-	-	4	10
Treasury & Finance	1	1	-	3	2	-	7	14
Works	-	3	-	-	-	-	3	4
Total	6	31	4	9	8	4	62	

* including Commerce and Agriculture

state public servants or holders of a non-departmental statutory office. In other words, they may be long-standing public servants when appointed as secretary, but not in a departmental position. But, excluding those, it may be expected that, in a non-mobile public service, a substantial number spent ten years or more in the SES before their appointments. In fact, the opposite seems to be true. Promotion was fastest in the early days. If the figures for six or more years in the SES are taken as a benchmark, then 48 per cent of the Menzies to McMahon appointees, 50 per cent of Whitlam appointees, 61 per cent of Fraser's, 71 per cent of Hawke/Keating's, and 100 per cent of Howard's spent that long in getting promoted, though not all had continuous service in federal employment. More surprising is the fact that almost half the Hawke/Keating cohort spent 10 years or more, indicating of course they often had served in the previous government at senior levels. Internal promotion, after substantial experience within the public service, remains the most common route to a position of secretary.

The second sub-set relates to experience in central agencies. There is an assertion that experience in central agencies has become an asset in a route to a secretary position. Again we have only considered SES level experience in these calculations (Kelleher 1988). Table 3.9 bears out the belief that, for those who selected secretaries, there was an increasingly recognised benefit in central agency experience. Under Fraser, over 40 per cent had that advantage and under Hawke and

Table 3. 8: Years from SES level to head of department by first appointment

When appointed	N	None		< 2		3–5		6–9		10+	
		N	%	N	%	N	%	N	%	N	%
Pre-1950[a]	15	6	40	3	20	5	33	1	7	-	-
Menzies to McMahon[b]	60	10	17	2	3	19	32	16	27	13	22
Whitlam[c]	18	7	39	-	-	2	11	6	33	3	17
Fraser[d]	23	2	9	1	4	6	26	9	39	5	22
Hawke to Keating[e]	45	6	13	-	-	7	16	10	22	22	49
Howard[f]	9	-	-	-	-	-	-	3	33	6	67
Total	170	31	18	6	4	39	23	45	27	49	29

a 2 missing   b 4 missing
c 2 missing   d 5 missing
e 1 missing
f Barratt and Moore-Wilton did not continuously hold office in public service prior to becoming heads of department.

Keating 60 per cent, several of whom had experience at SES level in more than one of the three principal agencies. Incidentally, of the 27 Hawke/Keating appointees with central agency experience, six had been in Treasury, seven in Finance and one in both.

Central agency experience may indeed have real advantages. An understanding of how government works as a whole may be beneficial to a person later running a line department. But of course so can the reverse. Experience of delivering substantial government programs brings its own insights too. The senior committee that manages that top echelon, trying to ensure a suitable supply of potential secretaries, may deliberately rotate people into a central agency to broaden their experience.

Changes in groupings of departments

In order to discover whether these changes were common across the public service, the secretaries were arranged into five broad groups of departmental functions (see note 2), and then the data reanalysed in the same way, government by government. An obvious problem is that such small numbers are found in some categories that not too much weight should be put on those particular figures. The Howard government was excluded as the total there is too small to divide in any meaningful sense.

In the Menzies to McMahon governments, those secretaries who headed infrastructure departments show different career patterns.

Table 3.9: Central agency experience by first appointment

When appointed	N	None	Ex N	Ex %	PM&C	Tsy/Fin	PSB
Pre-1950	17	14	3	18	1	2	-
Menzies to McMahon[a]	62	53	9	14	2	7	-
Whitlam[b]	19	15	4	21	3	1	-
Fraser[c]	26	15	11	42	5	6	1
Hawke to Keating	45	18	27	60	20	14	5
Howard	10	5	5	50	2	3	1
Total	179	120	59	33	33	33	7

a 2 missing
b 1 missing
c 2 missing
Note: PM&C = Prime Minister & Cabinet; Tsy/Fin = Finance and/or Treasury; PSB = Public Service Board

They were more likely to be without a degree and the majority were over 50, and often over 55, when appointed. A consequence of that late age was that many more of them had short terms of under five years than those in other groups and, since a significant minority had continuity of promotion within the second division to the secretaryship, they seem to fit the traditional image of a closed bureaucracy, with gradual promotion within a department. Less than 10 per cent of those outside the central agencies had experience there. This presents an image of semi-independent fiefdoms (the Canadians call them 'silos'), rather then an integrated and single public service. This distinctiveness of the group declines under Whitlam and Fraser to the extent that no secretary in the group is an internal promotion.

Under Hawke and Keating, the trend towards similar career characteristics across all groups of departments became even more marked. Central agency experience was widespread, continuity of promotion rare and turnover of appointments common. The departmental silos had melted into a more integrated pattern, as the idea of a single service, managed for the broader whole of government interests, became more accepted, particularly at the centre. The presence since 1993 of a central committee managing the careers of potential may have strengthened the trend.

One category perhaps justifies particular attention, given the weight attributed to the prevalence of economics in the debate over the future of the public service. In the early years, economics degrees were thinly spread. Then those with degrees in economics became more specialised. Partly under Fraser (70 per cent), and notably under Hawke and Keating (80 per cent), those with degrees in economics — often after experience in Treasury and Finance — were appointed to the central agencies and to the economics and trade groups of departments. Two conclusions are possible. If economics was to be the language of policy-making, then possibly further advantages were being given to these areas in the policy debate; however, second (and less conspiratorially) these may just be the areas where, once degrees were the norm, economics graduates could be expected to be found.

Some tentative conclusions

The concept of a career service has never been tightly defined; it is at best a loose description of the way that the APS was organised. But if it has some characteristics, they would include the ideas of a single career, a commitment to public service, and the belief that officials would rise to the top and retire, or perhaps take another government post. It was never a precise concept and examples could always be found of lateral appointments from outside the service to top positions. More recently, the wide range of redundancies and the number leaving voluntarily at all levels across the service have perhaps undermined any old notion of career.

Nevertheless, those assumptions would provide a fair description for most of those who reached departmental secretary status across the service. They were long-term employees who had been in the service for decades. In the early years, they may have been part of closed departmental careers, rather than part of an integrated public service, but the general assumptions were accurate.

What has changed? The silos have been reduced and there has been more lateral movement, so that careers are now within the public service, rather then in an individual department. Attorney-General, Foreign Affairs and Treasury remain the principal exceptions to the concept of a single public service.

Promotion to secretary is still normally from within the APS, and often after a substantial period in the SES (rather longer then it used to be). Even those not in the service when appointed have a substantial record at senior levels in the service. There is no record of *secretaries* leaving for the private sector and returning, and even those recruited from outside (such as Barratt and Moore-Wilton) have not been in the private sector for long. Both made their reputations in the public sector, rising to the level of deputy secretary in Trade before moving elsewhere. The route to the top is almost exclusively internal.

But whereas the departmental secretary position was once the pinnacle of a career, now appointment may remove the secretary, from the career stream by being placed on a term appointment. There is a career up to and including the SES level, but no guarantees beyond. As secretaries leave earlier, as termination rather then redeployment becomes more common, and with alternative careers in the public sector no longer being available, so the career patterns have clearly changed.

More often now, a position of departmental secretary may be a stepping stone to another role, either by choice or by force of circumstance. Secretaries may regard the public service as a first career, with their eyes always open for new opportunities. In this respect they reflect the changes in the career patterns of their political masters; there has been a tendency for politicians to enter politics younger and, particularly after a stint as a minister to prove their capacity, to leave younger for greater — and better paid — opportunities elsewhere (Weller and Fraser 1987). This profile suggests that similar patterns may develop for departmental secretaries; they are often career public servants, appointed younger, serving less time as secretary and leaving earlier. That is a substantial change in the nature of our public service.

Notes

1. Castleman, Beverley D. 1992 'Changes in the Australian Commonwealth Departmental Machinery of Government: 1928–1982', PhD thesis, Deakin University.
    Commonwealth of Australia Gazette (Public Service) (various to 1998).
    Curriculum Vitae of Departmental Secretaries (various).
    Departmental Internet sites (various, 1997).
    Departmental Annual Reports (various).
    McAllister, Ian *et al.* 1990 *Australian Political Facts*, Longman Cheshire, Melbourne.
    Ministers and Permanent Heads from 11 July 1972 to December 1983 (nd).
    National Archives of Australia (Internet site, accessed April 1998).
    Public Service Board, *Annual Report* (up to 1986).
    Public Serv.ce Board 1973 *49th Annual Report1973*, AGPS, Canberra, pp.122–26. Secretaries of Departments, 1 January 1976–March 1989.
    Waldren, Laurie 1988 *Ministers and Secretaries from 2 December 1983 to 13 May 1988*, compiled 17 May 1988, Public Service Commission.
    Waldren, Laurie 1996 *Ministers and Portfolio Department Secretaries — from July 1987 to March 1996*, 16 February 1996, Public Service Commission.
    Weller, Patrick 1989 'Politicisation and the Australian Public Service', *Australian Journal of Public Administration* December 48(4):369–81.
2. *Central agencies*
    Prime Minister and Cabinet, Treasury, Finance, Public Service Board, Attorney General
    Economic/Trade
    Trade, Resources, Customs, Industry, Industrial Relations, Employment, Labour, Primary Industries, Business, Productivity, Agriculture
    Infrastructure
    Transport, Shipping, Communications, Postmaster General, Housing, Civil Aviation, Construction, Interior, Local Government, Administrative Services, Territories, Environment, Science, Works, Minerals and Energy, National Development, Media, Tourism, Urban and Regional Development
    Social
    Health, Social Security, Community Services, Education, Human Services, Immigration, Aboriginal Affairs, Repatriation, Veterans Affairs, Arts, Special Minister of State, Sport
    Defence
    Foreign Affairs, External Affairs, Defence, Defence Production, Defence Support, Supply, Army, Navy, Air

4

The rise to the top: Career patterns

Politicians go to Canberra with images of future glory at the forefront of their minds. They have already fought their way through the process of party selection and electoral success. Now they start to climb the next ladder, through the ranks of the parliamentary party to the ministerial benches. Some (far more than many imagine) even dream beyond that, to the Lodge and the prime ministership. But then they are already some way up the ladder of success; arrival in Canberra is at the mid-point of a political career.

Not so the future departmental secretaries. Their reasons for joining the APS are diverse. Some had hoped it would anyway be temporary, to others it was just a job. In the beginning, most had few expectations of reaching the dizzy heights of departmental secretary. Yet gradually they rose from out of the ruck, were identified as potential stars and were eventually appointed to head a department. In this chapter we will look at the patterns of the careers of these departmental secretaries: why they joined, how they progressed and how they became departmental secretaries.

Joining the APS

Few of the secretaries joined the Commonwealth public service with the stated ambition of becoming a departmental secretary. Ambition came later, fuelled by experience and opportunity. In the 1940s and 1950s, many future departmental secretaries joined the APS for the most casual of reasons and their early progress was little planned. One started as a telegram boy at Strathfield post office. The postmaster encouraged him to do his leaving certificate at night and then his degree. In 1949 he was told by a friend that there were good opportunities in Canberra and he went there to see what he could find. Within 12 months he was responsible for setting up the private office for Robert Menzies after the 1949 election. Another joined Social Security in the late 1940s; he had wanted to be an industrial chemist, but travel to work had cut into his social and sporting life.

Encouraged by a family friend, he joined the public service. After 18 years in Queensland he had crawled up the ladder to a Class 5, only to be told by his superior, who was just 10 years older, that if he kept his nose clean, he could have his job when he retired. The offer, however well meaning, encouraged him to move to Canberra to seek better opportunities.

To others, the APS offered a means of earning a living when completing a degree, a temporary position while considering career options or security of employment. With memory of depression and war still vivid in everyone's memory, security had its clear attractions. One lawyer came to work in Attorney-General's as a temporary position in 1953. It was to be a short stint before he returned to the Bar in Queensland and his target was the Supreme Court; he stayed for more than three decades. He emphasised how small the service was then. Attorney-General's had a few dozen people and was located in West Block with several other departments, including Auditor General's, the Treasury, the Taxation Office, External Affairs and half the Bureau of Statistics. An economist 'came up without any real understanding of what the public service did or what government did or what I would be doing and with no expectation of staying in Canberra either'. Wartime service led to opportunities in the APS, some directly, others by accident. There were a few exceptions to these stories of casual, even accidental, choice. John Taylor 'felt public service was a vocation — very much like a religious vocation, that one had an obligation and indeed a duty, to serve the nation; what was regarded as public interest'.

Recruitment was spasmodic; it was spread around the state capitals. The move to the small city of Canberra often came after a few years as they rose in the departments. Talent was unevenly spread. There was a limit (never actually reached) on the number of graduates that could be recruited in any year. Women were almost entirely excluded; the marriage bar, which prevented any married woman holding a permanent position, was not removed until 1965.

Only in the early 1960s was there any systematic attempt to recruit graduates outside the Treasury and External Affairs arenas. Then several other agencies became active. One was the Bureau of Statistics, which began to recruit bright graduates under the leadership of its deputy Keith Archer. The first cohort included Mike Codd and Michael Keating, both later heads of the Department of Prime Minister and Cabinet and thus head of the APS. Later the same system drew Vince FitzGerald, Neil Johnston, Chris Higgins and Andrew Podger into the APS. Archer took the view, enlightened for the time, that if he drew in good people, some would stay with the Bureau and the APS would benefit from those who went elsewhere. It did. Yet even here the motives were varied. Keating did not join 'the public service to stay in the public service. I certainly didn't join with the intent of becoming secretary'. Rather he had lost a part-time job working as a groundsman at a golf course. He sought vacation work with the Bureau and they offered him a cadetship that allowed him to get married while still a student. Codd made a more deliberate choice:

> I was interested in the public sector and public policy at university. I suppose that came partly from the economics course that I did and some of the subjects in that course. So I was looking, not just at the Bureau of Statistics, at the time I was silly enough to have a go at Foreign Affairs as well, and fortunately I was too uncouth for them; people who played football and that also went in the local university college annual review as a ballet dancer didn't quite appeal to Foreign Affairs. So, I was looking at the public sector as an area where there was, by reputation, very interesting, challenging work. And certainly in those days, a lot of the departments were very active on campuses, coming around and talking about the career opportunities and the sort of work you would be doing and that had quite an impact, I think.

Codd and Keating represent a distinct trend: most future secretaries who joined the APS after them came directly to Canberra. They may have had postings elsewhere — often overseas in Foreign Affairs, at the World Bank and the OECD, or on secondment in Whitehall or Ottawa. But they had little contact with the state branches of departments. There were exceptions. Bill Gray, later head of Aboriginal Affairs, began his career in the Northern Territory in 1961 as a 19-year-old field officer; he had walked into the Welfare department and asked for a job. One asset he had was his football; the head of welfare ran a football team mainly for Aboriginal people and they needed some additional players. Gray met a lot of people in the Territory by playing football against them. He only transferred to Canberra 20 years later. Tony Ayers started work as an education officer in Pentridge Gaol, where he spent time teaching the illiterate to read and write (only to find one of his star pupils later returning convicted of forging and uttering, an early lesson in the unintended consequences of a successful public policy). He only shifted from the Victorian to federal public service in 1969, some way into his career. Some joined departments whose head office was in Melbourne, and later transferred to Canberra when all the departments were concentrated there in the 1970s. But more and more, the modern departmental secretaries were recruited by graduate schemes directly to Canberra.

Even recruits to these elite schemes had varied motives. A couple had completed their PhDs in science and were looking for jobs when there were no research opportunities. 'I think I probably joined the public service by accident,' one reminisced. Another, a Rhodes Scholar doing a doctorate in linguistics, had a lengthy lunch with his former professor who tried to persuade him to join the private sector. Perversely, the lunch had the opposite effect: he decided he wanted to become involved in public affairs, gave up his doctorate and joined the APS. Others, too, decided to give up academic pursuits for a life that was more relevant. Often the reasons were simply a matter of opportunity: they needed some job, saw the advertising around their university, the APS seemed interesting and they turned out to be good at it.

In some cases there was more deliberation. Thus a departmental secretary of the 1990s decided: 'I had a degree in economics and had a great interest in economic policy, and I think family background had pointed me a little more towards government than the private sector ... But I certainly has a great passion about economic policy and that was why I wanted to come and work in Treasury' (Higgins). Another wanted to do something about drugs and joined the Narcotics Bureau in Melbourne; when that job disappeared, the only alternative offered was a position in Foreign Affairs where his law degree was of use.

But many of these bright young graduates did not see themselves as joining the APS at all. They came to specialised units and saw a career there, particularly in Treasury or Foreign Affairs. These departments had their own graduate trainees and encouraged them to see themselves as different. The new trainees barely saw themselves as part of a wider public service. Graham Evans, for instance, became a Foreign Affairs trainee and only gradually became conscious of the broader public service environment.

But the great majority of future departmental secretaries had joined the APS by the time they were 30. Whether they had been recruited as a career or by accident, they found an environment in which they quickly flourished. Their talent was identified and they were on the way up. Again there are exceptions, but very few. Occasionally an academic transfers into the APS at a senior level, as Hugh Ennor did in 1967 and Richard Johnston in 1985, both to Education, or as Peter Shergold did a decade later to as senior position in PM&C, and thereafter to a departmental secretary job. Only one person, Charles Halton, has been recruited directly from overseas; Whitlam headhunted him in Canada to establish an integrated transport portfolio. State governments have sometimes been recruiting grounds for experienced managers, although not often directly to the departmental secretary level. The private sector has yet to provide a departmental secretary; a few have been recruited from that sector but they all had extensive public sector experience before they joined the private sector. The only possible exception is John Menadue, who had worked for Whitlam when Labor was in opposition and only had experience as a junior public servant.

But interest in the APS does not typically transfer into immediate ambition. Departmental secretaries were often remote figures, long dominant in the 1960s when there had been no great change of style or direction for two decades. Most of the recruits had only a generalised ambition to rise; the top was a long way off. To deny a driving ambition to be a departmental secretary might be due to modesty. But few will admit to an early determination to rise that far. Again there are exceptions. Roger Beale was the product of a public service family; he had read C.P. Snow's *Corridors of Power* when it was first published in the early 1960s and decided that Sir Hector Rose was an admirable figure worthy of emulation. When he became an administrative trainee, he was determined to become a departmental secretary. Some of those who were recruited after some years elsewhere in the workplace, often from overseas where they had worked for international agencies, quickly developed the ambition to head a department; in a sense they were already mid-career when they started.

But, in general, it would be wrong to paint a portrait of a group entering the APS with a single-minded determination to reach the top. The pyramid is high. Those who reach the top are few: how then do their careers progress?

Careers

There is no one route to the top of the APS. Australia has no equivalent to the French *grand école* through which almost all top administrators will pass. There is no identified fast stream, as there is for the British élite. Careers are fashioned far more by individual initiative. Sometimes progress will be assisted by a yank from above from patrons who appreciate their skills. The routes to the top have been varied. Within the last fifteen years, it has been possible for a person who spent 20 years in a Queensland branch of Social Security or joined as a field officer in Darwin to rise to the head of a department. But more recent patterns of appointment suggest that long service in a state branch outside Canberra will be the exception. More and more, departmental secretaries are recruited direct to Canberra, usually as graduates; their service will be almost exclusively there, unless they are able to spend some time overseas, on exchange or at one of the international agencies. It is, of course, impossible to paint an ideal course that people have followed, but there are some career features that recur often as departmental secretaries describe their careers.

Early exposure to the influential patron helps a career, both in terms of contacts and as a means of understanding the way that the system works. The administrative trainee scheme initiated in the 1960s to recruit talented graduates gave some of its members an initial advantage; it provided some central training and rotations around two or three departments where the newcomers could make contacts and see where their interests lay. The Public Service Board ran the program and often kept some of the better people for itself.

The benefits in the provision of a quick education in the intricacies of the political/administrative interaction could be immediate. One person had the advantage of working with Sir John Bunting:

> He called me in, gave me a Cabinet decision and the day's newspapers showing a cabinet leak and told me to come back at lunchtime and tell him the source of the leak. I got it wrong. But it was heady stuff for a trainee and a marvellous way to fix their enthusiasm (Williams).

Others were able to make contacts in the Public Service Board and the Treasury and then return there after their initial year of training.

One of the telling positions, an indicator that a person was well regarded, was to be appointed as a personal assistant to a departmental head. Working for Wheeler, Tange, Yeend or Codd was an early mark of success. It also provided an insight into the way that a departmental secretary worked, the pressures that existed and, above all, a broad view of the way the department worked. Inevitably the horizon of any policy adviser is circumscribed by the narrowness of the arena across which they operate; only near the top do the sections of a jigsaw begin to fit.

But much of the time the APS operates on a system of self-promotion. High-flyers are not so much directed through a well-defined structure as make their own way. In explaining their progress, the single most common feature was the need for connections; mentors, patrons, supporters, advocates — the titles changed but there was an appreciation that support and encouragement was essential. These mentors came in several forms, all in effect interrelated. Some encouraged people to apply for jobs and backed them when choices had to be made. Others were rung and told to apply for positions. Indeed, some departmental secretaries say that they have only ever applied for positions when asked. Some mentors have a reputation as being good to work for; talented people are keen to join them and in some cases only accepted a job because their boss was a person they respected.

A few names constantly surface in these discussions with the departmental secretaries. In the 1960s, Wheeler at the PSB and Westerman at Trade are commonly listed. In the 1970s, Bill Cole in Finance was seen as supportive and keen to develop talent. He wryly commented, when people opposed the appointment of Helen Williams to the Second Division: 'I appointed a woman. Somebody said it would be over his dead body, so I appointed her and he didn't die'.

Two names — Ian Castles and Tony Ayers — stand out among more recent appointees as departmental secretary. Ian Castles, both as a deputy secretary in Prime Minister and Cabinet and as secretary of Finance, was both mentor and preferred boss; he was regarded as intellectual, stimulating and supportive. He was not interested in management; even as a departmental secretary, he left the running of the department to his deputies. He would take on some intractable and large problem and work through it with a team of officers; he allowed people to have their say. More than anyone, he was responsible for collecting the economic talent that allowed PM&C to act as a counterbalance to the Treasury. When he had shifted there from Treasury, the transfer was seen as a surprise; PM&C had not previously been noted for its economic expertise. But his presence encouraged others to come. Visbord, Keating, Fitzgerald and Charles all worked under him there. Indeed, they went to PM&C largely because Castles was there.

Tony Ayers was seen as another who provided opportunities. Take this account:

> John Taylor, who was a commissioner of the Public Service board once said to me: 'If you had your choice, who would you like to work for in the public service?' I said: 'I've heard a lot about this bloke Tony Ayers; I'd like to work for him'. Taylor responded: 'Well, you'll need to go out there and get some real line experience in the not too distant future. Tony is a mate of mine; I'll organise it'. Taylor rang me up a week later and said: 'Ayers won't have you'. This was a blow of course and I said: 'Why's that?' He said: 'You've never delivered a bottle of milk'. I said: 'What does that mean?' 'Well, you've spent all your life in a central agency'. I said: 'That's why I want to get out'. 'Well, you get your own way out, that's your bloody problem' (Hawke).

But after he had two years in a line agency, Ayers was on the phone to offer him a chance and thereafter he only applied by invitation for specified positions that he got. In one case, when Ayers changed departments just as he had accepted a position there, there was some disquiet when he chose to immediately move on; he was reluctant to move so quickly, but it was all arranged between departmental secretaries and his transfer went through.

Another recalls:

> When Tony called me, he said; you are going to be a secretary one day; you're going to have to broaden your experience; if you stay in this place, you'll be deputy of Finance and then you'll be really locked in. You've really got to try something different. Come and join me (Podger).

Ayers was open about his approach: 'I'm a headhunter. I won't just wait for people to apply; I will go and talk to them and persuade them to apply'. In this he was very different from Castles; he was an energetic, enthusiastic person, brash, up front and down to earth. His irrepressible character, his willingness to delegate and his personal support made him a boss worth pursuing. Many who worked for him regard that support as crucial in their rise through the senior ranks. Both Ayers and Castles were seen as great bosses.

The secretaries of PM&C are often named as mentors too. In part, they sit in the crucial position as they are responsible for making the recommendations to the prime minister on appointments to departmental secretary positions, but they have also taken seriously their role as head of the APS with the responsibility to develop the next cadre of potential secretaries. PM&C has often been seen as a training ground for departmental secretaries — indeed, a substantial number have worked there. But the role of head of PM&C has often been more than just talent spotting. Those who are departmental deputies and who by then aspire to the top job may ask for an audience to discuss their prospects. Not surprisingly, almost all the heads of PM&C have a reputation for discretion, for playing their cards close to their chests. They may be helpful in their advice, but in the last resort they know that they cannot guarantee anything.

At times, careers may have been shaped by animosity. Not everything went smoothly. At least two people left the Treasury because they believed they had no future there while Wheeler was head of the department. In another case, an associate secretary left as soon as possible after the 1987 amalgamations when all the problems were heaped on the previous regime. In these cases, a change of department gave a new lease of life to their careers.

Being in the right place has always helped too. The significance of Canberra has already been noted. So too has the need to be noticed. Luck played its part; one person recalls that the minister took a dislike to the obvious candidate, so he was pushed into the position. As mobility increased and the notion of a generalist group became more distinct, so too did the advantages of being in sight. Experience in Treasury, later Finance, the Public Service Board and PM&C have always loomed large among the departmental secretaries; so has Foreign Affairs. In part, these departments recruit and keep the talented. In Treasury, it was argued that an officer stayed there until it was clear there was no future, and only then left to head some other, lesser place. Elsewhere, the progress was more two-way. Experience in Finance as a deputy secretary was regarded as valuable. PM&C gave an officer insights into the cabinet process and the problems of maintaining a whole-of-government view.

So did the Prime Minister's Office. Many career officials have had a stint there. Lansdown and Yeend served under Menzies, Wilenski under Whitlam, Rosalky under Fraser, Evans, Sedgwick, Coneybeare, Hawke and Calvert under Labor. One recalls that a minister had rung him to ask if he wanted to be a departmental secretary; he had said he would love to take it. But instead he was sent to be principal private secretary to the prime minister. It was not an entirely successful period; he was perhaps too much the public servant to fit comfortably in such a politically charged environment, but he reflects:

> I never regretted it from the point of view of the insight that I got into the private office and the way in which governments make decisions and how the system really works. Public servants rarely get the opportunity to see how it works from that point of view (Hawke).

There is always a potential risk for a senior official in working in a minister's office, and all the more so when working for the prime minister. Will the opposition regard such a move as an indication of partisan commitment? Perhaps a year or two is seen as reasonable, whereas more might be seen to be too much. It is difficult to tell. Fortunately — and properly — this secondment has not led to the automatic assumption of partisanship by later governments and several of those who have worked for the prime minister have been retained or promoted by a later government

Was there a central conspiracy by PM&C to colonise the departmental secretary cadre? There is a distinct growth in the number of departmental secretaries who have experience in the department of PM&C and in Finance. Yet the accusation is hard to sustain if the whole career of many departmental secretaries is taken into account. They do not fit into any conspiracy hatched in PM&C to dominate the APS. Rather, experience there can be interpreted as a necessary part of development to produce the next cadre of potential departmental secretaries. It provides experience at the centre where there is a need to see across the range of government responsibilities, and crucially gives ministers a chance to see them in action. Often the direct contact between ministers and senior officials is limited to their own departments and to those who help to service cabinet. They, not surprisingly, will choose those who they have seen in action, rather than a person who is recommended to them but whom they do not know. In 1993 a senior committee was created to plan the careers of those officers seen as having potential: did they need experience here or there, had they been too long in the one position? That process made explicit what had already been a matter of concern for senior officials: how deep was the pool of talent from which the next cohort of departmental secretaries could be drawn?

This picture may seem enclosed and cosy. Within a small group some are anointed for greater things. Departmental secretaries in their turn note those who helped them on their way. It is worth noting again that these people are the successes. Their route to the top was far from ordained. The hurdles they jumped, the challenges they overcame on the way were seldom easy. They were promoted because they delivered what was required and then got the breaks. Others were identified and fell by the wayside. Some left the service, took statutory appointments, chose not to seek further promotion or were finally deemed not good enough. For every successful appointee, there are many cases of thwarted and unsatisfied ambition, whether due to lack of talent, ill-chosen enemies or just sheer bad luck. The top levels of the APS are highly competitive, often ruthless. As one person suggested, merit might succeed up to the level of Division head, but 'after Division head, it is in the lap of chance and the politicians' (Charles).

Ambition

The departmental secretaries themselves will admit they were lucky. Opportunity called and they were in the right place. Many felt that most of the time they were too consumed with their existing challenges to think far ahead in their careers. Certainly, many of them initially did not intend to stay in the APS, seeing it as a temporary job; they just stayed and prospered. When asked when they first thought they might become a departmental secretary, several longstanding departmental secretaries denied that they had expected the promotion:

> I didn't at all. At no stage of the game would I have dreamed of being a secretary, and as for staying head of whatever it was, a number of departments including Defence, I would have laughed at you (Ayers).

> Oh I hadn't really thought about it. I didn't really think in those terms. I did think by the time I had applied for the deputy job in Finance, that it was time I became deputy. That was after eight years as an FAS (Keating).

In some cases there was even a sense of amazement:

> I have to say I am way beyond my ambition, never had an ambition to be a secretary, I never dreamt of being a secretary, but when the offer came, it was so gratifying to be offered a job at the top of your career structure. I didn't hesitate for a split second (Departmental Secretary 1990s).

At times, people noted that others anticipated their success before they expected it themselves and even then viewed the prospect with a degree of uncertainty:

> I didn't really think about the possibility that I might hold a senior leadership position in the public service. I guess I'd been in the public service a dozen years before I realised that was possible. There were a couple of things that brought it home to me. One was while I was working at the Embassy in Washington. I worked with two former Secretaries of Foreign Affairs who were ambassadors during the period I was there. I formed the view that with a bit more experience and maybe some exposure in different environments that that was an attainable objective. Also by that stage in terms of the promotion pattern through that department, I was in the top category, so clearly they had decided that I'd be one of the people with a better chance of being a high achiever, subject to what I did in the intervening period. Beyond that, I spent a period of time in Treasury and I worked in the PM's Office, and working in the PM's Department exposed me to all the department heads. I guess that reinforced the view that I thought I could do that job at some point in the future (Graham Evans).

> Many people seemed to think that I'd become a secretary years before, well a year or two before I ever conceded that to myself. And there were some signals I suppose that I should have been more alert to. But being a prudent, pessimistic, cautious fellow, I never really opened my mind to them (Mathews).

Is all this modesty credible? This is, after all, a group of high achievers, many of whom glisten with ambition and a desire to achieve. They climbed more effectively than their counterparts. Quite possibly it is, especially in the early years because the pyramid is steep and promotion uncertain. Most people who serve as a FAS in the key departments at a young age may think about the prospect, and even more so if they are a deputy secretary. 'I think a fair number of my peers would have said, he was always ambitious, but it wasn't my image of myself or what I was trying to do; I wasn't spending my time trying to position myself' (Podger). Many who are at that level never make the final step. Indeed, as the position of departmental secretary seems to be more burdened and less secure, so some of those at the level below are suggesting that they do not want the final promotion.

Some acknowledge their ambition. Not all the aspirants were as surprised at their promotion; to be a departmental secretary was a real target set early in their careers. One person tried to calculate the best route to the top: 'you see the competition and assess your comparative advantage'; even so, many of his moves were more a response to opportunities than the result of calculations. Another at the age of 31 set himself an objective: to be a departmental secretary by the age of 39 (Charles). (He had selected the target of 39 because he was working in PM&C and had heard of the example of Alan Brown who became head of PM&C at 39; he made it at 41). A third hoped to end his career as a departmental secretary because the pension would be that much higher. There is no shortage of the confident and the ambitious. Sometimes explicitly so, for others a more generalised ambition:

> I don't know that you actually set out to be a secretary, but you want to move up the line and there is an assumption that at the end of the line you become a secretary and that's the target (Volker).

Once they were there in a position of authority, they believed that they could actually influence the way things were done.

Selecting the departmental secretaries

Promotion to departmental secretary is never entirely predictable, either in its timing or its format. There is no single route or method of selection. Before 1987, the responsibility for making a recommendation lay with the chair of the Public Service Board. Prior to 1983, he would convene a committee that always included the departmental secretary of PM&C:

> The list usually had several names, though on one occasion there was only one and on another as many as ten. Sometimes we ranked the names, sometimes not. Twice that I can remember we were urged by a minister to name an individual we were not keen on. Once we refused and once, because we thought there was a case of sorts for the individual, we agreed. In the latter case Cabinet picked that individual who we had ranked last on our list.

> I usually sent the recommendation by courier. I remember once I handed it personally to the prime minister because they were in a hurry — he came out of cabinet to receive it. Normally I just sent

it over and waited to see what happened. We did not often follow up with a discussion. The relevant minister would sometimes ring. I was fairly careful then (Cole).

Of course, who else discussed the appointment with the prime minister is open to speculation. It seems likely that the head of PM&C continued to play a significant role.

Since 1987 there have been three players in the selection of the departmental secretaries: the prime minister, the secretary of PM&C, and the minister of the portfolio where the vacancy is. And finally, of course, there is the person who is being offered the position. The prime minister is always significant; no selection will be made without his approval and prime ministers have jealously guarded their rights to the final say. The secretary of PM&C must now be involved since a report has to go the prime minister. That report may or may not include a number of names; it is not required under the legislation, but some secretaries regarded it as a useful practice.

Ministerial participation may depend on the occasion. Directly after an election when the party has just won power, there may be little consultation. If there are machinery of government changes, then several departmental secretaries will be moved. Some may have their contracts terminated; others will be found jobs elsewhere. And all the changes have to be done in a hurry. Filling positions, whether those of ministers in cabinet or the departmental secretaries who support them, will be like fitting together a jigsaw; some pieces naturally fall into position, others take longer to find a niche. It all must be done quickly so that the new government can quickly hit its stride and implement its program. After the 1996 election, several of the new ministers had never met their new departmental secretary. The partnerships were determined at the centre.

To an extent, ministers may also be less heavily involved when there is a reshuffle of departmental secretaries during a government; at times, several may be moved simultaneously, whether to reduce areas of tension between a minister and departmental secretary, to improve performance in a department, to give an portfolio higher priority or to take advantage of the opportunity to rotate departmental secretaries towards the end of their term. The changes after the 1987 election were one such example. Ministers may be consulted about their preferences by the secretary of PM&C, but the need for a complex set of arrangements may mean that some do not receive their preferred solution.

When a single vacancy occurs in the normal process of government, ministers may have the greatest input. Some have views on who they want, others rely on advisers to point them in the right direction. Occasionally a minister may hold a series of interviews. Often the first a departmental secretary knew of the vacancy was when a minister rang to ask if they were interested in the position (presumably, but not always, after some discussion with the secretary of PM&C who provided a list of names). The more senior the ministers, the more likely it was that their choices would prevail.

What role did the potential departmental secretaries play? If the ambitious have their dreams, do they then have a choice about where they might go and which departments they might head? There are, of course, two sides: the qualities the selectors are looking for and what the candidates think they might want. Most aspirants thought they had very little choice in the initial appointment:

> To my knowledge people don't get offered alternatives. It's an offer that you can't and don't refuse ... In a very real sense it was a culmination of all that I'd ever done and aspired to in a career sense (Mathews).

> No, you're just told where you are going. I suppose there is an opportunity to say no, but then you would be stupid, wouldn't you? You wouldn't be thought of again (Volker).

> There was never, do you want to apply or are you interested. Lo and behold, I ended up with the job but there was never an approach, do you want to be a secretary or if you were which one would you want, none of that (Podger).

The experience could be abrupt. A departmental secretary was told by a PM&C secretary he had been selected and should go interstate in a hurry to see the minister. He said thanks but pointed out it was the eve of a holiday and all the planes were full. 'He said: "That's your problem" and hung up'. It was an interesting initiation, solved eventually by fixing up the details on the phone and arranging a later meeting.

In very few cases, people recalled that they had said no because they felt that their skills were not appropriate to the position. In other cases, seeing that a vacancy was about to occur, they tried to send out messages to show that they would like to be considered; whether that process had any influence is debatable. They got an offer, though there may be some doubt about how significant the initial feelers were. Some were concerned about whether they were ready for promotion:

> I had wondered whether I was ready. I had only been a deputy for a year. I didn't get a surprise; I was a logical appointment. But I was wondering whether I was ready (Keating).

A few people had sought discussions with the head of PM&C when they felt they might have been overlooked. In those discussions, they had mentioned the areas in which they might like to work. One at least turned down an offer in the hope, later satisfied, that he might be appointed in an area that he felt more comfortable in. But that was indeed very rare; half a dozen at most mentioned such a decision and sometimes then with encouragement from the centre that had other plans for them. Another was asked by a minister to head a statutory authority; he accepted and then was persuaded by the secretary of PM&C to change his mind in the expectation of better things to follow. Such career advice was most useful.

As an election neared, some departmental secretaries may have been asked where their interests lay. No promises were given; after all, the final decisions were made by the prime minister. But it did give the secretary of PM&C some indications of people's ambitions.

In part, the process of selection depended on the circumstances. When there had been a change of government, individual ministers were unlikely to know much about potential — at least not much first hand. There are few contacts between the opposition and the public service in Canberra. There may be — indeed, often are — a series of rumours about incumbent departmental secretaries, often to the effect that they are too close to their current political masters. These rumours are usually malicious and often wrong; sometimes they may be planted deliberately by other public servants. Some shadow ministers may have suggested that they did not want to work with the existing departmental secretary. But the choices at that time were likely to be in the hands of the prime minister. One exchange described by a departmental secretary illustrates how it works:

> I was sitting in the office on Friday after the election, about to go out to a regular lunch, when the phone rang and I was told the Secretary of Prime Minister's was on the phone.
> 'G'Day, Allan, Congratulations, on Monday you go to the new department of Transport and Regional Development. Be there at 9.00 a.m'.
> 'Can I ask some questions?'
> 'I suppose so'
> 'Who decided this?'
> 'None of your business'
> 'Who is the minister?'
> 'You'll find out this afternoon. Now, get off the phone, I've got other people to ring'.
> So I told my personal assistant: 'Get some boxes; we're moving to another department' (Hawke).

Just like that. Whether this is an accurate or a coloured version (as the secretary of PM&C insisted), the flavour is clear.

All positions have to be filled and in effect a jigsaw has to be completed with an appropriate person found for each position. It meant that, at a reshuffle, there was often little time for anything but agreement. On another occasion a departmental secretary recalls:

> My immediate reaction was 'Well, why me?' I'm just sitting here thinking about what I want to achieve next year in this department and I don't want to move. But I think it's beyond recall. So I thought: 'Oh well, if it's got to happen, it's got to happen' (Rosalky).

Others have felt that they were being shifted too quickly. Codd had only headed Community Services for a couple of years when he was asked to return to PM&C. After a career spent largely in central agencies, he did not want to move as he was enjoying the actual delivery of services. But he did, as he had felt it was useful symbolically. Having been pushed sideways in 1983 because it was felt he was too close to Fraser, it was a lesson that a public servant who continued to maintain the necessary standards could regain the confidence of a different government. Mike Keating did not want to shift to Finance at the time the offer came; the position had great appeal, but not then. He still moved. And he applied the same logic when he was secretary of PM&C; the general interest took precedence:

> Mike Keating rang me. I said to him: I'm not sure that this shift makes much sense; I have just got this job, just started to get an idea of where we are going. Wouldn't it be better if I stay where I am?' He made it abundantly clear it was not my decision. My thoughts on the issue had no bearing on the matter whatsoever. I moved (Podger).

Some were very relaxed. They regarded it as given that they would go wherever the government chose to use their skills, even when in one case a person was moved three times in a few days: 'Bill Cole asked me on the Friday what department I would like and I said: 'Look Bill, I've always said I will go wherever I'm sent, I won't express a view'. Then he was caught up in a constant reshuffle. 'On Thursday I was running Employment, on the Friday I was acting secretary of Defence Support and on the Monday I was appointed to Transport and Construction' (Rae Taylor).

The pattern is clear. The process is not a measured exercise in advertising, shortlisting and interviewing candidates; such formal processes were rarely used (and then sometimes most ineffectively when the successful candidate did not adapt to the demands of the job). Nor, of course, was it random. It was based on extensive experience of working at a high level with people over a long time. There were lists of those who were seen as suitable — unwritten maybe, but always in the minds of the prime minister and his department head. The actual process of selection reflects the environment into which the new appointees were thrown: rushed, ambiguous and demanding a variety of skills. Experience, not formality, was the test of the selection process.

It could also be unforgiving environment. There has only been one woman appointed as a departmental secretary: Helen Williams was made head of Education in 1985. Two years later she went on six months' maternity leave, returning just as the 1987 reduction in departments took place:

> Comments in Canberra quickly get back to their subject so it didn't take long before I heard that several fairly senior people in central agencies had said that 'she was given her chance; after this she'll never get another job'. Even some parts of the women's movement attacked me on the grounds that, by going off on maternity leave, I'd let the side down. Added to that, I came back from maternity leave in 1987 almost on the day that the 28 departments were amalgamated into eighteen. It was hardly surprising that I wasn't given one (Williams).

Perhaps the lack of an appointment at the time (she was promoted back to departmental secretary rank in 1993) was not surprising, but nor did the attitudes expressed reflect well on the acceptance of gender equity at that level.

For the chairs of the PSB or the heads of PM&C there is a different perspective; they have to advise the prime minister on the best people for particular slots. Many of those proposed the PM will not have met, or will only have seen briefly, particularly when there is a change of government. What do they look for? A chair of the PSB noted:

> A track record of good management, including people management, was usually the first criterion. Creative ability was highly desirable. Ability to both work within the system and work the system was important. Sometimes a person without top-level management skills would be recommended because they had exceptional creative ability, knew their management skills weaknesses and could delegate, and the department was one where the second level of management could supply those skills. You never find the perfect person and you have to decide how to weight the pluses and minuses. These might be articulated in our report so ministers could give their own weighting, plus bringing their own knowledge of the candidates to bear (Cole).

Mike Codd suggested:

> If you are talking about Treasury, then you're looking for somebody who is a quintessentially very highly respected economist — a person who is able to lead a group of professionals in advising

on tax policy, fiscal policy, monetary, etc. You know you want somebody who can command that respect and somebody who has the personality to work constructively with ministers, including their Treasurer, and to lead people generally — but not huge management strength. I mean the management strength is important but on the scale of things it's like two-thirds of the way down the list. If you're talking about Education or Social Security or huge program running departments or indeed Defence, then the leadership skill and experience in financial management of a very large organisation, they're up the top of the list. The policy — the personal policy capacity as distinct from drawing other people in to do the advising — shifts down to be two-thirds down the list. So it depends on the job, the portfolio — but fundamentally, you're talking about people who are committed professional public servants, who are, or are willing to be if they're from the private sector. And who will manage their way through the labyrinth of being a secretary (Codd).

Max Moore-Wilton sought slightly different skills of being a secretary.

You not only have to be a good policy analyst, you also need to be a good communicator and be able to show that you can run a well managed organisation which is, I think, a significant shift. There are generic qualities. Firstly they need to have a fair degree of common sense because you shouldn't be accident prone. You require leadership ability and need to be able to demonstrate that you can lead. You've also got to demonstrate that you've got some competencies which are relevant to the task that's going to be carried out. If you're going to be in an economic department, most of them now require some familiarity with economic framework. You've got to be able to show that you have been able to deliver outcomes — achieve tasks (Moore-Wilton).

Another secretary explained how they thought that skills should be developed:

Yes I think there are generic skills — which isn't to say there aren't specific skills which can be picked up in one portfolio, but they are — well I can make a distinction in policy management. In a policy sense I wouldn't argue that every secretary is a great policy adviser and a great manager. I wouldn't say that there is the expectation that every secretary does every job equally well, but there certainly is the expectation that within that theory of competence, if you like, they should be able to move, they should be able to manage, one place or another place, or should be able to provide policy advice in one place or another place (Stevens).

A minister had a slightly different perspective:

I look for a secretary who has a first-class capacity to contribute to policy development; who brings out the best in people well and who has an eye for ability and quality and brings that on in the department. And who is very alert to the government's agenda and is effective in bringing forward policy advice which clearly advances what the government is looking for in terms of policy outcomes.

When ministers are in office for a number of years, they are often more heavily involved in determining who the departmental secretary will be. After 1984, the requirement to consult the minister was included in the legislation. On several occasions under Labor, ministers were given a short list of potential candidates; they were then able to interview the select people and indicate their preference. How much influence the minister had would depend on their weight and seniority. When Keating was seeking a replacement for John Stone as Secretary of the Treasury in 1984, he asked the two potential candidates to write a 12-page essay on how they would see economic policy develop if they got the job. Bernie Fraser was selected that time and the other candidate, Chris Higgins, succeeded him five years later. When ministers changed portfolios, they sometimes tried to take their departmental secretary with them; thus Vince FitzGerald moved from Trade to Employment, Education and Training when Dawkins got moved to the larger department.

Political connections?

How far did political connections help in the selection of candidates for a departmental secretary position? There are two types of connection that can be noted: the clear links with the party in government and the links with a particular minister. There were clearly occasions when the party affiliation was useful. Menadue's appointment to head of PM&C was a consequence of his relations with Whitlam; he had only been a public servant for a few years at a junior level. So too were the promotions of Wilenski and Spiegelman; the latter had never worked in the APS. Wilenski worked as a departmental secretary exclusively for Labor governments at either state or federal levels. More recently, Peter Boxall's selection as secretary of Finance occurred when he was on the Treasurer's staff. He had earlier worked for opposition leaders Andrew Peacock and John Hewson, had been an SES officer in the Treasury and head of Treasury and Finance in South Australia. One person with political experience commented:

> There's no question that the fact that I'd worked with the Opposition ... in the federal government helped ... I believed I got it on merit, but there's no question that because they knew me,

because people knew of my work with the Liberal Party in Canberra, that I got it (Departmental Secretary 1990s).

In these cases, there were explicit links with the party. That is a contrast to those who were career public servants who were sent by their department to work on the staff of a minister or, more noticeably, in the Prime Minister's Office.

Several departmental secretaries had served on the prime minister's staff. Positions there vary. Sometimes the head of the office is a partisan appointment; on other occasions it may be a secondment from the APS and designed to keep the processes running smoothly. That was certainly the intention in the days before 1972 when the office had comparatively little policy impact. It changed under Whitlam. Fraser continued the practice of a substantial and powerful staff. Hawke's first office head was Graham Evans, whom he had met briefly in Washington. Later Coneybeare and Sedgwick served time there. Under Keating, Alan Hawke was briefly the head of office and Ashton Calvert a foreign affairs adviser. No one suggested that they were not career public servants and three of them have continued to serve and gain promotions under a Coalition government. They all went there as career public servants; the links between the public service and the Prime Minister's Office were seen as being crucial to the smooth running of government; the secretaries of PM&C saw it as essential to put good people there. It should not be surprising that several of them continued a successful career under another government.

Harder to categorise are those who are selected for their style. There is a legend that Margaret Thatcher used to ask before making an appointment as permanent secretary in Britain: 'Are they one of us?' The implication was not so much whether they were members of the Conservative Party, but whether they had a style that emphasised action. Similar comments can be made in the type of choices made of departmental secretaries at different times in Australia.

Alan Carmody, selected by Fraser to head PM&C in 1976, was a long-term public servant with a reputation for a can-do philosophy that emphasised getting the PM's wishes done (although that should not be taken to suggest he did not tell the PM what he thought at appropriate times). Perhaps that style is epitomised by a comment he made in the early 1960s to a group of his officials: 'I think my batting average is about 70 per cent; and on the 30 per cent where I'm wrong I just dig myself out of a hole as quick as I can'. That was taken by the listener as an important lesson on the need to keep the system moving. It was Carmody's approach to take risks to get things done. Max Moore-Wilton, appointed by Howard to the same position in 1996, had a reputation — epitomised by his nickname, Max the Axe — as a tough administrator. Both Carmody and Moore-Wilton were regarded by their prime ministers as suitable for the roles they had in mind for them. These types of appointment have been described by Richard Mulgan as a type of managerial politicisation. It allows the government to indicate its determination to appoint its style of people, possibly those who are identified with administrative or policy approaches.

It was always easy to be labelled as political even while doing a good job. Codd's career is instructive. He had been executive assistant to Sir John Bunting in 1972 when the Labor government was elected with grave suspicions of Bunting that were transferred to him. After a time in Whitehall, he was brought back to Canberra:

> I shall never forget going over there one day and I ran into Gough in the corridor of his office, and he paused and he looked at me and said: 'I hear you've been reconstructed'. So I mean, it's an interesting story because it does show that you can, even in those days, perhaps more so now, if you're intent on just being a good professional adviser and so on, your career can be brought to a very smart halt by some people forming a view that's based on ideology or misconception, and particularly by assuming some sort of political allegiance — which I've never had and still don't — to any party (Codd).

In 1983, he was pushed sideways into the Industry Assistance Commission by a Labor government suspicious of his close connection with Fraser before his appointment in 1981 as departmental secretary in Industrial Relations. In 1984, Yeend persuaded Hawke to bring him back to Community Services. By 1986 Hawke chose him as Yeend's successor in PM&C:

> It wasn't an easy decision; it wasn't something I said an immediate yes to. I needed to spend time thinking about that and talking to my wife about it before I finally decided it was probably the right thing to do — one of the reasons being, funnily enough, that I thought it would send a signal through the service that sometimes the vagaries of political leadership meant that you are pushed into the cold, but if you stuck to your last and just kept being a professional that could turn back again. So there was a symbolic significance, I think, about having been sent by Bob Hawke out to grass after three weeks and for him to actually draw me back. I thought that was quite an important thing for the service as a whole, not just for me personally. One of the reasons, I felt if I said no, it ran all the risks of getting out, as these things do, and it being a negative and indeed possibly making the Labor government feel they were right in the first place and that I was really not one of them (Codd).

Ironically, when Bob Hawke was replaced by Paul Keating in 1991, Codd offered to stand down. He had been the principal architect of the new federalism initiative that led to the special Premiers' Conferences and the later creation of the Council of Australian Governments, an initiative of which Keating had been very critical but on which he would energetically build. Keating accepted his offer.

One point of debate resulting from these changes is whether they will increase politicisation. The term 'politicisation' is itself contested. In 1989 I defined politicisation within relatively narrow parameters (Weller 1989a): politicisation occurs when appointments and promotions are motivated by party politics instead of the merit principle and when the public service is used for party purposes, as distinct from government objectives. Mulgan (1998), by way of contrast, has sought to broaden the meaning of politicisation. In addition to my definition, Mulgan identifies two other forms of politicisation. First, there is policy related politicisation where people are appointed because of their association with a particular policy position. And second, there is managerial politicisation. This is where incumbent public servants are replaced and new people appointed simply because a new government wishes to stamp its authority on the public service by putting in place its own personnel (Mulgan 1998: 7). What these cases have in common — and this is also Mulgan's justification for placing them under the politicisation banner — is that they undermine a secretary's capacity to serve alternative governments. The ability of a secretary to be employed by alternate governments, for instance, should not be confused with the issue of whether a secretary has been employed for partisan reasons or if she or he is working on behalf of the government. It is this sort of differentiation that Mulgan's classification blurs, yet it lies at the very heart of the politicisation label.

In assessing the period since Howard had come to office, Mulgan found that:

> [o]f all the new secretaries appointed [following the change of government in 1996] ... all were career public servants who had had successful careers under Labor (with the half exception of Paul Barratt who had left the APS in 1992 to work for the Business Council of Australia) (Mulgan 1998:4).

There are very few secretaries who have been appointed in the APS who do not fit this characterisation. Two notable exceptions are Wilenski and McGuarr, appointed under the Hawke Labor government, who had strong ties with the ALP. There is a popular impression that Max Moore-Wilton, employed by the Howard coalition government to the position of secretary in Prime Minister and Cabinet with the objective of reducing the size of the public service, would fit into this category. It is certainly the case that Moore-Wilton's identity as a secretary is tied to the Howard government and a specific set of policies which makes it highly unlikely that he will survive a change of government (Mulgan 1998: 5). He does not, however, have partisan links with the coalition and had been appointed in the past by the ALP in a senior position. If Moore-Wilton's appointment is problematic, this is due to a separate set of issues to those that would be raised if he had been appointed to this position because of his connections to the Liberal Party. In particular, the principle of merit is not challenged in the same way as it would have been had Moore-Wilton been appointed because of party patronage rather than his capacity to achieve a specific government outcome.

While Mulgan's broadening of the term 'politicisation' might be problematic, his approach does highlight those instances when appointments are made in ways that deviate significantly from what we would expect to find in a career public service. Furthermore, he provides a method of classifying these deviations. While Moore-Wilton's appointment is not best understood as an example of politicisation, Mulgan's argument that it is an appointment made with a specific policy outcome in mind is useful. Similarly, the Howard government's replacement of secretaries immediately after an election was not based on partisan politics and therefore does not classify as politicisation, yet it does represent an instance in which a government has employed a specific strategy in an attempt to increase its control over the public service.

Is there a better way of defining these types of appointment? One suggestion is that the desire to appoint people with whom the minister can comfortably work puts a premium on the personal characteristics and working style of the departmental secretary. As ministers become involved in the selection, so their opinion counts for more, particularly if they are senior. They may be looking for people who have policy views that are similar to their own, or the right style. In 1983, Mike Keating speculated that a possible reason for his selection as departmental secretary for the Department of Industrial Relations was that, at a sabbatical at the University of Melbourne two years earlier, he had written favourably about the benefits of a wages policy. Since most leading economists in the APS opposed a wages policy, that made him rare. Another departmental secretary argued:

> Ever since Whitlam, Labor and the Conservatives have tended to appoint people to be Secretaries of departments who were generally

supportive of, or at least accepted rather than opposed, the world view of the minister. If you have five or six professional public servants who have a range of views, you can appoint a good one who can do that. It's not as if they are political appointments of hacks. Rather, ministers have taken over more of the running of policies and thus want more hand picking of appointments. The pure Westminster version doesn't seem to fit the modern world (FitzGerald).

In many cases, the ministers did not know the departmental secretaries before they interviewed them. They had seen them in action or they had been recommended by the departmental secretary of PM&C. The interview was designed to get an idea of whether they could work together. Ministerial involvement might be on the increase, but for many it might only be of marginal significance. The removal of departmental secretaries will be discussed later, but there is enough evidence to show that the selection takes in a number of factors, which sometimes include a view of the minister.

The prime minister has defended the need for impartial advice as an essential value of the APS, but has added that, consistent with that end:

Any government must, and should, reserve the right to have in the top leadership positions within the public service people who it believes can best give administrative effect to the policies it was elected to implement. Governments of both political persuasions have recognised these realities (Howard 1998:8).

He is correct in noting the bipartisan attitude.

Could it be another way? In Canada, for instance, there is some evidence that deputy ministers (DM — the Canadian term for departmental secretaries) have been appointed by the prime minister because he did not trust the minister and wanted someone safe in the DM position to keep an eye on the minister. Indeed it was made clear to one deputy minister that that was why he was there. Such an appointment may be possible at state level in Australia where the quality of ministers is often low and where premiers tend to dominate their ministerial colleagues and the local politics to a greater degree than occurs in Canberra. It is not unknown in Australia, although it will never be announced in those terms. But there is no explicit evidence of such an appointment in Canberra. Nor is there a strong case for such an appointment as it might make life hard for both minister and departmental secretary. If the minister is to be involved, then some weight must be given to their opinion. How much depends on their position, on the strength of countervailing views, on the degree of support given by the secretary to one candidate or another and, of course, on the views of the prime minister. Some departmental secretaries are much more explicit: 'Every minister has a right to choose their secretary in consultation with the prime minister' (Departmental Secretary 1990s). Ministers were the customers.

What is clear is that, whatever the circumstances, the great majority of appointments still come from within the APS. There has, indeed, been much greater mobility between federal and state services in the last two decades, particularly as some states have offered much higher salaries, especially in public enterprises. Several senior officers just below departmental secretary level have shifted and in that area mobility is likely to increase more as the incidence of contracts expands. But the state services are only one source of loss of talent from the federal service. Many others are moving to the private sector at even greater salaries and prospects — some double their APS packages. If there is an image of a career that straddles the public and private sectors and sees a potential secretary going from public to senior private positions and then back as secretary after experience as a CEO, it is wrong. Indeed, it is most unlikely to happen. Secretaries are much less well paid than positions in the private sector, and anyway a person with experience running a substantial company will soon realise that secretaries are not CEOs because final decisions on policy will lie with the minister. Although there may be a great intrinsic excitement in the shaping of public policy, the personal and financial sacrifices will often be great. Nor is there a history of the successful shift of people with exclusively private sector experience into the public sector. In fact, the reverse is true. Most attempts have failed as the different requirement of accountability and politics make it hard to adapt to the more intrusive public sector reality. All secretaries have spent the substantial part of their careers in the public sector. That is unlikely to change in the future.

It is likely, though, that remuneration and other terms of employment will improve as compensation for greater insecurity. There is already evidence among Commonwealth agencies that, where executives have been headhunted, they have demanded remuneration and conditions beyond those provided in the standard package — and have been granted additional incentives.

Nor should the changes that have occurred be interpreted as a deliberate move towards the situation in Washington and be justified on that basis. Mobility there is commonplace. American business and universities work comfortably with the notion that senior executives move between the government and private sectors. Their Australian counterparts do not yet do this. Nor should debate on the need for constant changes at senior level to ensure the appointment of responsive officials be justified on the grounds that it is done regularly in the United States. Appointments of secretaries in Australia are made by the executive without reference to the legislature. It would be easy to appoint only party hacks, without regard to their expertise or professionalism. Executive power in parliamentary systems has few limitations in the shaping of the bureaucracy. By contrast, Washington has a number of safeguards that can protect the service from too many whimsical appointments. The Senate must confirm most senior appointments and thus ensure their suitability. There is also a much larger pool of talent to draw on, with almost an administration in waiting in the think tanks and universities. The contrast with the US practice is barely valid.

Before accepting the argument that partisan processes in the United States provide a model for Australian developments, there is a need for a careful debate on the benefits and disadvantages of those processes. The APS's practice is evolving slowly (unlike some state services where spurious tests of political reliability will undermine capacity). But if there are to be greater moves in the partisan direction, then the introduction of suitable checks and balances will need to be considered.

Implications

The significant point is the degree to which new styles of appointment have led to a different class of departmental secretary. Some clear findings can be made. Departmental secretaries still largely come from within the APS; even if more members of the service are leaving at an earlier point of their career, in search of the better benefits that come from the private sector, there remains a pool of talent still capable of providing good people, though some question whether that pool is being replenished adequately.

Most of those who come through to be promoted to departmental secretary have now had a career spent mostly in Canberra, sometimes with a period overseas. It is unlikely that many new appointments will have been working in the regions for 20 years or in the field in the Northern Territory. Such people, already rare, will become more so. Careers are narrower, more circumscribed.

There is some increase in ministerial involvement in the selection of departmental secretaries — indeed, since it has been included in legislation by both sides, that involvement can be seen as bipartisan and unlikely to be reduced. The change should not be exaggerated; it is difficult to imagine a McEwan or an Anthony not making their own choices. Junior ministers will usually accept whomever the centre of government proposes. Only after an election, when several changes need to be made in a hurry, will the interests of the whole override the wishes of the particular minister. The selection may still be regarded as a process of anointment, sometimes mysterious, often opaque. But there are more actors involved now and at least there is a process that needs to be followed.

A departmental secretary was cited as suggesting that Westminster did not apply in the modern world. Certainly the system of selection is more inclusive than in London. The characteristics of a successful departmental secretary may be changing somewhat as personal style that makes the minister feel comfortable becomes a significant factor in their selection and, as we will see, their possible removal. But there are still some common characteristics: they are public service careerists, male, Canberra based and reared, ambitious high achievers. They do not fit a neat disciplinary background, and are not chosen through any *grand école*. They do not have a common social background. They are selected because they offer the promise of a good service to the minister. The question, then, is whether those factors have changed the dynamic of the relationship between the departmental secretaries and their ministers.

5

Advising ministers: From monopoly to competition

Ministers are the focus for much of the life of the departmental secretary. Some ministers may be a delight to work for, giving direction, leadership and weight to the department; others may have to be led carefully, even rescued daily. Regardless of their talent, the role of the departmental secretary is to advise the ministers on policy matters and to be responsible 'under the minister' for the general management of the department. The words 'under the minister' were added in 1984 to emphasise the constitutional seniority of the ministers. Ministers may play a part in the appointment of departmental secretaries and can certainly influence their continued employment. Talk to any departmental secretary and they will explain how significant this relationship is. Whether the interviews were undertaken 20 years ago in the late 1970s or in the late 1990s, the centrality of the minister was always there.

Perhaps the first classic statement of the position of the departmental secretary was given by Sir John Crawford in 1955:

> In order to best assist the Minister, the civil servant must give honest opinions and advice drawn from all the relevant data he can muster. If that advice be accepted, well and good. If, and I remind you, the responsibility is his and Cabinet's, a Minister rejects advice given in good faith, the role of the Permanent Head includes the final duty: to pocket his own prejudices and judgement and to make the policy, adopted by the Minister and Cabinet, work to the best of his ability (cited in PSB 1974:30).

> Since even within a department views differ, the Permanent Head must accept the responsibility for final advice to the Minister. Pros and cons: yes; but come off the fence, too. It is the Permanent Head who takes the jump. True, the Minister finally may decide not to jump on his side: it is the task then of the Permanent Head to accept the situation, climb back over the fence, and loyally support his Minister (cited in PSB 1974:35).

This formulation of the relationship was written at a time when the influence of the mandarins was reputedly at its highest. Crawford was and remains a man of the highest reputation. But often in those days there was a single channel of advice to the minister through the departmental secretary.

However, there is another view, expressed by a minister with long experience of government, that emphasises change more than continuity:

> There has been a transition over 25 years from the final days of an imperial public service to a public service which is focused on policy advice and service contracts, as an enterprise operating in a competitive environment where governments have alternative sources of advice and service provision ... it was an institutional struggle between the democratically elected governments and the public service for control over the public service. And in that struggle the elected governments have won.

The emphasis is on governments, rather than any single government, and it gives the initiative firmly to the elected. The question then is: to what extent has the relationship changed? What are the implications of any change? At the core is the increase in the competition to be heard, a competition that has removed the monopoly of the APS as policy advisers and challenged the notion that their expertise should be either given precedence or even be listened to at all.

Establishing a partnership

Departmental secretaries will often refer to their operations as a partnership with a minister. But many of those partnerships are fairly short. Table 5.1 illustrates the point. Over 80 per cent of the partnerships lasted less than three years, or one term of parliament. About a third lasted less than one year, as ministers and departmental secretaries were shuffled between positions, as machinery of government changed and as governments rose and fell. Of the 61 that lasted more than four years, 40 can be found in the Liberal governments of 1949 to 1972. They can be found across a range of portfolios and reflect the stability of a settled cabinet, long-serving ministers and the extended tenure of senior officials. Life was settled and often comfortable.

However, after 1972 that pattern was broken forever. The only partnership that lasted more than five years in the Fraser government was that between Doug Anthony and Jim Scully (although the caretaker government of one month in 1975 inflates the short-term partnerships and makes the government appear more unstable than it was). In the post-1983 Labor governments, Paul Keating and Bernie

Table 5.1 Partnerships between ministers and departmental secretaries by length in years (rounded percentages in brackets)

Years	Total	Coalition 1949–72	ALP 1972–75	Coalition 1975–83	ALP 1983–96
0–1	205 (35)	65 (29)	40 (56)	63 (48)	37 (25)
1–2	162 (28)	59 (26)	13 (18)	28 (21)	62 (41)
2–3	110 (19)	40 (17)	19 (28)	27 (20)	24 (16)
3–4	44 (8)	24 (10)	0	7 (5)	13 (9)
4–5	26 (4)	10 (4)	0	6 (5)	10 (7)
5+	35 (6)	30 (13)	0	1 (1)	4 (3)
Total	582	228	72	132	150

Fraser in the Treasury, Bob Hawke and Mike Codd in PM&C, and John Button and David Charles in Industry lasted for five years. (Ralph Willis had Mike Keating as his departmental secretary for five years, but over two departments and with a substantial gap between the two periods.) All were senior ministers. In the four- to five-year range again, most of the partnerships were with senior ministers too, and two of them with prime ministers. In these cases, it was unlikely the ministers were going to be moved from their favoured position and, as long as they were continuing to work well with their secretaries, change was less likely to occur. In the long-standing cases above, one departmental secretary chose to retire at 55, two sought and took other government positions and in the final case, Hawke lost his position and thus terminated the partnership.

If some ministers were able to keep the same departmental secretary for a time, in other cases departmental secretaries were faced with a moving kaleidoscope of ministers. The most extreme case was Sir Richard Kingsland, who was a departmental secretary from 1963 to 1981; in that time, he served thirteen ministers. His departments were seen as junior (Interior and Veterans Affairs) and represented the first position for many ministers who were often impatient to be promoted to departments they perceived as more interesting. Sir Arthur Tange was departmental secretary from 1954 to 1966 and then from 1969 to 1979 and worked for four Ministers of External Affairs and six Ministers of Defence. Bob Lansdown worked for nine ministers over three departments. In more recent times, Tony Blunn and Graham Evans had to support eight each and Evans was a departmental secretary for only nine years. Tony Cole, as secretary of the Treasury, had four Treasurers in six months in 1991. Further, these figures refer only to the portfolio secretaries; after 1987, departmental secretaries also often had to deal with junior ministers, not all of whom were intent on providing support for their senior colleague, yet they all needed to be serviced in the way they found comfortable; given these additions. Evans may have dealt directly with 12 or 13 different individual ministers in those nine years.

The two figures, on the limited period of most partnerships and the regular turnover of ministers that some departmental secretaries must accommodate, have some obvious consequences. It is often difficult to build up a partnership when there is such a regular change of people. If each time the minister or the departmental secretary changes, a new confidence has to be negotiated, then in some areas that process of negotiation is almost continuous. No sooner have working arrangements been established than one partner moves on and the process must be begun again. If trust is to be the crucial factor in ensuring that the processes of government work smoothly, then it is hard won because of the frequent changes.

There is a further challenge for departmental secretaries. The more ministers are served, the more likely it is that at some stage the departmental secretary will work with a minister with whom trust is difficult to build. It may be a matter of personality rather than competence. Two people may get on one another's nerves or may be unable to find common ground for discussions. Sometimes a departmental secretary who can work for almost everyone else finds that their approach and style is suddenly wrong. Some ministers are just difficult to please because they do not like what they get but do not know what they want, and consequently trouble ensues. These departmental secretarys may envy the colleague with a long-term and settled partnership with a senior minister, but must do the best they can. Regular change makes it hard.

In each case, it is the departmental secretary who is likely to adjust, not the minister. Departmental secretaries must work to develop a sense of trust. The task for the departmental secretary starts as soon as the minister is appointed:

> When a new minister arrives, your antennae are up and you are learning about that person in every depth that you can. There is a lot of judgment that needs to be made, not just judgments about interpersonal relations, but shades of gray in policy advice and how to communicate unpalatable advice (Mathews).

It is the minister who determines the structures of the relationship. The way they are briefed, the style of presentation, the frequency of the meetings will depend on their interest and skills:

> It's up to the secretary to make sure he has a personality transplant if he needs one to get on with the minister. I think the last thing any head of department should do is try and convert a minister to a different style. I mean if the minister prefers to deal with things face-to-face, you respond to that. If they prefer not to see you unless there's a piece of paper in front of them you respond to that (Codd).

> You adjust — you quickly pick your markers to what their style is (Ayers).

> The psychology of working with ministers is extraordinarily different. There are some ministers who don't want much paper for example, they'd just like to have a chat about things. There are some ministers who really like paper, you know, like lots of paper and they like to sit down and read and they like to do things on that basis. So if ministers want paper, you give them paper as long as it's reasonably clear what you want out of them. And there are some ministers who like to have a chat about how things are going so you usually have a regular meeting (Volker).

Without a working relationship, it is difficult to make the system work. This point was constantly emphasised. In some cases, the two would sit down to discuss the way that the minister liked to work and have meetings once or twice a year to review progress. In others, the adjustments were made on the run, as the departmental secretary learnt the minister's preferences. Sometimes a departmental secretary might ring the counterpart from the minister's former department to gain some ideas about the best way to serve and, in addition, to learn of any idiosyncrasies that the minister might have.

Consequently, there are no guidelines that can determine how often a departmental secretary should see the minister. A few will have a regular weekly meeting:

> I had an arrangement with all the ministers I worked for that we would get together on an informal basis usually once a week during parliamentary sittings and at other times when the minister was available in Canberra. I would have my list of things to talk about and he would have his. Either of us could include other people for some or all of the meeting. I could promote the things he wanted to do along with some of the things that I wanted to do. I would hope that the minister would tick off some of mine when I had already ticked off some of his. It was, of course, not unusual for other meetings to take place on specific current isues of relevance to the portfolio on an as-required basis (Tanzer).

They may speak once or twice a day on the phone, to answer a query, to provide an opinion, to make a point. Others would meet as required; they wanted to avoid the danger that a meeting became routine and that ministers might find them a nuisance. They met seldom and briefed primarily on paper. How dependent a minister is will depend in part on the experience they have. A departmental secretary who usually had novices as ministers argued that he tried to contact them quickly after their appointment to persuade them not to speak to the media until they had been briefed on the functions and problems of the department. Inexperience can lead to reliance, as ministers unaware of the details of the portfolio, combined with the nervousness that comes with a first appointment, seek a crutch to support them. That problem may have been alleviated by the machinery of government changes of 1987. Now most portfolio ministers have some experience in a junior position, where they must work as part of a team under a senior colleague.

The style of the departmental secretary may have been significant too. Some see themselves as crisis managers and will be in and out of the office. Others want to think about longer term issues and will see the minister only when one side deems it necessary. Ministers may not be so set in their ways that they can work with only one type of secretary. They may be happy to adjust to different styles too. Peter Walsh notes that, even before he was sworn in as a minister, his departmental secretary was on the phone. He compared the style of his first two departmental secretaries:

> Alan [Woods] was an activist Secretary, in my office with other officials about twice a week, and on the phone in between. (By contrast, the next Secretary I had — Ian Castles in Finance — I hardly ever saw) (Walsh 1995:81).

It did not appear to undermine his effectiveness as a minister. Both sides of the relationship could adjust. What mattered was what worked.

The hardest time, of course, is when a new government is sworn in. The political turnover is now so high that few incoming ministers have previous experience. In 1983, only Bowen, Hayden, Uren and, for three weeks, Keating had prior ministerial experience among the Labor ministers who had lost office in 1975. In 1996, Howard and Moore were the only survivors of the Fraser cohort. Every new government brings with it a suspicion that the departmental secretaries were too close to their predecessors, that they had become Labor or coalition puppets. These suspicions are usually based on nothing but rumour as there is often little contact between the opposition in Canberra and the senior officials who are, after all, serving their political opponents at the time. One departmental secretary who had worked for a time for the opposition noted that he never saw his public service colleagues and that the two worlds, of public service and opposition, never met, except perhaps in parliamentary committees where they were arguing the case for the government. When a new government is elected, departmental secretaries have to work hard to illustrate their credentials as non-partisan officials. A few are not given the chance; they will be shifted or terminated as the new government is sworn in. The others will meet the new ministers for the first time in the days after the election.

They ought to be well prepared. Departments prepare a brief for all eventualities: for the return of the same minister, for the advent of a new minister when the government is returned and for a new minister from a new government. In the last case, the department will have trawled through all the statements of the opposition leader and shadow spokespersons to see what the party proposed to do in office and then present the new minister with a set of proposals about the best way to implement those promises. New ministers have often commented on how impressed they were by these briefings, and the constructive support they received on their arrival to the office, particularly as they had believed that the officials really supported the other side.

It is, of course, just the first stage of an elaborate and necessary 'courting' of the ministers as the departmental secretaries prove by their support that they are professional public servants who are non-partisan. To be professional and non-partisan means simply that they are prepared to serve any elected government to the best of their ability. They are not neutral between government and opposition; they will serve the people the electors choose. Most ask to be given the chance to illustrate that they are perfectly capable of working for the new government. Proving their competence, showing that the senior officials have something they can add, takes time: they must learn the style of the ministers even while quietly training them in the demands of government and the requirements for running a department with its constant flow of decisions, delegations and meetings. The rhetoric of opposition does not prepare them for the daily rigours of office; in that, the departmental secretaries must be a help and a guide, while never overplaying their hand.

Eventually the level of trust will depend on the two people. Effective departmental secretaries have served ministers with very different styles. Conversely the same minister may be comfortable with two departmental secretaries who approach their task in different ways. Good relations are an unquestioned asset in making the process work:

> I suppose it's always been the case that the relationship between a permanent heads (as we were then called) and the minister is a very important one. How well it works depends on both of them as individuals, and particularly on the chemistry between them (Castles).

> Look, the relationship between department head and minister is essentially a personal one. If you can't make that personal relationship work, you are not going to get anywhere (Blunn).

> I think a key to performance for a secretary is the relationship they have with their minister and if that relationship is not based on trust, if the minister does not have trust in your judgment and ability, then I think you can't perform effectively and therefore I think you go (Shergold).

Some doubt whether that early level of trust still exists. Menadue tells of the time he briefed the opposition party room on immigration policy:

> The Minister didn't think it necessary to send along one of his personal political staffers to check on what I said. Things have changed now. Trust is not the same (Menadue 1999: 222).

But being close should not mean becoming to close. Often departmental secretaries felt the need for some continuing formality:

> He said: 'I want you to call me Tom'. I said: 'Well, Minister, there will be occasions in public places where it would be appropriate to call you Minister'. He said: 'I want you to call me Tom'. I said: 'Yes, Minister' (Departmental Secretary 1985–95).

Another said it was not necessary to be 'bosom buddies, but they did need to understand each other'. Many had a preference for retaining a degree of formality, particularly in public where the minister was only ever called 'Minister'. If that kept the departmental secretary at a distance, then so be it. 'A departmental secretary has a lonely job. Those who are good keep it lonely'. Wheeler explains the way he saw it:

> The Permanent Head should also remember that with the passage of time, he will be required to serve another minister either because of ministerial reshuffles or changes of government. For me, it follows that a permanent head should never fall into the role of medieval courtier; instead he should take the role of loyal baron. He should avoid fraternising, should maintain an appropriate degee of aloofness and always ensure the obsevance of due process (Wheeler 1980:171).

That relationship, after all, provided the foundation on which policy advice could be offered with a degree of objectivity and authority.

There were views on what made a good minister. Ministers 'must have ears' and be prepared to listen. Another identified the best ministers as those:

> who delivered; they can actually deliver so that they can get cabinet to agree to the things that are important to them; that they can

articulate what's important to them, they can give you a stong
message about what's important; that they will listen to you, that
they will tell you why they disagree with you and where they
disagree with you. And then in the last resort loyalty is a two-way
street (Blunn).

Consistency was particularly desirable:

> Because you knew where he was and the mental process that got
> him there. He would say what he wanted, he would talk about
> what he hoped for, you could interpret with certainty ... if you
> saw him going down the track you knew it was totally predictable
> without reference or twittering (Scully).

The same departmental secretary also noted the potential problems:

> I would hate to be a permanent head in a bad relationship with a
> minister. All of us have relationships that were indifferent or less
> than you'd hoped for, but I think if a senior public servant has a
> bad relationship with a minister there's only one thing to do. You
> go for the door, not him (Scully).

But he was talking of a period when there were possibilities of
alternatives. That bad relationship might be even harder to take if
the consequence was dismissal. Even so, there are not many obvious
examples where departmental secretaries have fallen on their swords,
even if some may have opted for an early retirement.

Some ministers were hard to work for. They might never make
decisions. They might distance themselves from anything
controversial to leave themselves the ability to deny they had ever
given the idea support. They might just be inconsistent and hard to
pin down. One account can give the flavour:

> XX was a man for the day, whatever happened on the day you ran
> with it and he had people around him who effectively spoke on his
> behalf in relation to policy. Which is a bit frustrating for us. We
> prefer to get that from the minister, rather than his advisers. There
> was always someone at [his] elbow or someone at the door who
> was a gatekeeper, whom one had to convince to get a direct
> discussion (Gray).

Another minister with whom the same departmental secretary had
to deal was:

> Impossible to deal with, totally unpredictable, erratic, someone
> driven by what I always saw to be totally impractical and often
> incomprehensible motivation. Extraordinarily difficult to work
> for. Ring every hour with new priorities (Gray).

The qualities of ministers are always variable. There is nothing new
about that. Hasluck commented that 'the major weakness in

constitutional democratic government in Australia during the 30 years or more during which I observed it at close quarters is in the quality and capacity of ministers' (cited in Tange 1982: 9). Many of them are not appointed for their talent but for factional or representational reasons. Every ministry has a number of duds, a fact that can influence the appointment of departmental secretaries and the ministers' influence over their appointment. Tange looked back over his career with a degree of realism:

> In my short or long experience with each of about 20 ministers or acting ministers, I found not every one was as competent as the theorists seem to suppose at defining what the government policy was to which I should work. Some needed occasional reminders of what their own cabinet, or what the prime minister had been saying. While one would forbid any departmental action until directed, discourage policy suggestions, and remain relatively inaccessible, another was almost excessively available to give decisions provided the department came up with the policy proposals. Another left much doubt whether he understood what was put to him and was correspondingly ambiguous in his policy and managerial directions. Contrary to theses popular with some reformers that all options must be presented, one minister complained about the practice as confusing and asked for a sole recommendation. Some were impetuous with decisions, others vacillating. Some were considerate about and cooperative with other ministers concerned with a field, others were all-possessive. One was not a little frivolous. Few read serious periodicals in their field. Capacity to read and absorb varied greatly. What to one would be enough material short of 'snowing' him, to another would represent wrongful withholding of needed information (Tange 1982:10).

That range of ministerial styles and abilities should never be forgotten in discussing the way that departmental secretaries interact and the conditions under which they work.

In one area nothing has changed or is likely to. Ministers must hold their own in cabinet, they must stand on their own. No amount of good advising, no coaching, can take the place of an effective minister. Give me a winner, a minister who delivers, was the constant demand. One statement from a 1990s departmental secretary can stand for the unanimity of opinion:

> If your minister can't win in cabinet, you're at a real disadvantage. I can make up for a lack of political weight to some extent, but cannot fully compensate. I can work the secretaries' network; I can make sure our processes are fine; I can encourage the minister's office to talk to counterpart ministers' offices. But in the end the door closes as the minister goes into the cabinet room.

So say they all. It is entirely appropriate, too, that the ministers should stand on their own. That is why they have the final word. It does, however, starkly show the limitations on the departmental secretaries' influence.

The end of the imperial bureaucracy?

Ben Chifley had his 'official family', a group of public servants, 'perhaps a dozen senior officials and nearly as many fast-rising younger men' (Crisp 1963:257). Not all were departmental secretaries. They provided advice and support. The prime minister gave the group a sense of identity. Menzies had 'the boys', another inner group with whom he worked closely, often including the same people as Chifley's advisers (Bunting 1988:96–127). He told his new ministers: 'Make use of your department. You should not be the prisoner of their advice, but if you go ahead without knowing what the advice is, you put us all at risk' (Bunting 1988:59). These groups may have been in part a product of the time; there were few people living in Canberra and they could provide both intellectual and social solace to a prime minister marooned there. Nevertheless, such an arrangement would now seem inconceivable: prime ministers would not have a key group of advisers so clearly identified. Nor is it likely that they would be reliant on such a group drawn from across departments for much of their policy advice. Times have changed.

So perhaps has the style. One future departmental secretary went to a meeting with Harold Holt with Sir Henry Bland:

> 'Now listen here', said Bland to the prime minister! That was described to me as how you have got to deal with the minister; you just got to tell him (Rae Taylor).

It might have been a matter of age and longevity in those days. As one departmental secretary notes, in the 1960s:

> Older secretaries had ministers who were younger than them and who they could subtly be paternalistic towards, unless they got a really strong character like Malcolm Fraser. Later governments were comfortable having people who were relatively young and inexperienced (in the worldly sense in which the Geoff Yeends were experienced), but nevertheless able to run important parts of government (FitzGerald).

Few departmental secretaries now would describe a minister as a delight because 'he let me do what I wanted'.

There is a need to be careful not to create caricatures in describing these earlier periods. As Bunting said in 1988, while systems will change, there should be 'one article of faith for governments: that their predecessors were not only not necessarily imbeciles, but almost certainly were not. Therefore their ways and ideas deserve study and understanding and not simply the waste paper basket' (Bunting 1988:68). He was clearly applying the comment as much to his successors in the public service as to governments. They may have been men of their time, but there are new demands, both up and down.

Earlier departmental secretaries could be 'more imperious in nature because public service culture was more traditional ... it was a reflection of a different Australia, where to an extent they reflected a relatively small minority of well-educated people operating in a strict hierarchical framework outside the professions' (Moore-Wilton). Talent was limited. In those 'good old days', said one cynically, 'one or two secretaries were top of the pile, knew it and kept everyone in place. But the problems were lesser and did not seem to matter so much. If there was that kind of set-up now, when everything's so much more complicated, it would be a horrible mess, it would just not work' (Fraser). Of course, those secretaries would doubtless have adjusted too to the new demands and conditions, but at the time their position was strong. Ministers also were more limited in their education and perhaps less able to challenge the expertise of their officials. There was an acceptance that, at the end of the debate, the experts had the techniques and knowledge that should prevail.

That belief gave power to the technocrats, to the permanent advisers. That culture has largely gone. Expertise is no longer given such predominance. A greater breadth of opinions and wider educational backgrounds have provided a basis for the challenge. An ingrained scepticism of the experts, based on an appreciation of the values that underlie expert solutions, and on the failures of policies based on their advice, have undermined the position of the mandarins.

There is now a change in approach, too:

> The whole concept of the public service as the partner of the government, rather than now as the servant of the government changed. I don't think a lot of public servants think they owe very much loyalty to the public service (Blunn).

The change can be reflected in two areas in particular: policy advice and the growth of the ministerial office.

The policy advice they want or the policy advice they need?

Departmental secretaries in the 1970s were inclined to preface their discussions on relations with ministers with the comment: 'I believe in the Westminster system. Ministers make policy; public servants implement it'. By the 1990s, the evocation of the Westminster system might have been less common, but the sentiment continued. Indeed, it was expressed with even greater force, coupled with a scepticism that their predecessors were giving lipservice to a distinction they did not practise.

But what of the stories of that imperial bureaucracy? The most frequent target of criticism was the Treasury, which had built up a reputation for providing the 'right' advice and no alternatives. Let Treasury officers speak for themselves. One recalls that the Treasury challenged the right of other departments to give economic advice:

> Wheeler took the view that a department should speak with only one voice. In the interdepartmental debate that preceded the run-up to the November 1974 economic statement, he set out to prove that PM&C had three different opinions: those of Fred Gruen, Austin Holmes and myself. This may well have been true in that the three of us hadn't bothered to develop a common position; we saw the presentation of our somewhat differing views as providing alternatives and as assisting the debate. It was my impression that Fred did not realise that his success in proving that PM&C advisers were not unanimous only served to increase Whitlam's concern that the Treasury's advisers always were. I believe it was the presentation of a single view by Treasury, as if it were the only possible view that an intelligent person could take (or, if there were other views, that it was preferable that ministers not know about them) that upset the prime minister. He believed that well-informed experts would inevitably hold differing views, and wanted these to be exposed and debated (Castles).

Another was disillusioned when he got close to the top of Treasury: 'It wasn't the Westminster image of frank and fearless advice and integrity in dealing with one's colleagues'. The backstabbing 'destroyed my starry-eyed concepts of all the Westminster tradition'. Treasury options were as much to preserve the 'policy of the Treasury as to assist the government of the day' (Fraser). That conclusion can be documented in an account of the 1974 budget, where the Treasury sought to persuade the government to adopt a particular line by giving only one set of figures and then provided no help when the government chose not to adopt the advice proffered (Hawker *et al.* 1979:Ch. 9). There were seen to be some problems with the advice, but there were not often powerful Treasurers either. Bad habits were easy to develop. Malcom Fraser's response was to split the Treasury in 1976 in order to provide an alternative source of economic advice.

The acknowledgment that ministers must have the last word is of course standard. In the comment of Sir John Crawford with which this chapter begins, it is the departmental secretary who climbs over the fence when he and the minister disagree about the preferred policy option. Given that he worked as departmental secretary to Sir John

McEwan, the dominance of the minister is not surprising. It is, further, never asserted that ministers make policy on their own — that could lead to a series of disasters as they often know little of the subject when they begin in a new portfolio. Rather, it is a combination of minister and advisers who develop policy in an iterative interchange, with the proviso that where there is a difference of opinion the minister's view stands.

For that process to work effectively, the departmental secretaries must be able to argue with the ministers, to take them through the strengths and weaknesses of the options and, where necessary, to point out why the minister's preferences are likely to come unstuck. There is a difference between arguing a case and being obstructive. That is why there must be a sound relationship between minister and departmental secretary. Only when that is achieved can a regular and free exchange of views take place. The essence of the relationship was the belief that the departmental secretary was there to help the minister and the minister knew it:

> If a minister knows that you're trying to be instructive and helpful on a whole range of other things and then you walk in the door with a problem, then you're entitled to a reasonable hearing. If you're all the time turning up telling them they can't do this or their policy on that is wrong and you don't have any suggestions about how to tweak it so that it's better ... If you've built that kind of relationship then obviously you would suffer. You wouldn't be able to effectively raise issues like that (Codd).

> You clearly have to try to develop a relationship which is going to be cooperative and constructive and usually if you've got that sort of relationship as well, you can say 'Look Minister' (and I've always referred to them as ministers in official relations I must say, even though you knew them well but always call them Minister), 'Minister, there are problems here'. They'd always say to you: 'Look, things aren't going too well', but it wasn't putting the stake up you or anything like that. Most of the secretaries I think who have done well have been people who have had that sort of relationship with ministers (Volker).

There is a familiar ring to these comments. They would have come as readily from the mandarins of the 1950s and 1960s. Certainly there were occasions when the ministers did not give direction and when the initiative was left to the senior officials. But that was seldom regarded as ideal because it was seen as difficult to deliver anything new, and certainly to get cabinet approval for a new initiative, if the minister was not up to the task of taking it through the cabinet process. Besides, there was less pressure for constant initiatives then. The message was essentially the same throughout the 1978 interviews:

how should the senior officials relate to the ministers, how could they build up trust?

Of course, there are times when the departmental secretary feels there is a need for review. Not all ministers are either amenable or smart:

> What do you do with ministers who don't accept your policy advice? Well, it's the old question — you persist if you've got enough moral stamina to the point where you become a bloody pest and then you stop short of that. And that's the judgment that every senior adviser has to make in his own conscience. When is it the time to say: 'Well, I'm just wasting the minister's time?'. But whether because of decided policy or his convictions or for whatever reason, and they are good reasons, he may decide not to accept advice and this course of action. So you don't need to apologise for that. You just have to have enough savvy I think to know when to lay off (Tange).

Some may be more persistent than others. Wheeler (1980: 168) recalls one occasion where 'the rectification of the situation required me to ignore the initial refusal to discuss the matter and to wait on a chair in the corridor for nigh on two hours'. Would such a tactic be regarded as possible now?

In 1978 the chairman of the Public Service Board argued:

> Public servants must understand that Ministers may have different perspectives. What appears to be the epitome of logical reason and common sense to the public servant will not necessarily appear so to the politician; often it is a matter of judgement as to how forcefully and tenaciously public servants should press their own views. Certainly there are circumstances when officials should put their views pungently and with determination. However they should know when to stop and where the dividing line is between pressing an argument and nagging (Cole 1979:153).

Sir Keith Shann was more epigrammatic: if the minister was going in the wrong direction, 'To object once is obligatory, twice is necessary, three times is suicidal'. Public servants should be sure all the arguments have been put and should have the courage to raise issues if they have been overlooked, but with care. 'It is important to avoid an attitude that a minister should be free to find his own road to hell if he wishes' (Cole 1980:170–71). Wheeler:

> found useful colloquialisms such as 'the economic arithmetic clearly points to this conclusion but can you wear the political repercussions?' The colloquialism is, of course, somewhat artificial because economic arithmetic is also based on guesses about group behaviour. But the dichotomy has its presentational value. It is also a source of unpopularity. Ministers are human and do not like

the stark presentation of hard choices any more than anyone else. One aspect of style which I absorbed during my own apprenticeship can also be expressed in colloquialisms such as, 'always do your best to protect your Minister', and 'always do your best to make the Minister fully eyes open' (Wheeler 1980:172).

There were ways of giving advice that could push a view. Said one 1980s departmental secretary: 'I always believed that if you are pushing a view and wanted to spell out the implications where there were possible quantitative forecasts, you should be able to write it down'. Others did not feel that that amount of detail on possible outcomes should be committed to paper.

Records had their value. Others used the written nature of advice as a means of exerting pressure:

> If you are giving sensitive advice, you would often want to talk to the minister before you committed it to writing. But if your advice isn't being listened to, you would probably commit it to writing. You say: 'Well, Minister, I have got no option but to record my views for the file. I'm not threatening you, but I do believe it is important enough'. But in a sense you are threatening of course; you are saying there will be a paper trail that can be pursued (Blunn).

Menadue quickly learnt the importance of proper records to protect an official. When one statutory officer was being bullied by a Labor minister and the departmental secretary who wanted him to resign, Menadue 'advised him to make records of all discussions over a couple of months and then present them to the head of department and ask him to confirm his recollection of the discussions. He did that. Suddenly the harassment stopped' (Menadue 1999:122).

But there is a need for another skill in advising ministers: how to provide advice in a way that leaves the minister feeling that they are in charge, how to 'get your way without appearing to do so'. When asked if the departmental secretaries ever called the shots, one commented:

> One has to be very careful they don't perceive that is what you are doing — does that answer the question? Putting ideas in their minds as well as words in their mouth. An important skill is to have the minister accept your advice or the direction of policy without making them feel you are telling them what to do or how to do it. It's in their interest and in the department's interest (Blunn).

In the last resort, the ministers' performance is vital, both in their own eyes and in those of observers:

> Your minister has to win; he must be seen to be delivering goods. If he is negotiating overseas, you must be able to guarantee it to him before he goes and stage manages the great story. We are not

discussing politics. We are talking of the judgment of the secretary, whether it can be won or not, not politics. That is the discipline. To really explore, to sift and to have the minister realise that if you go down that track, these are the chances and the probabilities, this is the second-best option if you get rolled. Because few ministers want to go down, you have got to know the history. You've got to understand the people with whom you negotiate. It's a thousand things (Scully).

Even the best efforts could break down, often to the detriment of the minister. At times, ministers have got into trouble because they chose to act without getting departmental advice. Had they done so, the officials may have been able to assist in achieving their objectives, but not in such a way that they were left out on a limb and forced from office. For a departmental secretary to be frozen out is really a problem because they cannot do their job.

There are avenues if departmental secretaries have difficulties with their ministers. The first appeal for help would usually be the secretary of PM&C. One departmental secretary was asked to do something that he felt was 'outrageous from a public service propriety point of view. I went and had a word with Geoff Yeend and there was no more of that' (Blunn). Another felt threatened: he was being attacked in parliament and his minister was not defending him. He called PM&C. Fraser told his officials 'to ring the minister and tell him the PM expects him to be robust in his defence'.

There was another option: 'More formally I could of course approach the prime minister, but that would be a severely career limiting move'. Style will differ from minister to minister. The more senior the minister, the less likely it is that complaints will be taken to PM&C. New ministers are often hard to serve as they may be erratic, uncertain and still need to 'be broken in', as a prime minister said to a departmental secretary burdened with one such person.

The changes in the society, the economy and the environment obviously put pressure on the departmental secretaries because they put pressure on their ministers. They need to react faster, interact more — and all under greater scrutiny. But what has changed in this relationship over the last decades? Have these views that the departmental secretary has a right — even a responsibility — to press the point changed? There is a perception that the pace of government is faster and that makes it harder for both sides:

It is now a more intense relationship. The transaction levels have gone up exponentially, certainly much more intense in the sense of, again that acute realisation of the responsibility, and the speed of doing business, all of those things, the exposure, what we say about access to government information.

I think what has changed about them, the one thing I have seen is that on average they themselves are under much greater pressure than they were in 1967 ... On the whole, whatever the number of ministers there are in parliament, about 30+ ministers with parliamentary secretaries, they are all under close scrutiny not just by the media, but internally within the party ... It's a much more professional, much tougher, more accountable, assessable process (Rose).

Add the fact that there is a greater suspicion of the public service — a suspicion that has to be overcome — and ministers are no longer likely to assume that the officials, as experts, necessarily have the right answer. They may be listened to, but as one among many:

I get the impression that now ministers are far less positive towards the public service than they would have been 30 years ago (Ayers).

One consequence is that ministers feel under greater stress and that has implications for the departmental secretaries and has changed their relationship. They demand more:

I think ministers have become more assertive. That is not to say there weren't extremely strong ministers. This has got nothing to do with the strength of their will or personality; the extent to which they are involved in their portfolio is greater today than it was then (Moore-Wilton).

Yet, at the end of the process, there is a continuing recognition that the final judgment is that of the minister:

There is a skill in being able to put honestly and frankly on the table what you believe. Then if somebody wants to put a different value set on it and make different judgments, that's their prerogative, but I think the relationship has to be good enough to say these things (Higgins).

Public servants must accept outcomes they do not agree with — outcomes that may have, in the long term, an impact not on their commitment but on their approach. The departmental secretary has to be prepared to accept the outcomes, to not care too much. One of the most powerful of the old mandarins commented:

A departmental secretary has got to be a chameleon. I have never been passionate because I think for a departmental secretary to be passionate leads him into a kind of zealotry where you are not going to be useful to both sides of politics (Tange).

So the traditional line went. Departmental secretaries were prepared to accept policy direction from any direction. Can it be sustained?

Not everyone agreed. John Menadue was sceptical: he argued that, when he became a departmental secretary:

> I had a label on me. There was an assumption that senior public servants were neutral and I wasn't. The difference as I saw it was that I was open about my position. Furthermore, I have always been sceptical of the person who says 'I am non-political'. A person who is non-political accepts the status quo and is not attracted to political action to change it. That person is conservative and should acknowledge it (Menadue 1999:120).

That may be true in some cases, but is not necessarily so. Menadue himself is a good example of a departmental secretary who was able to serve different political masters. Others may accept the lack of passion, but consider it still hid a determination to get their own way.

From the political side, the formula has not changed. The current prime minister, John Howard, agreed that the APS which he found on his return to office was a marked improvement on the service he had known in the 1970s and 1980s. He emphasised the need for responsiveness to the policy directions of the government and argued:

> The need for responsive, relevant advice in no way removes the obligation on public servants to be comprehensive, informed and honest in framing their advice. Advice might have regard to known political implications, but all other implications must also be presented in a balanced way that enables the minister to make an informed decision. No minister wants to be told what is politically pleasing without being advised of legal implications, precedents and that constitutes good policy (Howard 1998:9).

The question, then, concerns the degree to which the circumstances have changed in a way that makes this traditional and desirable aspiration harder and more complex to exercise.

The pressures of the media and more immediate demands for accountability have made life harder. But that is only a start. There are several reasons for the perceived change in the balance between departmental secretaries and ministers. The two most basic are interrelated: the increased competition for advice in the community at large and the growth of ministerial offices in particular.

Competition for advice

The world of the departmental secretary in the 1960s was comparatively simple. Information was scarce; what there was was held in the APS, and often no one else had access to it. There were no policy bodies who were able to develop strategies for change.

Ministers had no staff, except those necessary to manage the office — and they often were seconded from the department. Canberra was isolated and communications were slow. Policy-making could be a dialogue between the minister and the department, a dialogue in which most of the advantages lay with the professionals in the department. They were more numerous, had often been there longer and may have felt more strongly about what directions were the more desirable. The Treasury, in particular, had strong senior officials and intellectually less able ministers for almost three decades from 1949. It would have been difficult for any of the Treasurers to reject their advice because there was no other body to which they could turn for informed alternatives; they did not have the knowledge to ask the right questions and, left to themselves, they would have been unable to devise any replacement policy. They had to rely on their officials.

By the beginning of the twenty-first century, those circumstances have disappeared. Expertise is widespread, alternatives abound and therefore the single official view has less weight. Even the monopoly on economic advice from the Treasury has been reduced. Policy institutes can provide advice. Banks and think tanks have alternative models of the economy. Soon after the budget, Access Economics will explain that they have modelled the economy differently from the Treasury and will therefore challenge its forecasts. Interest groups like ACOSS have become more professional, shaping their arguments within the context of an economic model. Large accounting firms have developed a public sector consulting capacity that puts few limits to the claims on their abilities. Outsourcing of service delivery has become commonplace, reducing the practical experience of the APS in advising what will work and what won't. Advocates suggest the trend should include policy advice.

To a great extent, that has already happened. The monopoly of the departmental secretaries has long been eroded. It was never complete; effective ministers always sought other opinions. What has changed is the professionalism of the policy institutes and the readiness of all bodies to enter the policy arenas. Advice from the departmental secretary will be just one opinion among many — perhaps the most persuasive when the ministers feel that only the departmental secretaries have their interests exclusively at heart, that they are the only ones who are 'rusted on to the minister'. But they will now never be the only source. Advice has become contested:

> I think that we live in a much more competitive world for advice. That's the difference really. Maybe the secretaries of the 1960s were more powerful because they didn't have as much competition and indeed one is led to believe they may even have colluded about

their advice. An oligopoly or monopoly may well have been much more powerful then in the marketplace for ideas. But we do not have that luxury — if you can put it that way. We live in a very competitive world for ideas not only from within government but without. The sources of advice are much more varied if the ministers want to get them (Departmental Secretary 1990s).

Alternative sources of advice became more and more significant and you had very professional organisations developing very professional techniques for advising government (Blunn).

A departmental secretary from the 1960s and 1970s could look at the current scene and identify not only new ideas but better informed ministers:

I think Cabinet is nowadays by and large better informed that they used to be and better educated ... There are more than in my day — public institutions, foundations, research tanks and things that didn't exist in the 1950s which can be tapped and probably are being tapped by parties developing their policies. So these alternative streams of ideas that are now available that didn't exist in the days when ministers were very dependent on departmental resources means from that point of view the relative influence of secretaries is probably reduced. And then of course there are the other deliberate steps taken by ministers in the form of their own advisers to work with or compete against departmental secretaries, and that started of course in the Whitlam days (Tange).

Perhaps the case can be taken too far:

I guess the competition for advice is certainly a significant development, but I'm not sure if you can't overstate that as well. I mean in reality there was always competition for advice within the corridors of parliament. The political part of the advisory process is just as important as the technical advisory role. But it is true now there's competition for ideas at the technical level as well (Departmental Secretary 1990s).

Indeed, it is the last point that can be seen as crucial. If ministers had once listened to anyone on the politics of an issue, and properly so, they had then relied on the departmental secretary to give advice on the technical processes required to put those ideas into effect. Now even that is contested.

But departmental secretaries still have a distinct advantage. They have the opportunity to engage in a series of discussions with the minister as a policy develops. Initially policy is often ill-defined — it almost always needs clarification and development. Before advice is sought (from anywhere, but particularly from consultants), it is useful to know what is to be achieved; that is not necessarily always obvious. Departmental secretaries can work with their minister to determine what it is they are actually after and can therefore know how best to frame the advice in the way that is most persuasive. They have access to considerable analytical capacity in the department and will typically (but not always) see the competing advice.

It is difficult to argue that contests for ideas are necessarily harmful to government. There was in the past extensive criticism of the Treasury Line, a process by which cabinet received only one set of economic forecasts as a basis for policy advice that was often drafted in a way designed to inform cabinet that there were no alternatives. As prime minister, Malcolm Fraser sought to break that monopoly over economic advice both by splitting the Treasury in 1976 and by building up economic expertise within his own department. He wanted more than one view to come to cabinet. Contests over information, options and policy directions are continuous. Sometimes ministers struggle to get on top of the implications of new technology and need constant explanation; only one view may be misleading. If contestable advice is seen as desirable, then it must have an impact on the way that departmental secretaries interact with their ministers.

The growth of ministerial staff

The second change was the development of ministerial staff — 'minders' in the local parlance (Walter 1986). They were born of the suspicion with which the Whitlam ministers approached the APS in 1972 (although Gorton may have been moving towards that end when he reshuffled his office on becoming prime minister). The Labor ministers wanted their own people to assist in making policy. Gradually, the advisers became more institutionalised — indeed, the ministers' offices became seen as a route to parliament itself for the young and the ambitious who were intent on making a early mark. Over the years, departmental secretaries have come to accept their existence, sometimes reluctantly, on other occasions seeking to use them to their own advantage. But they must all face the reality that the staffers are now a potent, if not always effective, addition to the policy scene.

There are several reasons given for the emergence of the minders. In part it is geography. A characteristic of Canberra is that ministers almost never work out of their departments, unlike their British counterparts. When the new Parliament House was built, the ministers were each given comfortable suites of offices in an executive wing that includes the Prime Minister's Office and the cabinet room. Any incentive to shift to the departments to give direct access to officials was finally removed. If the departmental secretaries want to see them, they have to travel across Canberra to Parliament House.

If parliament is not sitting, they may have to travel interstate. Yet in contrast the minders are always on the spot, just outside the ministers' offices, on the plane, around the electorate. Proximity provides the immediate capacity to exercise influence. This was given as one of the reasons for the rise and rise of the private offices.

> I think one of the things that happened was new Parliament House. Because they used to be terribly crowded, you've never seen anything quite so crowded as a minister's office in old Parliament House. And because the private office had to be with the minister, it just didn't work to have it separate, because to work with a minister you have to be there when he says 'Joe, find out about this'. The bloke who works on it has to be outside his office in the adjacent office and walk straight in. That was the most effective curb on private offices. When they expanded to the new Parliament House, private offices simply expanded to fill the gaps, to fill the space available ... And ministers could get what they always wanted from politically loyal people who effectively have come between them and their departments. I think departments have been weakened there because you have this other tier now which is splitting them (Visbord).

Departmental secretaries had an additional group of people with whom they had to negotiate. There was little point in trying to ignore them; they were there, they had the potential to exercise influence and so they became part of the orbit of the departmental secretary. A good departmental secretary had to establish good working relations with them:

> I found that, as there were increasingly more and more people in ministers' offices, if you wanted to stay with or ahead of the game, you had to make sure you personally knew more about them ... I took the line that they were there — you may not agree that they should be there — but you'd better damn well find out what they were up to and what makes them tick (Halton).

The existence of the private offices made it harder for the departmental secretary to develop a close relationship with the minister and destroyed any possibility of the departmental secretary maintaining control over policy advice:

> The creation of private offices for ministers through the MOPS Act ... further reduced the monopoly power of the secretary over informed policy advice — these days a secretary that insisted on giving a minister only one option and only allowing the minister to deal with the department through him, would not last very long unless he was in tune with the minister. And of course, the ministerial office has meant that a lot of those things you used to do as a public servant are now handled in the office and the relationship with the minister has become less intimate (Beale).

At times, it also changed the attitude of a number of ministers to the development of policy. In some people's eyes, ministers no longer felt they needed the public service:

> When in power, I think most [parties] are quite satisfied with the view that they have people much more aligned to them and much more supportive of their political ideals on whom they will rely for policy advice. And they see the bureaucracy very much as their tool to give effect to that by way of administration of programs. You are not now, in a sense as a department, the initiators of policy thinking any longer. You are effectively informed as to what it is the policy will be and in a sense, you are to try and implement and give effect to the administrative aspects that will put those policies into place ... I think we're much more seen as tools of government and that we are there to give effect to policies and programs that are devised by others (Gray).

But not all thought that the increased size of the offices had this effect. Even if, with the assistance of their staff, the ministers could develop a better view of what they, as ministers, wanted, (and not all could), thereafter the departmental secretaries still had plenty of opportunity to advise on the policies required to achieve the ministers' objectives. The private offices have limited capacity to develop policy (as distinct from political) advice. Their influence is in the questions they ask and the options (developed in departments) that they espouse. They might even be better than the minister in getting multiple views out of the department itself.

But there were also advantages in the maintenance of good relations with a competent staff; they could reduce the political demands of public servants:

> The more competent the political advisers, the lower the heat, simply because you have a far better signalling capacity, far more effective input doing the political thing well, asking for the information, but not seeking advice on how that final political part of the decision-making process, the public presentation, is actually run (Rose).

Another did not see the increase in staff as necessarily undesirable 'because it seemed to me to be a safety valve to preserve the political neutrality and objectivity of the public service' (Volker).

Yet there is also a need to consider the possible alternatives. When Labor came to power in 1983, its platform proposed that 10 per cent of the SES should be appointed by the government. They would not have been the bottom part of the SES either. A compromise that strengthened the ministers' offices was more desirable than more direct political involvement in the senior ranks of the APS. The change may have made the competition for attention more vigorous but it also protected the essential nature of the service.

There is another fear, less related to the day-to-day management of policy advising, more concerned with the image and attractiveness of the public service as a career. Those who join the APS because they want to have an impact will be less inclined to stay if they see that, even if they reach the top, they may still have to play second fiddle as advisers to the ministers:

> It's a really fundamental change for us ... And it does mean that departments are having views, robust advice and one thing or another filtered, and the frustrations creep in and it has the potential I think to damage the quality and fabric of the public service in the end. Because people who are very good and who want to have some chance of influence [of the kind I was talking about earlier in relation to myself] those sort of people will not stay. Especially given the poor remuneration at senior levels compared to the private sector, they won't stay if their influences are being muddied and their views filtered and so on by people, some of whom are very able, but others who frankly are not (Codd).

Even then, there is always likely to be dispute about how much difference the advent of the minders has made. One account suggests they have taken over the field; a second proposes that too much influence was credited to the old mandarins:

> I think it's the gradual wresting of power, or perhaps more accurately influence from departmental management to ministerial offices. If you look at the way it works today, it's clear that the advisers have had the better of that struggle, but obviously taking contributions from both areas (and other pertinent sources where appropriate) in a cooperative partnership works best for everyone (Tanzer).

> It is sometimes easy to exaggerate the power of the mandarins in those days. In more contemporary experience, I think there's no doubt we compete now as sources of advice with a much wider range of alternatives (Departmental Secretary 1990s).

Competition led to the reality that departmental secretaries and their staff were just one of several sources competing for the ear of the ministers. If they were to be the principal adviser, that position had to be earned and then kept against others. Combined, it meant that the departmental secretary had to operate in a more fluid environment in order to achieve what earlier departmental secretaries had taken for granted; they had to 'battle through the noise level'. What was the general impact of these changes?

> Just generally greater insecurity — not just for you but your department. Really knowing that you're in a contestable,

competitive environment that you do have to explicitly or implicitly benchmark what you do, knowing that you've always got ministers asking you if you can do it better elsewhere, doing it outside the public service. So it's insecurity, not for myself but the insecurity of the public service environment, I think that's a profound change. A second profound change in my view is the growth in importance of the ministers' offices. I think that has fundamentally transformed the role of a secretary. I constantly have to compete for the policy attention of the minister with those in the minister's office. No two ways about it; I have to fight for my position at the table (Departmental Secretary 1990s).

Terminating contracts and the implications for departmental secretaries

The explicit ability of the government to terminate the contract of a departmental secretary raises more disputed consequences. After all, in the last decade the list of casualties has been long, and they can be found under both sides of government.

The rules in the *Public Service Act 1999* state that 'the Prime Minister may, by notice in writing, terminate an appointment of Secretary at any time'. He is required to act with procedural fairness, which in practice seems to mean giving them due notice, even if not adequate reasons or explanations. He must first receive a report from the secretary of PM&C. The requirements are stark and minimal.

Two questions are raised: does the new legislation change the relationship between departmental secretary and minister and does it alter the nature of the advice that is given, whether in form or in content? There are problems in seeking to answer these questions. It is unlikely that any departmental secretary would agree in an interview that *they* were scared, even if they agreed that some of their colleagues were. Further, those who have been a departmental secretary only under contract are used to no other system; how they would have reacted when they were guaranteed tenure, or how the earlier departmental secretaries would have worked under contract must be a matter of speculation. The most useful comments may come from those who moved from one circumstance to the other, but they are rare, as the process of change was gradual and the tenure of departmental secretaries became briefer over a decade or more. Three long-standing departmental secretaries see the dangers in the process in two forms: the reduction in the professionalism of the APS that assumes a capacity to serve either side of government; and the problem that the messages the process will send to the lower ranks of the service will discourage potential departmental secretaries from staying:

> I certainly think the sacking of those departmental heads when the Howard government came in marked the public 'loss of innocence' of the public service. The assumption that if you had done a reasonably good job then an incoming government would respect your professionalism and not punish you for having worked for a particular minister could no longer be easily made. We had earlier seen changes even with a change of prime minister. I mean it just keeps people off balance. You are not quite sure where things are coming from and so you must be, even if only subconsciously, less inclined perhaps to be as frank and fearless as you would previously have been. Now the counter to that is a lot of people recognise that and are pretty careful to protect the concept of frank and fearless advice (Departmental Secretary 1990s).

> I don't like it because I think it has the potential fundamentally to take away from a career professional public service and that's the bottom line. As soon as you have a perception that people will be changed, not because of your professional performance but for other reasons, whether it's political, perceived political allegiance or some ministerial peculiarity or obsession, as soon as people perceive it is not their merit on which their tenure at the top is based, then it will discourage the best people from wanting to join and stay in the service like that (Keating).

> I think there must be a temptation under those circumstances for people to be very wary in rocking the boat ... The problem of people without an institutional memory will have an impact in my opinion. If half the department heads go, you are going to have a public service of very little experience at the top, and the danger there is that people underneath will decide whether it doesn't matter if you perform well, you get done. Why do I need to work for this lot, any lot? And they would go out and work for the merchant bank and get paid ... the danger is that you lose all the really bright people and you're left with the bums (Ayers).

But perhaps the most damning comment came from a former departmental secretary and chair of the PSB:

> How do you have a career public service when really able people, the people who are going to come to notice, feel that their jobs can be terminated for no good reason. When Howard came in and they shifted a lot of people, some of them, in my judgment, didn't deserve it. Now in the private sector that can happen, but in the private sector the board is responsible to shareholders and if they're appointing the wrong managers, as BHP did over the years, then the odium falls on you. So it's a dilemma for the public service. I solved the dilemma in a personal sense by advising both my children not to work in the public service. They accepted my advice and with hindsight, in the light of their subsequent careers, correctly

> so. But that was serious advice. In other words, although I had
> what you might call a successful career, I would not advise a bright
> young man or woman to go into the public service unless they
> were doing it on the basis of getting training and experience; they're
> in treasury for example and when 30 go out and join a merchant
> bank (Cole).

Terminations at political whim undermine the notion of a career
service because life at the top is so precarious. The question, then, is
whether people still aspire to the top positions. There is evidence,
mostly reported by departmental secretaries, that some of their
deputies do not want to take the next step. Some see it as too
dangerous a career, others as too great an additional responsibility
for the comparatively meagre increase in pay. Ministers will doubtless
say they are unsuited for the role if they are so risk averse.

In addition, there was the question of how new the circumstances
really were. Insecurity was traced back to 1972: 'When Hal Cook
went, it made a lot of people think: "Well, you're not safe and when
there's a change of government you may be out"'. (Cook had been
pushed out of the Department of Labour because the new minister
was not prepared to work with him; it was the most contested of the
changes to departmental secretaries by the new Whitlam
government.) Over the ensuing 20 years before the introduction on
contracts, a number of departmental secretaries were sent overseas
or found statutory positions — some willingly, others less so. Before
the decision to provide five-year contracts with specified termination
payments, several departmental secretaries had lost their position in
the APS. Graham Glenn and Ron Brown, for instance, had been
peremptorily removed. The idea that people had tenure was seen to
be in tatters, so some believed that all that contracts did was provide
a guaranteed payment if it was cut short:

> 'I don't think it makes life more precarious; it just makes the exit a
> bit different, the trapdoor is a bit more sudden' (Higgins).

The previous understanding was that a displaced departmental
secretary would be found an alternative position (even if of lesser
stature). As one departmental secretary from that era commented: 'I
drew great solace from permanence. Unless I did something
unthinkable, I knew I would have been placed as a senior trade
commissioner or whatever. When you have got kids at uni that is a
source of comfort'. But as he also commented: 'Given the choice, a
government should pick the current system every time over the old
system. The ability to place your misfits overseas in a nice quiet alley
is too expensive to the Commonwealth' (Scully). A former chair of
the PSB thinks:

> Was the old system of keeping people on the books better? I think probably I'd have to say the answer is no. I mean theoretically those people could have sat around for ten or 20 years or something like that without doing any work. It's not good for them and not good for anybody else. Whereas the current system does enable people to get a lump sum (Cole).

A current departmental secretary made the same point: open discussion of performance was 'better than to deal with poorly performing secretaries as perceived by the government in an opaque fashion by sending them to the OECD or finding them a high commission somewhere. I just think that's outrageous for a taxpayer'. Both have a point: it was perhaps too easy a system on those who did not perform adequately. But that assumes that it is the departmental secretary who has failed and that, quite obviously, is not always the case. Sometimes it is just the chemistry that does not work. Sometimes the minister may be unwilling to try. A departmental secretary recounted the way a minister sought to remove one of his colleagues who had served ministers well before and was to again:

> As soon as he got in, he started telling people and the business community that he was going to get rid of [his departmental secretary]: 'he's no good'. Now the silly thing is you get an absolute dill coming in and chucking out a competent bureaucrat for no good reason; and in the present day he would simply be good-byed (Visbord).

There are some checks, and in this case the minister could not shift his departmental secretary immediately and a reshuffle was eventually arranged. But there are cases that should provide concern, where there is no lack of performance or efficiency by the departmental secretary but a lack of chemistry or a silly minister. How does that affect advice?

At times it is argued that the possibility of termination has a direct impact on advice:

> I think the lack of security of tenure, it does mean the department — the permanent heads in the department — can't give frank and fearless advice. If you know you can be chucked out if the minister takes a dislike to you or if what you suggested is unacceptable, you're going to be careful. And most of these guys don't have private incomes. They have become a little younger and they've got young families ... I think because people tended to be a bit older, it also didn't matter as much to them if they left, or if they fell out with their ministers. They didn't have young families and responsibilities and they weren't really thinking of going anywhere ... I think it is much harder for people in their forties (Visbord).

Another view suggested that the contracts and larger salaries altered the attitude towards departmental secretaries and this in turn had an impact on the way they approached the sensitive parts of the job:

> The salary increases that came with contracts were not particularly large but the perception in this area had jumped ahead of the fact. Constantly you heard 'well with their large salaries they can expect to take the rough with the smooth'. The secretaries themselves sensed this. Several were quite frank. 'You can't expect me to put my head on the block' (Departmental Secretary 1990s).

John Menadue, whose appointment was, in his terms, a 'major break from the traditional 'non-political' service, had a different view. In asking whether the changes had affected the capacity to give frank and fearless advice, he concluded:

> Do better salaries and contract appointments rather than permanent tenure promote honest advice? Frankly, I don't think they do. Neither am I convinced that appointments from outside the public service are inherently better or worse. The evidence doesn't seem compelling either way.

> In my experience as a CEO in government and business and as a board member, the issue is one of personal authenticity and experience rather than one of tenure or money or even management training. By personal authenticity I mean being publicly true to one's private values. I am confident that it is within that authenticity that frank and fearless advice is most likely to be found (Menadue 1999:185).

The two alternatives were most colourfully put before the Public Account Committee when it was considering the new *Public Service Act* in 1997. Sir Lennox Hewitt argued on 7 August that tenure was essential to the provision of frank and fearless advice. He commented that he could not be sacked:

> There are more ways of skinning a cat than hanging it ... I have been dismissed by a prime minister. You can be abused, you can be exiled and you can be sent to coventry, but the only thing they could not do to you would be to throw you in the gutter.

The tenure made a departmental secretary safe, even in exile.

In response, a few days later on 28 August, the Committee asked Max Moore-Wilton to expand on his comment that 'a number of people ... have confused frank and fearless with just being a bloody nuisance. He argued:

> I think frank and fearless in some people is a sign of hubris and stupidity. Frank and fearless in other people is a sign of well-reasoned argument and debate ... I think that tenure, whether it be in the public sector or whether it be in the universities ... has little to do with intelligence and honesty ... I think the prime minister

uses the word 'robust' when he talks about my advice, if that is the
word, instead of frank and fearless. But let me also say this, that if
one's advice is constantly at odds with the direction in which your
employer wishes to go, one has to question then utility of you
remaining in that particular position.

That has nothing to do with your honesty or the honesty of the
person you are working for or with. It has something to do with
the ability to work in an environment where you have to interrelate
with both juniors and seniors and, at the end of the day, the
responsibility — the buck — still stops at the level above you. There
are a number of people who have confused frank and fearless advice
with just being a bloody nuisance.

Later in the hearing he said:

I do not think you grow into being frank and fearless. I think you
are born into being frank and fearless and it is encouraged in you.
You either have intestinal fortitude or you have not.

Perhaps these are the two extremes. Both can be criticised. One
suggests that any humiliation is permissible as long as the
departmental secretary is not 'in the gutter'. But is that reasonable
treatment for senior officials who have just fallen from favour, perhaps
through no fault of their own, and might not a desire to escape such
humiliation flavour the advice even from a tenured departmental
secretary? On the other side, people may be born with guts and lack
of tenure will not make cowards of them. But to suggest that the
possibility of capricious removal has no impact on the way they
serve seems unlikely too; sometimes it may be true, often it will
affect the judgment of when and where they might push a valid case.

These are general views of how the system may work and the
impact that the changes will have on the process of advice. They are
seldom then translated into a description of the individual
relationship. That will depend on the individual character of the
departmental secretary: 'it is not possible to legislate for backbone'
was one comment.

Ministers, too, would not accept that the new procedures will
make the departmental secretary fearful. Government minister David
Kemp commented:

I don't accept that's the case [people unwilling to give advice because
of terminations]. I mean that suggests they are basically people
without courage.

We will return to the issue at the end of the chapter.

Has the process of advising somehow become more politicised?

If the debate on politicisation is slippery when applied to the appointment of departmental secretaries, it becomes even more so when asking whether the advice is now more political than it was. What are the criteria for judgment? Some clear boundaries need to be set for the debate. To be politically neutral did not mean that departmental secretaries were neutral between government and opposition, or that they espoused some notion of an ideal policy to which they should be committed. It meant that they served the elected government to the best of their ability, regardless of its political colour. Departmental secretaries were never unconcerned about the political environment; they needed to understand how their political masters appreciated the situation and from where they came. They needed to understand what the impact of a policy would be. In the 1960s, Hasluck argued that 'the public service cannot avoid politics any more than fish can avoid the water in which they swim' (1995:91). As Mike Keating (1996:65) has said:

> Of course we do not work in a political vacuum and while we should not provide partisan political advice, it is not expected that we should be politically naïve either ... for a public servant to be aware of the government's mandate, philosophic approach, and of the political constraints is not to be political; it is part of being professional.

None of his predecessors would have demurred from that sentiment; they argued that their role was to give relevant advice to the minister. At the very least, good advice required that advice needed to appreciate the uncontested links between politics and policy:

> When you're giving advice they do want you to bark, but they want you to bark in a way that understands all that, that politics and policy are absolutely inseparable; if they're ultimately to work, you've got to understand these links (FitzGerald).

Has that changed? In these terms, very little. Advice was just as sensitive in the 1960s when the issues concerned Vietnam, the battle between the Treasury and McEwen's Trade empire.

Some people do take the view that the situation has changed:

> Well, I have no direct evidence but [the process of advising] cannot be other than politicised because how do you unfailingly expect frank and fearless advice from somebody who is a career professional administrator and policy coordinator if you can summarily sack him [or her] (John Taylor).

This opinion reflects a common view outside the service: that the capacity to sack has led to departmental secretaries only telling the ministers what they feel they want to hear politically. Most people inside have a more cautious and more nuanced view:

> There appears to be an expectation on the part of the government that their senior executives, particularly their CEOs, in a sense share their commitment to their policies and their ideology ... There is certainly a perception amongst some of my colleagues that more is required of them in terms of a commitment as it's referred to. But it seems to be not a commitment to giving effect and getting the outcomes that the government wants. It's a little more than that. It's an acknowledgment that this government has an ideology of a kind that you support (Gray).

In other words, ministers want not just service but commitment. This did not necessarily mean commitment to a particular party — though, as we have seen, a few departmental secretaries have made their party allegiance clear. It did propose a degree of commitment to the policy directions. Indeed, some may have been selected because they were identified with a policy style or direction:

> Max was chosen not because he used to be a public servant. He was chosen because of his attitude and his views, and the perception about his ability to deliver change. And that implies that somebody had a view about the sort of change they wanted delivered. So if you call that politicisation, I mean that could be political, or it could be managerial and maybe managerial isn't all that far from being political (Blunn).

Sometimes departmental secretaries have moved from one portfolio to the next when their minister was shifted. The ministers knew their capabilities and liked their style; they felt comfortable with the way they were operating. Comfortable, of course, is not the same as political.

Not all would agree. For some, the advice remained primarily technocratic, even if it had political overtones:

> One of the advantages of all those confidential stamps was that you could say things in a fairly unvarnished way. You were giving technocratic advice on the economy, even though it might be highly sensitive material if it got out to the political domain (FitzGerald).

Ministers were conscious of where the line was. As a 1990s departmental secretary commented: 'If they find you were trying to do their job for them, rather than your job, you might find objections mounting'. And they knew the difference:

> One minister said to me; your job is to provide the best policy options because good policy is good politics. On another occasion

a different minister said to me; you worry about the policy and I'll worry about the politics (Graham Evans).

Not every minister was as clearcut, to their own disadvantage. But it is still a modern refrain.

A second way in which the departmental secretaries have apparently been politicised concerns the need to explain policy in public. Accountability has become more public. Should the departmental secretary explain enthusiastically or deadpan? One view was:

> I think I am not doing my job if I am not actively promoting [the government policy] and how it operates, and how a program works and what the outcome should be ... Now the difficulty I have is that when I speak in public on issues, I tend to be quite strong, forceful and passionate and therefore it is often assumed that I'm *supporting* 100 per cent the policies of the government of the day whereas I think I am *communicating* 100 per cent the policies of the government of the day. I think there is a lot of misunderstanding on politicisation of the public service (Departmental Secretary 1990s).

Others would prefer a *lack* of passion! Some were quite happy to explain what the government was doing. If the government wanted to push a line, they would not waste time on boundaries. They were 'less hung up on being apolitical' and were quite prepared to talk to groups to explain, even support, the policy, a practice that they recognised as a 'no-no' in times past.

Indeed, it is in the explanation of policy that many of the problems seem to emerge. Departmental secretaries naturally work most often behind the scenes. When they appear in public, they have no right to differ from the government policy. Parliamentary committees are a basic part of the system of accountability; there many departmental secretaries will be required to explain the administration of policies that they are implementing on behalf of the government. That has its costs, as many observers assume that public support for one set of policies could not be transferred into public support for another if the government were to change.

But the process of communication is much broader than that. Because media and public demands can be so immediate for ministers, the department has to assist in them in that process. It is part of their supporting role as advisers:

> One of the things I think is rather more intense now is the nature of the communication task. There has always been a demand for us to assist a government to put its case in the best light in the public domain but my sense is that the breadth of the

communication task and the immediacy of it has certainly increased in recent times. Issues need to be managed much more closely now compared to fifteen years ago and that is putting a greater premium communication skills within the public service compared to the past (Departmental Secretary 1990s).

Some secretaries were entirely comfortable with the change; they accepted that the expectations had changed. Others were concerned about the potential misunderstandings that could follow.

There is one area where Australian departmental secretaries are not faced with great problems. In Canada, the deputy ministers and even their deputies are sometimes required to attend meetings of cabinet committees on behalf of their minister and argue the case there with other ministers and even with the prime minister. In Australia, the ministers guard their special status. As one person with experience of both systems recalls:

> In Canada I was often in cabinet committees and occasionally in cabinet, sometimes without the minister who just walked out. I knew a lot of what was going on, so I could at least handle part of the political side of it, which I was careful to do with great discretion. But I was never comfortable with all of that. When I came here I was relieved to discover that, although you would occasionally get invited in, you were usually expected to tell them the facts. That was one area where, at least at that time, I was in no doubt the Australian approach was better (Halton).

But of course departmental secretaries had to rely on their ministers to deliver. When they could not, there was a real sense of frustration.

The distinction does not seem to be one of dramatic change, but rather of emphases. It leads to the most basic question: have these changes led to a change in the nature and content of policy advice?

Frank, fearless or in the national interest?

There are two related propositions that concern the debate, both of which are contentious. The first argues that the APS once accepted a higher responsibility than simply that of advising the government. It also maintained the integrity of the national interest in the development of policy, an interest that went beyond the concerns of any one government. The mandarins of the 1950s and 1960s — men like Crawford, Wilson and Bunting — it is argued, were the nation-builders whose vision transcended the immediate political and electoral interests of the day. By contrast, the modern departmental secretaries are too subservient, too responsive and less brave and visionary.

The second proposition suggests that the advice given to ministers was once frank and fearless. Ministers were told what they needed to hear; the advice given was the best policy that ministers ought to adopt — even if, for reasons of political expedience, they did not always do so. Now ministers will not listen and departmental secretaries are too scared to tell them any bad news or to argue with them if they think the policy chosen is not the best available.

There is a need for some caution here in not creating straw figures based on nostalgia. Many of the arguments are implicit and polemical: the public service was once full of giants and nation-builders, compared with the modern responsive Uriah Heaps. Certainly it is a basic assumption of Pusey's book on economic rationalism, as it is entirely about the ideas of senior officials and not ministers. Yet it is subtitled *A Nation Building State Changes its Mind*. By implication, it is the change in the views of officials that affect outcomes. But there is a problem with this analysis. First, it is difficult to find any departmental secretary of that earlier period who would argue that they had the right to determine policy over the wishes of the minister because it was somehow in the national interest. Some frustration with the capacity of ministers certainly, which might lead to the initiative for developing policy to the senior officials, but no claim to superiority. Tange, for instance, would accept reference to broader interests only when it is the only criterion available:

> When ministers fail to define what policy they want applied in a situation that arises or, not exceptionally, remain silent (or even occasionally disappear from contact) and give no direction as to how to respond to events that have their own inexorable timetable, departmental officers will fill the void. They will not do it for reasons sometimes suggested — love of power, or to indulge their own value system. In my experience they will apply what their judgment tells them the Ministry would want, extrapolating from available evidence. If that source yields no guidance they will fall back on what the reformers disapprove as suspect inspiration. That is, the public interest, as seen by an officer's own value system. It is of course right to prefer to have responsible ministers applying their own values; public servants prefer that too (Tange 1982:10).

So this application of the national interest is only a last resort when no other guidance is available, not a driving motive for a departmental secretary. Indeed, the ideas expressed by Crawford at the beginning of the chapter provide a good summary of the prevailing view and there is no reason to doubt their practice either.

The second problem is that most of the national interest claims are essentially selective. The Snowy Mountains scheme and the immigration drive are often cited as examples of nation-building that the mandarins are given credit for. But such credits are essentially selective. Both these programs were highly contested at the time and were both supported and defended by politicians and were in the midst of the political arena. They were not just the invention of officials. If the mandarins are to be given credit for success, should they not be held responsible for the less admirable policies of the time: a 'white Australia' policy until 1966, high protectionist barriers, and of course Australia's commitment to the Vietnam War and the conscription of 20-year-olds that followed. Within its own bailiwick, a bar on the employment of married women as permanent public servants was continued until 1965. None of these policies would now be regarded as acceptable, but they were continued during that time when the 'national interest' mandarins were at their most powerful.

Occasionally these contrasts were explicit and, to recent departmental secretaries, often aggravating. At the height of the debate on the adequacy of the tendering process for pay TV, one recalls:

> A paper said: it wouldn't have happened in Sir Arthur's day or something like that. I was really offended ... the inference was that under a certain style of leadership you didn't have mistakes being made. You can't have it both ways; you can't say that the senior public servants were more powerful and got to take decisions in their own right in that period and then, when you point to problems, say, oh no, that was the politicians. You have to have the accountable process going both ways. The contrast is unfair (Graham Evans).

Of course, it would be as unfair to belabour those departmental secretaries with exclusive responsibility for those policies as it would be to give them exclusive credit for the policies that in retrospect were seen as great successes. They may have played a large role in developing these policies, but they needed political endorsement and support to get them accepted and some public support to maintain them. It would be as absurd to blame them for 'white Australia' as to credit them alone for the expansion of the university system.

Even if it were true that everyone gave that 'frank and fearless' advice (which several recent departmental secretaries doubt), there was a view that too often the advice proffered under that auspice would take no account of the political situation. 'A lot of the frank and fearless advice was frank and the minister would be pretty bloody fearless if he took it. It was fearless because the consequences were removed' (Beale).

In those terms, the modern departmental secretary is not so distant from the views expressed by Crawford. Departmental secretaries have a responsibility to provide good advice that ranges across all the implications but, unelected, they do not have the right

— and they do not claim the right — to have a greater understanding of the national interest than their elected political masters.

> The guardians of the nation are the politicians who are elected by the nation to govern. That's their role and no self-appointed guardian should usurp that role. If you believe in democracy then nobody else should seek to take from the elected politician that fundamental role to represent the people (Moore-Wilton).

> Most of us actually still do believe that the elected person should have the right to call the shots and most of us would say that is one of the pluses from all these changes (Blunn).

> Mine's a fairly simple model. That is, we serve the national interest through the minister and through the government of the day, and that gives me all the freedom of movement that I need to say to a minister: 'I don't think that's in the national interest' or 'I don't think that's the best way to go'. But in practice it's uncommon to get that situation (Mathews).

More explicitly, there was an acceptance that it was not just the right of election that gave politicians that right of final decision. Because of the different backgrounds and experiences, they might even have a better idea of what the people want and will accept:

> This is a bureaucracy and by and large I trust politicians better than public servants to understand what the people want, as long as they have advice in the dangers that might be involved in taking the popular path (Beale).

> I'm a great believer in the democratic process. I've never expected that a democracy or market always get the right solution; it is just that they get the right solutions more often than other systems (Departmental Secretary 1990s).

That view is commonplace. Even if those outside the APS argue that departmental secretaries have a responsibility to protect the national interest against the self-interest of ministers, it is not a role that they want to take for themselves. And that is *not* a new development: it was just as consistent when they were tenured because they regarded it as part of their professional responsibility that they served, not dictated to, the ministers (as long as ministers could be persuaded to make a decision).

But perhaps there were some reservations. In Attorney General's, by one account, 'they really did have a view that they knew what was the right thing to do and it didn't matter if the government agreed ... we're not here to help you; we are here to tell you what to do'. Treasury at times believed that, whatever the internal debate, it should stay in-house. One departmental secretary who thought the Treasury options 'were as much to preserve the policy of the Treasury as to assist the government of the day' and were often 'pretty extreme', later argued they 'could be as hard as they liked as long as they could defend the case and kept the government's objectives in mind; there had to be a balance' (Fraser). Only one departmental secretary put it explicitly:

> The perceived waywardness and expediency and all the rest of some politicians, if borne out in practice in ministerial office, could make good permanent secretaries and other senior advisers appear enemies rather than guardians. The corps of permanent heads — and indeed I felt the whole of the public service — while loyally supporting governments, was really in the best sense of the phrase 'a permanent opposition', regardless of who was in power. It was the informed, sceptical force, interested in the long term, suspicious of the quick fix and therefore, despite its loyalty, all the more infuriating to some politicians (John Taylor).

It was unique for the view to be expressed in such stark terms. Yet that is indeed the role ascribed to the APS by those who demand that it should have a separate and additional role. They get little explicit support from within, and almost none in the late 1990s.

Ministers will argue that frank advice is in their own best interest. David Kemp, the minister responsible for assisting the prime minister on public service issues, believes:

> Well, frank and fearless advice means that the advice may be advice that the minister may not be terribly happy to receive, but is the secretary's best analysis of the consequences of taking a particular action. In other words, what ministers expect from secretaries is the same quality of advice that the PM expects from them. It is quite counterproductive for the secretary and the minister to have anything other than frank and fearless advice. It is the merest self-interest, if you like, of both the minister and the secretary. It protects the secretary and it provides the minister with the best possible opportunity to take the right decision ... I think that's the only sound basis on which government can operate.

The prime minister has made that case too, as cited earlier in this chapter.

Several departmental secretaries recount similar requests from ministers. They are told that, even if this advice will not be accepted, the ministers still want to keep saying what they think:

> I have had some pretty vigorous discussions with the minister, but what I try to do is to preserve that personal relationship that I see as an absolutely threshold condition. They expect me to tell them if they are going to get into trouble (Mathews).

Others say that their ministers have never been left in any doubt about what they think.

Senior officials will put it in similar terms; ministers need to be told what they think is likely to happen. It is part of their professional responsibility. Mike Keating expressed it well by explaining the balance between professionalism and responsiveness:

> The key ethical obligation upon advisers is to ensure that the decisions are fully informed and ministers are not misled. The APS can only fulfil this role if it has the capacity to give its advice frankly and without fear or favour. Good advisers will find the balance between being responsive to the policy objectives of the government and exercising their responsibility to draw attention to the possibly undesirable implications of policy proposals. Advisers should complement political leadership by questioning and probing the apparent constraints to better policy ... in effect while public servants are expected quite naturally to have views of their own, they are also expected to be sufficiently detached so that they can advise in terms of what they understand to be the government of the day's objectives. Indeed it is arguable that the capacity to adapt and respond in this way, whenever there is a change of government, is what defines an impartial and truly independent public service (Keating 1996:65).

This requirement has been sometimes put with great force. Recounting the story of how once Fraser told him: 'I don't want to hear that', a departmental secretary said: 'I'm not paid to tell you what you f'ing want to hear. I'm paid to tell you what you f'ing ought to hear' (Ayers).

> I understand that the essence of the task is to tell ministers what they really need to know in terms of making a decision and that clearly includes warning them. Things that could go wrong. I never felt that was terribly difficult, it somewhat puzzles me that people feel they could be under threat. I would just sort of say well why would they expect to be under threat? My experience is that most ministers are rational, and they would prefer to be forewarned about what could go wrong before the event rather than after the event — and forewarned by somebody who essentially they can trust. You won't be in the job if they can't trust you (Keating).

There is a confidence here expressed by senior public servants who have become sure of their position. Several others would agree:

> My view about all this is that the job's not worth doing unless stuff like that [the possibility of losing your position] doesn't make a difference to you. So if you are going to get worried about the fact that you might lose your job, it's time to give it up. That's been a view I've had since way back. And you just get used to managing that ambiguity. At times you say to the minister: 'Look, you are not going to like this. Nonetheless, this is what I have to tell you' ... Most ministers will understand where you are coming

from and they will respect your view. A good minister will tell you whether they agree or not. A less forthright minister might hear you out and ignore you, but typically they know that you have a job to do and they respect that (Sedgwick).

The implications of the changes

Trying to define with any accuracy the relations between departmental secretaries and ministers is always going to be impossible because much of it is undertaken behind closed doors. It may be possible to speculate on the way that the introduction of contracts or the growth of ministerial staff has affected the ability of the departmental secretaries to do their job by drawing out principles of behaviour. Often that has been done, as people assume that practices have changed even when everyone denies it. Interviews may not be individually reliable, but they can begin to give some ideas of the way the system works.

At the core there has been little change. The relationship between the minister and the departmental secretary is vital. If the minister is to get the best out of the department and utilise its knowledge, then the departmental secretary must be trusted and work cooperatively with the minister. Good advice is direct advice. But such a relationship does not always occur, and in recent years it has become more difficult to develop because of the advent of the ministerial minders and a greater range of well-informed advice from sources outside the government. The departmental secretaries are no longer the only principal advisers, and certainly not the final source of advice that they could once be in more leisurely days. Ministers will listen to more people, both in structured and relaxed environs. There are simply more ideas out there in the market, more challenges to the orthodoxy, more solutions for the picking. Technology has provided instant access to data and plans for anyone to access. The world of advice is thus more free-wheeling and competitive. That must have an impact on the way the system works.

Does it matter? In democratic terms, obviously not. It is appropriate that the elected ministers should be able to gain access to as many ideas as could be useful in determining a policy. It is desirable that they not rely exclusively on their official advisers. They are the ones who have an authority founded on election to decide what is best for the country. It is desirable that they listen to their advisers and necessary that those advisers spell out the likely consequences of the policy, both in the short and long term. In that circumstance, the departmental secretary has a responsibility to identify the outcomes that may not be, in their view, of national benefit. The relationship between departmental secretary and minister needs to be robust enough for that exchange to take place, but the final choice will lie with the minister. None of the departmental secretaries would quibble about that distribution of responsibilities.

Nor should debate be couched in terms of the rights of the departmental secretary to be heard. The APS is there to serve the ministers. If its services are seen to be of little value, then it will not be surprising if the government chooses to go elsewhere in search of advice. Departmental secretaries must earn their keep. The potential problem comes when ministers make little effort to see what benefits they can gain from careful advice that appreciates the political environment, understands the government's priorities and rigorously works through the possible alternative solutions. Then the fault lies with the ministers. It is worth recalling the comment made by the most powerful of mandarins, Roland Wilson:

> Advice from all quarters can be of help to governments, and in certain areas it is essential. But 'taking five minutes off' or even five days or five months, is not going to produce solutions to the more vital problems of public policy and economic management. We must continue to rely heavily on the full-time advisers who staff the various agencies of government.

> There is no problem in getting advice, whether from inside or outside the regular channels. It can be good or bad, or it can be like the curate's egg; it can be self-seeking or objective; but it is never in short supply. The real problem is for ministers, not themselves always technically proficient, to select the good from the bad and to relate it to their own broader appreciation of political and economic realities and their own philosophical approach to the task of government. It is to assist in this that the policy units of government departments exist (Wilson 1976).

That should indeed be the test. Are the relations between the departmental secretaries and the ministers strong enough; are the departmental secretaries skilled enough to provide that bedrock advice on which well-informed public policy can be built?

Such relations are certainly harder to develop and more onerous to sustain in the 2000s than they were in the 1960s. There is more competing 'noise' that interrupts the message. At times the quality may suffer under pressure of greater speed, more intrusive media and impatient demands. Insecurity may amend the way in which the message is delivered. Ministers may have less respect for the messengers. All that is true in places. But the basic element remains. Unless both sides appreciate the need for the relationship to work, the policy process is likely to be worse. One thing clearly *is* in the national interest: that policy is well considered and well informed.

6

Management: The invisible art

On 14 July 1975, Sir Lennox Hewitt responded to a request from the Royal Commission on Australian Government Administration for a copy of the objectives of his department. He commented: 'I had not previously encountered the suggestion of objectives for a Department of State. The Royal Commission would presumably not need anything more for the Department than a copy of the Administrative Arrangements'. A few days later, Sir Frederick Wheeler made a similar point: 'The function of the Treasury is to advise and assist the Treasurer in the discharge of his responsibilities ... The objectives of the Treasury are, in essence, to carry out its function as efficiently and as effectively as possible'.

Twenty-five years later, in February 2000, a new departmental secretary in Defence, Dr Allan Hawke, complained that, when he came to Defence, he had hoped to find 'an overarching corporate plan, derived from government policy and objectives, setting out our purposes, our future directions, our priorities and our values'. He expected business plans for each functional unit, a 'plan on a page' for each person, 'a record of achievement and progress against the Government's policy platform and priorities'. 'I hoped to find them but I didn't', he commented (Hawke 2000).

The two views reflect how far the APS has changed in its approach to management technique and rhetoric. What once was regarded as unimaginable is now seen as routine. The language and practice of the manager is part of the armoury of the modern departmental secretary. This chapter will examine the changes to the management position of the departmental secretaries and see how it affects the way they work and the influence they wield.

The management framework

Historically, departmental secretaries have had an enduring role as administrators or managers of departments: a function that was made explicit in the *Public Service Act* 1922, which states:

> The Secretary of a Department shall be responsible for its general working, and for all the business thereof, and shall advise the Minister in all matters relating to the Department (PSB 1974:2).

Under this Act, administrative responsibilities for the department are placed squarely on the shoulders of the secretary. The minister's presence, however, cannot be missed within the legislation. The reason is both constitutional and conventional. Section 64 of the Australian Constitution states: 'The Governor-General may appoint officers to *administer* [italics added] such departments of state of the Commonwealth as the Governor-General in Council may establish'. The doctrine of ministerial responsibility, within parliamentary democracies like Australia, considers the acts of officials 'as the acts of the minister: officials are seen as agents of the minister's will' (Emy and Hughes 1991:352). Even if Westminster rhetoric says ministers make policy and public servants deliver it, the Constitution is more expansive. There is no doubt about the rights of the minister to administer a department, even if at times those rights are restricted within legislative limits. Departmental secretaries have the responsibility for staffing, and some departmental secretaries have statutory responsibilities defined by law, for individual social security decisions or air safety, where the minister cannot intervene.

Thus, while the administration of a government department might be considered the duty of the secretary, any actions are, in fact, being undertaken on behalf of the minister. The power relationship between ministers and secretaries is further defined in favour of the former by the notions of accountability built into the convention of ministerial responsibility. As the democratically elected members of the executive, ministers are directly accountable to parliament and by implication to the electorate for their department's operations, and are therefore empowered to determine the direction that it takes. So, while many ministers choose to delegate their administrative power almost completely to the secretary, such power is a consequence of choices made by ministers, not secretaries. If problems emerge when formally delegated power is exercised, or if there is evidence of systematic mismanagement, the minister can review and change that delegation.

As Spann observes, the association of a departmental secretary with administrative matters is:

> mainly a sober statement of the realities, and one with which (it seems) nearly all Ministers have been content. Of course, there have been occasional Ministers who have dominated their Departments, but more by the incessant pressures of new policy-making than by taking a great interest in the administrative arrangements. Very occasionally a Minister has extended his

influence markedly into structural matters and even senior appointments, but usually at the cost of exciting considerable alarm (Spann 1976:25).

A secretary with long experience in the 1960s believed:

> there was an instinctive theory of resistance alive in the public service in the 1950s and 1960s that ministers are there to give us direction on policy but for God's sake don't let them mess around with the public service because they have no experience as managers; they have been school teachers and they have been union secretaries or lawyers or whatever, but what would they know about running anything? (Tange).

A more recent departmental secretary observed:

> When the 'real mandarins' were there — the Buntings, the Tanges and the Wheelers and others of that group — who were 'kings' in their departments, they guarded extremely jealously anything to do with public management and internal departmental operations. The convention seemed generally acceptable to ministers at the time, probably because these departmental secretaries were in office for lengthy periods during long periods of same party government. But this did not remain the case. The convention appeared to sour somewhat when there was a new government with a substantial reform agenda. There was a feeling that their reform agenda could be frustrated if the convention was allowed to continue unchanged (Tanzer).

Perhaps it was a reaction to that attitude, and the consequent assumption that minister should not be involved with administration, that led to the 1984 amendment to the *Public Service Act* which added a vital phrase to section 25. Now the act stated that: 'The Secretary of a department shall, *under the Minister*, be responsible for its general working ...' (emphasis added). The addition of the words 'under the Minister' made it clear again that, even where the minister chose to play a negligible role in decisions on administration and management, they had the right to be involved where they chose, unless there was a specific legislative ban on their involvement (as there was, for instance, in decisions about public service appointments within the department). As one departmental secretary put it: 'Dawkins' reforms really put the responsibility for managing the department with the minister, with the secretary as principal agent' (Blunn).

The 1999 *Public Service Act* defines the responsibilities of secretaries:

1. The Secretary of a Department, under the Agency Minister, is responsible for managing the department and must advise the Agency Minister in matters relating to the department.

2. The Secretary of a Department must assist the Agency Minister to fulfil the Agency Minister's accountability obligations to the Parliament to provide factual information, as required by the Parliament, in relation to the operation and administration of the department.

The minister's role was re-stated even more emphatically.

Even so, many ministers were still not interested. In 1976, Spann's explanation for why ministers delegate administrative responsibilities rested on a number of points. First, ministers usually see themselves as party political actors and policy initiators, not administrators. Ministers have, as Spann explains, 'manifold political duties to distract them, attending parliament, cabinet, party meetings, looking after their own electorate, and so on', leaving them little time for the administration of a department. Second, ministers (unless they are elected from the ACT) do not live in Canberra, whereas secretaries do. Thus the day-to-day workings of the department are less likely to be effectively undertaken by ministers (Spann 1976:26). The points are still valid. The fundamental elements of the political system still direct ministerial attention elsewhere.

> Most ministers are not managers, and even were they managers, it would be a poor use of their time. Because being a politician is a pretty full-time activity in its own right. By and large, it demands different skills. There are not too many public servants that become very good politicians (Beale).

Different skills should ideally be complementary with the greater responsibility for daily management in the hands of the departmental secretaries.

For a long time, the tools of management adopted by secretaries as they performed their administrative functions received only limited evaluation. For instance, in Spann's (1976) *Report for the Royal Commission of Australian Government Administration* on the role of secretaries, considerable emphasis is placed on assessing the degree to which secretaries manage their departments compared with ministers, with little said about the range of management techniques available in this process.[1] The reason can be found in the dominance of hierarchical approaches that had long been accepted within the Australian public service. As far as the secretary's role went, there were two basic dimensions of the power structure created by this approach to administration. Within the department, the secretary's power was considerable, as the controlling authority at the apex of a pyramid-style organisation. What the secretary could do in this position, however, was constrained by the fact that the power over most resources remained elsewhere. Particular government agencies, including the Public Service Board (PSB), Prime Minister and Cabinet,

Treasury (and later Finance), Administrative Services and, to a lesser extent, Industrial Relations, assumed the role of coordinating resources and regulated the activities of other departments.

The Public Service Board was a centralised personnel agency whose task was to manage Australian Public Service staff with 'responsibility for both the policy and much of the casework in relation staffing, pay and terms and conditions of service' (McLeod 1994:114). The PSB was the employer within the APS and the actions of secretaries, with regard to staffing issues, needed to remain within the parameters set up by the PSB (McLeod 1994:114). Treasury centrally administered the budgets of each department; departments had no capacity to carry funds over from one year to the next. Nor could they shift funds from one appropriation line to anther without permission. Prime Minister and Cabinet took care of procedural concerns for the running of cabinet. Within this framework, the administrative power of secretaries was severely limited, not by the minister, but a number of coordinating agencies. Of course, secretaries heading a coordinating agency had more power but were still restricted by the PSB and other coordinating departments.

Fundamentally, the nominal sharing of responsibility meant that no one was really responsible or accountable for results. This situation reinforced the focus on process: how resources were obtained and used, not what they were used for or what results were achieved. Under-spending the budget allocation, for instance, was seen as bad budgetary management and could have an impact on the next year's funding.

Management of people was never seen to be significant, at least not in the way that recent departmental secretaries understand the term. Many departmental secretaries would still not be seen as good people managers; they are more likely to be obsessive task managers. One of them served as executive assistant to a legendary departmental secretary, yet he thought his boss:

> knew nothing about people management Some of the best lessons I learnt as I grew up were lessons in the negative: how not to do it. People often have high aspirations for the organisations they work in — values, ethics and professionalism. He would not have given tuppence for all that, so I learnt a lot about people management and how not to do it by watching (Departmental Secretary 1990s).

Another complained that, as he came through the ranks:

> I wouldn't have known how to spell the word management, but what I observed was a total lack of management around me. I wasn't exposed at all to a sense of purpose. I had a sense of absolute worthlessness (Rosalky).

Since the 1970s, public service reform has altered the position of the secretary. The aim of the reforms was to assist governments to increase their output without increasing (and sometimes reducing) the resources used. It was a response to a variety of forces which are well documented elsewhere, particularly a continuing pressure to expand the role of the welfare state while there was a decline in the public's willingness to pay for these services. At the same time, a period of economic decline from the early 1970s and external pressures required governments to find ways of enhancing competitiveness; in these respects, the demands on governments were not unlike those pushing business to modernise. Reform to the public service was just one strategy which governments employed to deal with this situation.

This change in attitudes towards the management role of secretaries is the treatment of this issue is illustrated by two eminent practitioners. In 1974, A.S. Cooley, who was then head of the PSB and very keen to promote the secretary's administrative role, felt able to cover these activities in six relatively brief and highly general dot points (Cooley 1974:199). Undertaking a similar task in 1990, Michael Codd, a one-time secretary of PM&C, thought it necessary to write 15 pages of detailed prescription on the issue (Codd 1990:48–63).

Many of the reforms of the public service had significant implications for the way departments were managed. In particular, the public service's emphasis on inputs and due process, as well as its high level of centralisation, was seen as undermining the public service's responsiveness to both governments and their clients; as stifling innovation; as encouraging a public service culture where public officials believed they could define the public's interests; and as eroding incentives for staff to perform. It was believed that if these problems were addressed, principally through new forms of management, there would be an improvement in service delivery and taxpayers' money would be better spent; a more flexible public service would then emerge, one that would be more effective and efficient (Codd 1991). Andrew Podger (secretary of the Commonwealth Department of Health and Family Services) highlights the connection between changes in the wider political context and the need to manage departments in new ways. He also notes that this has led to a diversity in management techniques:

> The size and complexity of government, and the scale of change we are required to manage, have inevitability required the dismantling of many prescriptive processes and red tape. They have also required greater capacity for departments to go their own way to meet their program objectives (Podger 1997:11).

As a result of the reform process, there has been a restructuring of the public service, one which has give greater management responsibilities to secretaries. Codd (1990) has set out these changes in a systematic fashion (see Table 6.1), comparing the changes experienced by public service managers between 1980 and 2000:

Table 6.1: Changes experienced by public service managers, 1980 and 2000

	In 1980, a program manager had:	*In 2000, a program manager should:*
1.	• to contend with other departments with related interests;	• have broader, more rational and cooperative program arrangements;
2.	• to contend with detailed involvement of central agencies;	• have less detailed intervention and control by central agencies;
3.	• to put any program or involving expenditure legislation through an over-loaded cabinet system;	• be required to put only major changes to cabinet through the minister;
4.	• to submit and negotiate with Finance their 'bids' for budget;	• have published 3-year forward estimates and thus have a more simplified engagement in budget processes;
5.	• no flexibility to shift funds between programs and years;	• be able to shift funds programs and years;
6.	• a staff structure with too many occupations and levels and hierarchical work patterns;	• have a simplified and flexible staff structure;
7.	• to obtain central agency approval for changes to staff structure;	• be able to work with greater autonomy under the umbrella of a corporate plan with clearly specified objectives, goals and performance targets;
8.	• to accept property, transport and common services through other department;	• have a choice of fee-for-service for property, transport and other services;
9.	• to be accountable for a program when the emphasis was on inputs and process, and where control over resources was in the hands of others.	• be more directly in control of staff, with a clearer idea accountability and respon-sibility for results expected under the corporate plan, and have new challenges for staff development.

Source: Codd (1991:1–3)

This comparison draws out a number of the key aspects of the secretary's management role that have changed. All the points reflect the shift from the hierarchical and directive approach to management that prevailed prior to 1980 to the more devolved environment that was created by the reforms that took place throughout the 1980s.

Pivotal to this process was the Hawke Labor government's decision to give greater financial powers to the departmental secretaries, to relax the rigid systems of Treasury controls and to make them more directly accountable for achieving objectives (see points 3 4, 5 and 8 in Table 6.1). Financial management was devolved to departmental secretaries, as was resource management (points 1 and 2 in Table 6.1). Departmental secretaries became responsible to their minister for the financial performance of the department with the annual report used to identify the department's priorities, resources used and their outcomes. These changes in personnel and financial management were the result of rethinking how resources in the public service should be managed with a devolution of power from central agencies to the secretary aimed to increase its the effectiveness and efficiency. The rationale was that each department had different resource requirements and there was no one best way to organise a department: budgets and personnel needs would therefore be more effectively taken at the level of the department rather than at one centralised location. To allow for such variations, individual organisations needed to be responsible for their own management. Devolution meant that secretaries assumed new management responsibilities with the drive for efficiency demanding that their performance be monitored and that they should be held accountable to the minister for the outcomes achieved. The government retained the determination of the total budgets at the centre, as it was bound to do. But within those limits, there were fewer controls.

In the 1987 machinery of government changes, the PSB was replaced by the Public Service Commission (PSC). In contrast to the PSB, the PSC was designed to establish the broader principles within which personnel issues were managed, but the task of management was devolved to secretaries. The consequences of these changes are summarised by points 7 and 9 in Table 6.1. Now it was secretaries, not a centralised body, who were became responsible for finding ways of creating a more effective and efficient workforce. Their response was to simplify the department's staff structure and make it more flexible (point 6 in Table 6.1).

These trends were consolidated in the *Public Service Act 1999* (PSA), where departmental secretaries are given the power to employ non-SES staff without the approval of the PSC. The *PSA* also gave departmental secretaries responsibility for performance appraisal and gave them greater freedom to fire under-performing staff. Quite explicitly, the departmental secretary has assumed the position of the employer. Enterprise bargaining reconfirmed the role of departmental secretary as employer, taking on the role of negotiating agreements with unions. With regard to SES staff, the PSC might remain the formal appointing authority, but it can only act under the departmental secretary's recommendation. This gives departmental secretaries the central position in determining who their executives are, and what bonuses or relative rates of pay they might get. Thus, overall, the service has moved to a situation where departmental secretaries are now provided with freedom to determine the staffing structure of the department, with central control mainly exercised through a financial budget covering total running costs (McLeod 1994:114). The rationale behind this devolution of employment responsibilities to the departmental secretaries was to allow them to match staffing needs to the specific organisational structure of their departments.

Whilst focusing on efficiency and effectiveness in managing a government department, departmental secretaries were also given the responsibility for ensuring that public service values were build into the management framework. The PSC was to help in this process, as it was identified as having some over-arching responsibility for ensuring the maintenance of public service values. According to the *PSA* 1999, however: 'An Agency head must uphold and promote the APS Values'. These include a public service that is apolitical and ethical, accountable to the government and parliament, and responsive to the government in providing frank, honest, accurate and timely advice; where the merit principle is applied to employment decisions; that is free from discrimination; in which service delivery is fair, effective and impartial; in which the workplace is fair, flexible, safe and rewarding; and in which there is a focus on achieving results and managing performance.

These values had been developed over the previous decade. The MAB/MIAC publication *Building a Better Public Service* (1993:5) listed key public service values; the McLeod report added a variant. The new *Public Service Act* was prepared in PM&C as part of a long-term collaborative process. So the values listed in the 1999 Act are the outcome of long discussion and are widely accepted within the service. The expectation is that departmental secretaries will ensure these values are maintained within their departments; the Act therefore provides them with a broad range of responsibilities. Matching management techniques with the particular organisational structure of their department is a significant challenge.

The departmental secretaries are well aware of the impact of the greater requirement that they manage their departments. They are prepared to accept the additional authority, but see the problems they bring. Of course, from the centre, they were not to be given the option. The intent was not only 'to let the managers manage' but also to 'make the managers manage'. There is the view that improved management would occur only if the onus was on the departmental secretaries — and that meant giving them the authority to determine and utilise the resources they needed. The departmental secretary of Finance at the time many of the reforms were introduced commented:

> They are now required to manage. They have to focus on output, not just process, and beyond outputs they have got to really account for cost effectiveness and make decisions in terms of cost effectiveness. Prioritise and so on ... secretaries are under much more pressure to work out how best to spend the funds under their control (Keating).

The departmental secretaries of today accept that the situation has now changed:

> We actually do manage now — I wouldn't have said this a few years ago — we do manage because we can. We actually are now able to, and gain success from, engaging staff (Rosalky).

> I think the management task is significantly bigger (Higgins).

That is unlikely to change. Ministers will always require an efficient manager of the department, first to manage the development of advice across agencies, second to control the increasing supply of information and analysis, and third to oversee the implementation of their policies, whether they are delivered by the department or outsourced by contract and delivered by another organisation. The skills needed may change; the job will still be there:

> I think the secretary will continue to be a key management position: the arranger of resources, the securer of resources, a position in which the whole of government policies and networks are developed and maintained and a major policy adviser — but not the exclusive policy adviser to the minister (Beale).

For each departmental secretary, that role might be played across several departments. There may have been acceptance that distinct skill may be needed for policy development, but 'for management, there was an expectation that within that theory of competence they should be able to move, they should be to shift from one place to another'. Skills would be generic. Learning the management job often required on-the-spot training. As far as running a department is concerned, 'there is nothing, no substitute for actually being able to do it, through a period of different administrations'. The common route, working through PM&C at senior levels, might have made new departmental secretaries politically aware, but it did not prepare them for the rigours of running programs:

> You didn't get a lot of experience in PM&C because it's an office where you don't run things. You certainly get to know the way the whole machine runs better than anyone else; you know the parliament back to front and you know cabinet back to front ... but you have actually run some policy or program with a change in administration, so you can see how some of these different policies work (Rose).

Indeed, sometimes those who had spent a career in central agencies and then been appointed to run a line department were initially loathe to shift back to the centre, because they enjoyed the different process of actually delivering programs. Menadue recalls:

> The three years as Head of the Department of Immigration and Ethnic Affairs were the most personally satisfying of my public life. In such a line department I was very conscious of being part of nation building. This was much more so than as head of a coordinating department like Prime Minister and Cabinet where we didn't have direct responsibility for programs (Menadue 1999: 231).

Finance, too, provided a number of departmental secretaries but the transition from central agency to line department was often difficult:

> Moving to the Department of Education from the Department of Finance meant moving to a different world. Education at that time was incredibly badly resourced. I remember working to scrape together the funding to send one person overseas to deliver a paper at a time when other departments sent many more without a thought. The department had virtually no IT. A few months after I arrived, an argument in Budget Cabinet resulted in Education and Finance being sent away to produce their own estimates of Education Department staffing. Finance had completed its estimate at 8.00 p.m. We were still manually counting cards at two in the morning (Williams).

Managing was a constant learning process for those who had had limited experience in delivering programs.

How the departmental secretaries chose to manage would differ from person to person. One person emphasised the need to meet the three Ps: the publics, the planning and the people. In the first, he had to deal with the minister, private office and other stakeholders (departmental colleagues, parliament and industry). In the second, he had to ensure that the future framework was properly understood, so that there were clear sets of cascading plans which included every electoral commitment and were signed off by the minister; divisions had to report monthly on progress on business plans. Under people, he had to recruit, develop and keep competent staff and help them understand the corporate philosophy.

Another departmental secretary gave great significance to the corporate plan:

> We've used corporate planning here in part to try to help the translation of the general rhetoric into, well, what does it mean for us? So if you look at our corporate plan, you will see that it starts off as being, in a sense, an agreement between the minister and the department. What the department is doing for the minister, not so much the what as the how, but the two get caught up. So we say, what are the overall priorities, not so much the specifics but the general direction, and that would flow into a range of key result areas and directions (Podger).

Selling such a plan to officers in a department is not such an easy task.

One secretary thought that the greater freedom given to departmental secretaries under the new *PSA* actually allowed them to manage in a way that was much closer to the traditional CEO in the private sector, even if there were still restrictions imposed by the central agencies. When he took over a department, he held a series of open meetings, designed both to let people know how he saw the future but also to listen to the ideas that came from elsewhere. He wanted to allay the suspicion that he had a pre-ordained blueprint that he wanted to impose on the organisation. A reiterative development of a corporate plan allowed people to see where they fitted into the overall scheme and what they could add to the department's mission.

Some secretaries chose to emphasise the management task. When Cole went to Defence, he had spent all his career in central agencies; as a consequence:

> In Defence I decided I must concentrate on management — to get the department organised properly and operating efficiently. I had not come up through the Defence ranks and without that background I decided I would not try to become a military expert. There were plenty of such people in Defence, mainly military people but also some civilians. I did take an interest in the strategic and intelligence issues in the department but I never sought to do initial drafting of papers on these matters. It was a full-time job managing, particularly after the Department of Defence Support was absorbed into Defence (Cole).

Others talk less about plans and documents and discuss the people they recruit and the work they delegate. Ian Castles was described as 'not a good manager, absolutely fantastic intellect, the best intellect I've met in the country and to have that at the top was fabulous'. One departmental secretary wrote very little; he preferred to recruit good people and let them brief the minister. He was seen by his colleagues as a 'not a strong analyst, fabulous people person, wonderful intuitive thinking which is not just experience, it's beyond experience'. Another saw the role in two ways:

> I have two things in mind: it will be what will I be trying to get out of the department in support of you, minister, in support of the wider government, and what I will be doing, back in the portfolio, that will be less visible to you, minister, about people management, accountability, promotion and IT, all those management things that ministers find dull (Mathews).

Styles vary with roles; some departmental secretaries are distant, others more outgoing.

There is an appreciation of what has changed. In part it was the decline of the detailed control of central agencies. The PSB dealt with industrial relations on behalf of the APS as a whole. It decided what the staffing of departments should be in considerable detail. The Treasury had to agree to expenditure; if a department wanted to move funds from one line of the budget to another, it needed Treasury approval; if funds were not spent by the end of the financial year, they were lost. There was little managerial flexibility and a constant need for approval. There was also, of course, someone else to blame if the minister's wishes were not fulfilled. Someone else would not provide the resources or the personnel that the departmental secretary had insisted were required. When the pressure was put on the departmental secretaries, then the story changed:

> It is far more complex — that is, the matrix in which you operate is far more complex than it was in either let's say, 1984 or 1966 ... much more intensely since 1987, that the variables the secretary could actually play with rather than simply go to someone else like the Board or the old Treasury and haggle with, but know at the end of the day it wasn't your decision. You could influence and achieve results through influence but now you carry the can (Rose).

Another said the departmental secretaries now had greater apparent freedom, but they were operating within constraints that the older mandarins did not face: 'It is not as easy to be arbitrary' (Beale). There were too many external requirements for accountability. Parliament could be more intrusive in its questioning. Freedom of information could bring decisions into the public arena. Administrative review could challenge decisions. A less hierarchical approach might also allow greater debate.

But there was a sense of satisfaction that went with the responsibility:

> There's a sense of responsibility and accountability ... it is very clear who is responsible for the future ... it took away a lot of the ambiguity and it gave me a real sense of focus and of personal success (Rosalky).

> When you get there you become aware that at the end of the day it rests with you. A deputy secretary can still take an approach knowing the secretary is going to haul him or her back. He/she can afford to be 'purer' in policy prescription than the secretary. The secretary has to look at the broader whole-of-government position (Beale).

Some additional burdens made life harder. The demands that the departmental secretaries should handle industrial relations — a function that was once the responsibility of the PSB — certainly made the job much harder. In the past, departmental secretaries 'did not have to worry about any that. The wages were set centrally. Now there was a lot more autonomy' (Stevens). The reforms, said one departmental secretary, provided:

> More power, but more difficulties in some respects because first of all you had to handle your own industrial relations and in Social Security we were the first ones to have an enterprise bargaining agreement. People don't realise the amount of time and effort that used to go into industrial relations in those larger departments ... Really, I think one of the evolutionary processes which people haven't appreciated is how industrial relations has changed, very much so over the period from where you had centralised control through the PSB and to some extent the Industrial Relations Department, through to having some responsibility for negotiating within broad frameworks through to having individual enterprise bargaining agreements and now at the stage where there's virtually no centralised control. Similarly there were massive changes in terms of budgetary arrangements (Volker).

In the last few years, one of the few functional meetings of departmental secretaries was to discuss progress and problems in wage negotiations. Initially it was proposed that they meet only once, but by popular demand there have been regular meetings. It is simply a problem because it is a new and additional pressure on the departmental secretaries. But how independent are they?

> You've had all the rhetoric of recent years, particularly in the last two and a half, about 'you run your department, you're the CEO,

you've got all the flexibilities, no IR restrictions, live within your budget, you can do whatever you like, make things work'. The assumption is you will set your pay levels because your departmental labour market is different from other people's labour markets and the rest of the APS. There's an awful lot of ideology and a lack of reality in that. I've got no difficulty in dealing with flexibilities, but I do think in practice my main labour market rivals and competitors are other departments and the idea that I can set salary levels and conditions without being influenced by what they are doing is odd (Departmental Secretary 1990s).

Technology, too, played a substantial role in changing the style of management. Volker recalls the time when Sir Henry Bland, an old departmental secretary from the 1960s, visited his office 30 years later. He found several things amazing: the use by the departmental secretary of a PC to collect information (he used the old phrase of 'why bark yourself?'), the sheer volume of files, with 20 to 30 significant issues each day, the number of visitors (42 visiting ministers or heads of department in 1995 alone). While he was there, the minister, the junior minister and the parliamentary secretary all rang on direct lines (while he never had to deal with more than one minister). He was fascinated by the capacity of the departmental secretary to use the PC to get the live coverage of either the Senate or the House of Representatives. Just that day was an illustration of how far the position had changed as a matter of necessity.

IT innovations brought demands for outsourcing, an innovation that has let to new demands on the departmental secretaries. Whereas once the departmental secretary could be reasonably sure that most functions were under direct control, that is no longer the case. Finance, for instance, has outsourced much of its corporate management functions. Instead of management prerogatives, departmental secretaries must now deal with contract negotiations. Transport and Communications shrunk in size by almost 80 per cent over a few years as many of its functions were corporatised or sold off. Management has become more strategic, less hands-on in some departments. The Department of Social Security now has to oversee the delivery of services through Centrelink. The Department of Workplace Relations must determine the allocation of contracts within the Jobs Network. These changes require a management style that is less directive, as the departmental secretaries may not have the power to direct. Yet, at the same time, the ministers may want to know what is happening, why things go wrong and what can be done about it.

Since the government has chosen to act as a purchaser of services and does not necessarily deliver them itself, governments may now do less themselves, even though they maintain the same level of responsibilities for paying for programs. Programs may be delivered by the states or private companies, but the department still has to ensure they are provided efficiently and on time. That change brings new skills of management to the fore, without clearly reducing the pressure on the departmental secretaries to deliver. In terms of a job assessment, management had just become far more significant:

> You not only have to be a good policy analyst, you also need to be a good communicator and be able to show that you can run a well-managed organisation which I think is a significant shift (Moore-Wilton).

Even while all these changes occur, the departmental secretaries must work under the minister whose delegated powers they will still exercise.

Ministers and management

Ministers may have the right to become involved in management. Do they exercise it? Departmental secretaries must manage under the ministers. But do the ministers care about management? Despite the fact that over the last decades there has been a growth in ministers with a detailed interest in their portfolio, it is only a very small minority who want to play a direct role in decisions about the structure and workings of the departments. In the Labor governments, Evans and Dawkins were the principal two who were known as 'the management ministers'; Hawke played up their interest as though it applied universally to his government. But most of the rest were uninterested in management and left it to their departmental secretaries; several just assumed it was not their affair.

Yet initially they are given a set of instructions on what they should achieve. After each election, prime ministers send 'portfolio letters' to each portfolio minister, identifying a set of policy priorities and, in the cases where there are assistant or junior ministers, perhaps setting out a division of responsibilities and functions for those assistants.

How far can a minister go in determining the administrative arrangements? One departmental secretary believes:

> It is a reflection of society that, if you are a head of an organisation, you are increasingly expected to show you are in control ... because of democratic theory, because of community involvement and community interest in government, because of activism and better education, ministers have a much greater degree of involvement in the day-to-day operations of their department (Moore-Wilton).

Another thought it was 'entirely appropriate for the minister to comment on administration', but he thought there were limits: 'Sometimes he oversteps the boundaries by actually saying: "Look; don't you think that consultancy should be done that way?"'. The Dawkins reforms, argued anther recent departmental secretary, 'really placed the responsibility for managing the department with the minister, with the secretary as the principal agent' (Blunn).

But there might be a danger in the ministers taking the role too seriously. Not only would it massively absorb their time, but many did not have the expertise or the interest. A departmental secretary of the 1980s commented:

> A number of ministers see themselves as chief executives and indeed are frequently encouraged that way. However, I see the role of the ministers as analogous with the chairman of the board. It's a different skill. They have a skill in articulating policy, not in detailed oversight (Rae Taylor).

That has not stopped some ministers being determined to over see the revamp of a department and arguing that the quality of a minister could be seen from the effectiveness of the department when they left. A few departmental secretaries talked of the way they restructured their department in conjunction with the minister. Others merely noted that the minister had little interest in their management activities. It is reasonable for the ministers to assure themselves that the departmental secretary has set in place a set of arrangements and allocation of resources that will achieve their priorities, without developing those arrangements themselves. Like the chairman of a board, they may want to take a strategic overview. But few did even that.

Access to the minister was likely to be broad. Even in the 1970s, the departmental secretaries had given up the idea that only they should have direct access or brief alone. Wheeler recalled that:

> Prime ministers have railed at my practice of taking with me to ministerial committees one or two members of the team expert in the topics under notice. At times, arrangements were made to confine attendance to permanent heads. Except in special circumstances, I think such arrangements diminish the level of service provided to the minister ... A permanent head should not pretend to be an expert in all the matters covered in his department (Wheeler 1980:177).

The increased managerial emphasis has changed the role that the departmental secretary can play. Size and complexity have made it more unlikely that any departmental secretary can be the only policy adviser to the minister or even act as a conduit through which advice is directed. It has some consequences for particular positions too — for instance, the head of Attorney General's can no longer be both departmental manager and the principal legal adviser; some things have to be delegated:

> I would have to say from my own experience the administrative/ managerial element has become significantly larger and I suppose that challenges the idea of the secretary of the department also being the top lawyer of the department. We've got to the stage now where you wouldn't expect, if there's legal advice required in parliament, that it would be given by the secretary of the Attorney-General (Brazil).

Size had its impact:

> In a very big department like this we would have dozens of pieces of advice going over every week. There is just no way I can cover that. So what happens is I get a list of all the advices going over and I will ask for the minutes I want. For the most part at least one of the executive would have got a copy of it, but for the vast majority they would have got a copy after it was sent. They are signed off, as a rule, by the division heads ... The executive does not try to be a series of layers; it is more a quality control, quality assurance arrangement and on any major issue you would expect there to be quite a bit of interaction (Departmental Secretary 1990s).

But there could also be complications. In one case, the minister used to write such scarifying comments on the submissions that the departmental secretary tore off the cover sheet and relayed the message in more moderate terms; he was concerned not to undermine the morale of his staff.

Junior ministers make life hard too. Even if the usual practice was to identify a senior officer who would act as the de facto secretary for the junior minister and deal with the allocated programs, nevertheless there were occasions when every departmental secretary had to work with these ministers as crucial issues came to the boil. And sometimes they could be faced with antagonisms between the ambitious junior and a more tentative senior — not a comfortable role. One departmental secretary showed his new junior minister around the building; he was curtly told by the portfolio minister never to do it again; the latter feared the junior would be favoured by the department. Departmental secretaries had to be sensitive to the paranoia of the ministers.

Ministers have tended not to be interested in the planning mechanisms. In theory, they are required to sign off on the corporate plan that sets the directions of a department, but they often do so in a cursory manner. Forward estimates may set out the expenditure plans for the next years; but ministers will still not shrink from wanting new initiatives — why would they? Their incentives are not the same as those of officials. For them, a department is a means to an end, to provide a service and deliver the programs as required. Sometimes those who, from the point of view of the officials, seemed uninterested, will argue that was because they did not see it as their business or their problem.

There are some occasions where interest may be greater. In the making of appointments, for instance, ministers often want a say. Here there can be a conflict of interest. Under section 19 of the Public Service Act, agency heads are not subject to direction by any minister in the exercise of their powers over APS employees. Not subject to direction, certainly, but what of influence when they are about to make a senior appointment? Appointments were entirely the prerogative of the departmental secretary, but if they were senior they had to work directly to the minister on a number of occasions, so it was important that they were at least compatible with the minister.

Several attitudes can be seen: some chose to consult about the appointment of their deputies, but without giving them any veto:

> I would never ask my minister. For a deputy secretary level, I would tell the minister what I was proposing to do and would listen to anything my minister had to say (Beale).

> If the minister tried to select the SES, I'd handle it in a very delicate way, so that I wouldn't allow them do it (Departmental Secretary 1990s).

> It is quite right for the minister to want to know what I'm doing at senior levels to make it work. The minister accepts it's my decision, but he would expect to discuss it with me; if he's got some unease, for me to be able to respond to it. It doesn't mean I have to do what he says, but he would expect me to be able to say what I've done to handle the problem he's got. Now the pressures can be quite strong, you can go through a series of processes, drawing out the underlying concerns. But you must stand your ground (Podger).

The most strident rejection of ministerial input was the comment:

> Ministers were the least of your problems as long as you made clear to the minister: 'Each of us should stick to our own business'. You had to set down the ground rules, particularly with their staff, pretty early on, but as long as you were absolutely clear on it I never had the slightest trouble. The first time I promoted someone to the SES, I had this frantic phone call from the minister: 'What are you doing, you did this without telling us'. 'Well, of course I did it without telling you. Under the law it is my responsibility and there'd be big problems if you were involved'. 'Your

predecessor used to get my approval'. I said: 'Well, he shouldn't
have. I said I would consult you about deputy secretary because
that is the proper practice, that is the requirement, because the
argument is they would be acting secretaries and the minister is
entitled to at least input into it, to have a negative vote'. Of the
deputy secretaries I chose, I chose a number the minister didn't
want. He did not try to exercise a veto — he would have been in
trouble if he did, he was only entitled to express a view
(Departmental Secretary 1990s).

Some ministers — even prime ministers — did not see the public
service in political terms. Menadue relates Fraser's response to
information about appointments:

Despite the bitterness of the dismissal, I found little vindictiveness
in Fraser towards the public service — quite unlike the Howard
government years later. People were more likely to be judged on
their ability and honesty rather than what side of the political tracks
they came from. To properly inform him about the people he
would be dealing with, I insisted he be told of their party activities
if it was possibly relevant. His answer, with his chin sticking out,
was invariably, 'So?' He wasn't interested. He won the respect of a
wide range of senior officers in PM&C and I would include myself
in that category (Menadue 1999:171).

Not every departmental secretary would have told the minister that
much. Not all departmental secretaries would have been as fortunate
in the response they got. Still, ministers did not have the right to
choose their senior departmental staff, even if they could refuse to
talk to some of them. That circumstance provided yet another
situation that had to be managed.

A team of secretaries?

Is there a general service-wide approach to the issues of management?
Over the last decade, there has developed a tradition of monthly
meetings of departmental secretaries where there was an opportunity
to meet with colleagues and to compare experiences. Some drew
positive lessons from the more collegial relations of the modern cadre
and saw a contrast with earlier days:

This service has far less personality clashes, far less bitter disputes
between the Secretaries than the service I entered ... they had really
passionate disputes that would go on over an extensive period of
time. Then PAs would be given such demanding tasks as to find
some appropriate biblical or classical quotation to drive home a
point (Beale).

Another agreed that relations were better but was more sceptical of
the value of the meetings: there was, he thought:

a fading away of the mistrust among secretaries around the place. We all continued to go off to the monthly meetings that they have. But I don't think it led to any upsurge of collegial behaviour, performance or spirit or anything (Rosalky).

One person thought there was not enough of a corporate view, although enough 'to feel you were part of a collegiate team'. Before 1987, the chair of the Public Service Board held monthly meetings. Some of the departmental secretaries then chose to hold themselves aloof and mix very little with their colleagues:

We had meetings of permanent heads every couple of months. As chairman of the Board I would suggest an agenda and invite other suggestions, which I usually got. The meetings were very well attended. We did not make any decisions — the purpose was to talk issues through so that everyone knew what was happening and what views there were on those happenings. Some permanent heads were more collegiate than others. Some were very resistant to the role of the central agencies. Two in particular in my time were extremely difficult, but I think I had better not name names (Cole).

After the abolition of the PSB, the responsibility was shifted to the secretary of PM&C. How well the meetings ran depended very much on his personality and approach, and what purpose he saw the meetings performing. One attendee thought that Codd held the meetings to have discussions while his successors were more inclined to call meetings to tell people what the issues and policies were:

The meetings were not really conducive to argument, and often you would skip away from the serious issue, like maybe the PM's department needed to change; but it was very hard to tell Mike Keating that (Blunn).

On the other hand, the range of items expanded later. In addition, the departmental secretaries had an annual weekend retreat where they would sometimes meet with senior ministers. It gave them the chance for extended discussion of service-wide issues. There was at least a chance for some corporate agenda-setting.

As their positions became more precarious, and as it became obvious that the secretary of PM&C was to be the critical person in their performance appraisal, so participation in these meetings changed in tone. It was at a meeting soon after the 1998 election that the secretary of PM&C was reputed to say that the prime minister was only satisfied with the performance of half the departmental secretaries and named the three (or was it four, stories vary!) that were reputed to be doing a good job. When the story of the meeting leaked to the press, speculation began about which of the mandarins were duds, and hence the lemon hunt began. No one eventually lost their job and at another meeting a few months later they were told their positions were safe. But the episode may have changed the dynamics of the monthly meetings.

New management responsibilities added to the desire for some shared information. When the departmental secretaries were given responsibility for enterprise bargaining, they met to discuss the initial parameters. After all, most of them had no experience in industrial relations and bargaining. After they were given an initial briefing, they decided it was useful to meet regularly, under the leadership of the departmental secretary of Industrial Relations (later Workplace Relations), to hear about common problems and progress.

Even before that, several departmental secretaries thought that there was really little concept of a team. A few of the secretaries in social welfare departments based in the Canberra suburb of Woden had occasionally met for lunch to share experiences and common problems, but that was on their own initiative. Otherwise there was not a great sense of a team. One found 'no real cohesion, certainly no camaraderie, no sense of working together'. Another thought they were 'not an intrinsic team'. They were too busy and occasionally in a position to compete.

Mobility may have reduced the tension. Departmental secretaries were no longer in the same position for years and because few spent a career in the same department they understood better the alternative perspectives that were being promoted. They perhaps had a greater sense of where the government as a whole was going and possibly a greater preparedness to help others. They had common interests, and in relation to industrial relations, a need for some common understanding of what was happening. Their skills may have been exchangeable; most would see themselves as professional administrators, not as economists or lawyers. But their lives were dominated by the department and the minister.

Public and private management

The debate on the New Public Management assumes that at its core there has been an adoption of private sector corporate methods into the public sector. Indeed, much of the language of corporate planning, of missions and objectives, does apparently fit the bill. Over the last two decades, there have been a number of initiatives that seek to be more precise about what public servants are doing. Does this mean that there is a substantive change in the type of management that departmental secretaries now adopt?

In some respects there clearly is. The departments are often larger, and perhaps more complex as services and programs are taken across departmental boundaries. A wider series of techniques, created by the emergence of new technology, have made different styles of management possible. The private sector, too, has changed its style over the same period, sometimes contracting out all but the core functions. But the departmental secretaries themselves will still emphasise the differences, rather than the similarities, with the private sector. The public sector can learn from, but should not directly emulate, its private counterparts. It is a matter of both environment and attitudes:

> I think there are a lot of good techniques, which we can — and I do — borrow from the private sector. But I think it's very important not to lose sight of the fact that we have a different environment and, importantly, we have a different set of values that are really important among public servants. The occasions when people's eyes shine when I'm addressing staff are when I'm talking about values-based behaviour, public service as a calling, the contribution you can make for Australia. In the public service we deal with the big national issues; that's why people respond that way (Mathews).

Another secretary argued that 'there are still people who believe that working in the public service is a good and noble thing to do' (Blunn). There are values to be upheld.

But whose values? There is another view that is far more sceptical about any appeal to public service values:

> The question is who defines the integrity of the public service? The public sector is there, is paid, to assist; it's not an end in itself ... Some of my colleagues believe they are there to actually protect certain public service values, which they perceive as being different from private sector or other people's values (Departmental Secretary 1990s).

He did not accept that they had that right. He is correct in one of his assumptions. One departmental secretary expressed a broadly-held concern about attitudes in influential circles which questioned 'the thing called a public service in terms of a respected career' (Podger); threats to it concern him and many of his colleagues. The values that several secretaries espouse are largely procedural, non-partisan, equitable, fair values that are spelt out in the new APS legislation but which some fear may suffer from the *Yes Minister* doctrine of Inverse Relevance: put it up front so that it can be ignored in practice. As they see the APS as a profession, it is reasonable that they are concerned that the professionalism may be undermined — that is a common and normal reaction of any profession.

There were still seen to be distinct things that the public service did:

> There are very significant differences between a secretary of a department and a private sector chief executive. Whilst you can use many of the same skills, a secretary has to use them in different ways, particularly in regard to accountability and public presentation of policies. The minister assumes some of these essential functions (Moore-Wilton).

The differences come in several forms. First there are the factors that are fundamental to government and which loom larger the higher up the APS a person rises. It is essential to understand the place of the departmental secretary in relation to a number of legal and conventional frameworks that will always shape the way in which they will act. One departmental secretary sees it simply as part of the professional attributes of the public servant:

> To run any department, I think it is desirable to understand the elements of the public service, the professional ones ... And it ranges from the constitutional basis for what you do through to the way the finance system operates, through to the way parliamentary committees work and question time. All of those sorts of professional things that are peculiar to government as opposed to being the best structural engineer you can get (Blunn).

Then there are the different functions that they fulfil: a greater diversity of activities, more people to whom they are — directly or indirectly — responsible, less control over the immediate environment. A departmental secretary is not the same as a CEO, even if in places there is a tendency to call them that:

> The challenges for somebody running a department are more difficult than to be CEO of a major public company. And having sat on the Boards of public companies for a while, I still have that view (Codd).

John Menadue, the one person who had substantial private sector experience before becoming a departmental secretary, compared the two:

> Having worked in both the public and private sectors in my career, I found public officials much smarter in marshalling information, analysis and recommending action. Their intellectual horsepower was impressive. I found them, however, much more risk averse than their private sector counterparts, both as to career choices for themselves and what they would recommend. A predictable career path in the remote and privileged Canberra environment does not lend itself to risk taking (Menadue 1999:131).

Another departmental secretary who later had extensive private sector experience argued that 'every day at question time is your AGM'. The emphasis there is on the potential. Parliament meets around 70 days a year and some ministers get few questions. The significance is that parliamentary question time *may* suddenly explode in the face of the minister and there is a need to be constantly prepared for such an eventuality. The anxiousness and fear may be a means of accountability and the departmental secretary has to watch for potential problems and provide adequate information to counteract any threats.

In addition, the skills that the private sector values are different from those seen as vital in the public world:

> It is the decision maker, the profit maker in the private sector who is your most valuable man ... the profit maker can cut out what is dross and keep what is good. He would not be valued in the public sector and that is a huge difference. If you can produce the figures in business you are king within reason. If you ran the department economically, strictly, and watched the budget (I don't believe you can value the worth of a public servant) but if by 40 business efficiency yardsticks you were a whiz, it would hardly be noticed for that reason. Your minister must win, he must be delivering the goods to the country, to his party. He must be negotiating overseas. The access must come, industry groups must react: all quite different (Scully).

Secretaries face different publics, particularly in the range of people with whom they must deal. Community groups can be demanding. In a large department that delivers extensive services, the departmental secretary may have to be constantly available:

> In this place there are a huge number of interest groups, more than in any department I've ever worked in. Professional groups, community groups, consumer groups, industry groups, every single Australian has an interest. There is no other portfolio that has got that and it comes with the territory; it is far more high profile, not only for the minister but also for the department. Plus a requirement to be seen. I don't mean as a personality, but for the department to be out there; it's interactive, it's got huge numbers of committees, and there's no way the ministers could cover the ground, so you set up processes in the department for you and your senior people to be covering the ground (Podger).

Every citizen a client, every person a potential complainant: this is not business in action.

Another departmental secretary explained the difference in what had to be done:

> I think there is a difference. In terms of skills there are some you've got to have in respect of dealing with ministers and being prepared

to be accountable more generally and to the parliament. Doing things that in some respects as a private sectors person you would regard as not worth doing in terms of the overall priorities and a real pain in the neck. In the private sector, because time is so valuable and you're trying to make money for the shareholders or partners and so forth, you've got to have that foremost in your mind. I think the transition is actually easier from the public service to the private sector than the other way around, and I can see a lot of private sector people moving to the top levels of the public sector getting very frustrated (Volker).

The last point is significant. There have been no occasions when a senior officer from the private sector with no prior public sector experience has moved successfully into a position of departmental secretary. They have tended to find the restrictions too great and the expectations too high. In some respects they have less autonomy in the allocation of resources, even if it is much greater than it was when the Treasury and the PSB determined every detail.

Of course, on occasion a departmental secretary might accept some of the rhetoric of business. One commented:

> I would never criticise a staff member who has taken a risk and it's failed, subject to the one condition: that the innovation was surrounded by sensible risk management procedures (Mathews).

Whether parliament would be so kind might be another issue.

But several departmental secretaries suggest it is more the policy demands that are different because of the need to cope with ambiguity in intentions and outcomes and the requirement to calculate possible consequences over a range of arenas. Policy development, managing community demands and expectations, finessing the grey areas — these are the skills of the top departmental secretary:

> If you were chief executive officer of a private firm, you'd have shareholders and your major competitors. In the public sector you can certainly point to the accountability structure and transparency that's required of accountability. And I certainly think that's different from the private sector. But oddly I think the main difference, and where people who think about coming in from the private sector often lack in skills, is in the policy framework and the experience in working in a neutral sort of way with a range of players in the community and politicians and so on. It's those sort of general things about being a public servant. It's not just the accountability structure (Departmental Secretary 1990s).

Of course, it is possible to reduce the roles to fundamentals:

> The primary role of the secretary, as the primary role of the CEO of a private company, is to make the bloody thing work, make the organisation deliver its product and its product is good advice and good program management for the minister ... By far the most

important job of a secretary is to make the organisation run well and deliver for the minister (Rosalky).

The neatest distinction was drawn by one of Thatcher's advisers: a businessman working for a time in Number 10 and giving evidence to a parliamentary committee:

> If you are running a business in the private sector, to be successful you have to be right more often than you are wrong. If you are right 51 per cent of the time, you are just on the right side of that line. If you are right 60 per cent of the time you are doing better. Of you are right 70 per cent of the time, you are doing well. If you are right 80 per cent of the time, you are doing brilliantly. However, in the public sector, if you are right 98 per cent of the time, people are not interested in the 98 per cent; they are interested in the 2 per cent that you are wrong because the 2 per cent will be the ones that people are concerned about, where things are not being done properly, where things are not being done the way people would like to see them done. Therefore, I think the difference you mentioned is that you cannot say: 'I will not worry about the few per cent I get wrong', because clearly those few per cent represent very significant items which people do have to concern themselves about. I think that is the fundamental difference. That is why you cannot necessarily apply the same techniques which you would in the private sector because you cannot afford to just ignore things (Sir Peter Levene before the UK Treasury and Civil Service Committee, 26 October 1993, cited in Stowe 1996:97).

Remember this was not a civil servant, but an experienced businessman reflecting on his time working for the prime minister. Australian departmental secretaries would not disagree, for even as they have been given more freedom to manage, they remain under the demands of public accountability — and an increasing regime of accountability at that.

Note

1. One exception is Spann's coverage of management boards as a potential management technique that might be used by departmental secretaries and ministers. Yet even this discussion remains limited, with Spann citing the advantages one secretary accredited to management boards, but taking the evaluation no further. In general, however, Spann (1976), Cooley (1974) and the PSB (1974) — the three main relevant Australian publications of this era about departmental secretaries — are not interested in the different options available because they had more limited management responsibilities.

7

Performance and accountability: Who are the judges?

Amid the debates about the role of the departmental secretaries, there are two questions that still stand out as indications of the differences between the public and private sector; these are the questions of accountability and performance appraisal. If the principal difference between public and private is a matter of accountability, then how does it operate? For what and to whom are the departmental secretaries accountable? Further, given the snide comments about the performance of the public sector that are so common, how well do the departmental secretaries actually perform? Both would appear to be simple questions to answer, but they are not, precisely because of the ambiguity in activity that has already been mentioned.

This chapter will examine the performance of departmental secretaries. First it will explore the nature of public sector accountability, particularly the demands made by parliament. Then it will examine the issue of performance appraisal, asking whether it can be undertaken effectively and by whom this should be done. The first issue is the difficulty in assessing the quality of policy advice. Policy advice is at the core of the departmental secretaries' activities, but are there means for deciding how good that advice is? Then the chapter will review the processes and procedures adopted for the assessment of departmental secretaries' performance, including discussions of whether there should be connections between performance and levels of pay. It also raises an additional point: if prime ministers make the decisions about the future of the departmental secretaries, does that add a direct line of accountability to the prime minister? Finally it will ask what impact these appraisal procedures, and the nature of the performance contract, have had on the way that the departmental secretaries operate and how they may influence their future plans.

Changing means of accountability

The level and nature of accountability of departmental secretaries is always open to debate. In a study of Canadian deputy ministers, their equivalent of departmental secretaries, a former head of the civil service there started the study with the emphasis on the demands of accountability, the 'essential feature of parliamentary government' (Osbaldeston 1989:1). His study 'deals with one of the critical links in the parliamentary system of government — the accountability of deputy ministers to ministers and the government'. In the text, the accountability to government becomes accountability to the prime minister (1989:7). At this stage, Australian departmental secretaries will stop for breath. Accountability to the prime minister? They may admit that it is true in practice that they keep an eye on the opinions of the prime minister while arguing that in theory they are responsible to their minister, and only to their minister. But the variations of opinion in different countries that apparently have similar systems illustrate how each nation develops its own rules and conventions for accountability.

In 1991, the Management Advisory Board released a description of the system of accountability in the Commonwealth public sector. It was described as an 'exposure draft'. It argued that departmental secretaries were accountable only to their ministers. They may be *answerable* to parliament through their minister, but only through the minister. There was extensive criticism of the draft because it ignored the other people to whom outsiders thought the departmental secretaries should be accountable: the public as clients, the Auditor-General, the ombudsman and MPs (MAB 1991). The second and final version accepted that the lines of accountability were more complex:

> There is thus a continuum of accountability relationships between the electorate, the parliament, the government and the public service. Traditionally, the primary accountability obligation of public servants is to the government of the day. Ministers are accountable to the parliament for the exercise of ministerial authority, while public servants are accountable to ministers for the exercise of delegated authority. But these hierarchical relationships have now been complemented by public servants' duty to explain or justify their actions to various review bodies and directly to parliamentary committees where the minister neither knew nor should have been expected to know (MAB 1993:4).

Accountability, therefore, is not an uncontested concept. But it is widely accepted that there are increasing pressures being put on public servants.

Concepts of accountability are complicated by the operations of the public sector where, as Thatcher's adviser noted, the system more readily allocates blame than praise. That accountability has increased extensively in the last 30 years, in formal terms through parliamentary committees, through the introduction of administrative law and through the more immediate demands of the media. The bureaucracy of the 1960s was largely seen as unaccountable. Its procedures were largely carried on in secret. Information was restricted. Parliamentary review was no antidote to the mistreatment of individuals unless they became a *cause célèbre*. That was why a committee headed by John Kerr advocated the introduction of administrative law as an alternative means of review.

Gradually that monopoly over information was pared away. Freedom of information legislation gave citizens and the media an opportunity to gain access to files. The Ombudsman could review the processes and decisions of government and even recommend that a decision be overturned: he or she had the ability to report publicly to parliament. Administrative review could review process and in limited cases even overturn ministerial decisions on the merits of the case. Whereas once decisions could be made in the knowledge that they would be kept secure for 30 years or more, now there might be more immediate review, and in a public arena. That openness has had an impact on the way that departmental secretaries make, and certainly record, decisions: 'We have to assume that any decision may become public and be prepared to defend it,' one explained. It is 'less possible to be arbitrary' was a benefit seen by another. There was now a need to maintain a careful record that was defensible.

Any issue could always explode into a political dogfight. The 'sports rorts' were one such occasion. The minister was accused of favouring Labor marginal electorates in the allocation of grants. Instead of a defensible administrative process, the decisions had been recorded on a whiteboard in the minister's office. Her departmental secretary insists that it could have been done with due process in such a way that the conclusions were beyond challenge, but the minister's preference for a more informal procedure brought about her demise. The lesson was the need to ensure that the procedures were right; the warning was that any program could become an exercise in accountability.

The parliamentary capacity for asserting accountability has indeed changed. The Public Accounts Committee had long had a strong presence and tradition and, when required, departmental secretaries would appear before it to give evidence. Senate Estimates Committees were established in the early 1970s to give the senators an opportunity to review administrative activity. Slowly they developed some capacity and even teeth. Even if their questions were often bizarre, sometimes more concerned with the purchase of pot plants than the administration of programs, the departmental secretaries had to prepare extensively for them. A few declined to appear before them, arguing that they were often on fishing trips, rather than seriously reviewing government estimates; if the departmental secretary appeared, it gave them status. Instead they sent along more junior officers who could not be expected to know the answers and would therefore have to take the questions on notice and provide the details later. Whether they could still get away with such a strategy may be open to debate. After the appearance, they were conscious that they had to adhere to the public commitments that were made there. It gave the departmental secretaries a more public profile and added to the demands of the job. As one former mandarin put it:

> What developed in the 1970s that didn't exist so much in the 1950s and 1960s during the time I was head of one department or another was the creation and growth of parliamentary committees, investigations, you know the Labor reforms and Senate Committees and all that. Which meant a lot of time, more time, had to be spent by the departmental secretary in meetings of Parliamentary committees ... one doesn't complain about that, that's part of the democracy we have, what I'm getting at is it didn't necessarily improve sound government executive decisions (Tange; see also Tange 1982).

Others felt the expectation that their decisions could be challenged did have an impact on the quality of decisions. Public servants were not infallible; the possibility of the decisions being publicly reviewed forced a review of procedures and even their improvement. Anticipation of what might occur can be time consuming, and sometimes nerve wracking if the parliamentary committees contained those who were seeking to make a name for themselves by making life hard for the public servants appearing before them.

It certainly made life unpredictable for those who were brought in from outside and who were entirely unused to this form of cross-questioning:

> The people who we have brought in; a lot of them haven't worked because they can't get over coming to a parliamentary committee and having their arms torn off by someone who they are not technically working for. They are doing the job for the minister and having their arms torn off and they don't like it.

Sometimes, of course, the MPs — in the view of departmental secretaries — treated them quite unfairly:

> I got on very well with Bronwyn Bishop when she was my minister, but she virtually accused me of being corrupt in the Public Accounts Committee. Well, I mean, anyone who looks at my bank account

knows I haven't got anything and I get a security clearance, I have a regular audit of my finances and my wife's finances. I was supposed to be on the take from IBM. I said to the chairman of the committee: 'Well, let's adjourn the committee and let Senator Bishop go outside and make that statement and we will test it in court'. He said: 'I'm sure that's not what she meant' and Bob McMullan said: 'I thought it was exactly what she meant'. I can handle it; I'm big enough and ugly enough to look after myself. But others were badly affected and left because they didn't want to be part of that (Ayers).

Another departmental secretary objected to the probing in Estimates to find out precisely who made the decision: 'Typically I've drawn a veil around the identity of individuals involved in operations and I'm very careful not to reveal officers' names' (Departmental Secretary 1990s). Some anonymity ought to be retained. The minister (for policy choices) and the departmental secretary (for operations) ought to take the responsibility.

In general, the departmental secretaries accepted the inevitability of the changes. One departmental secretary commented that everything was written in the context that it could be tabled — an explanation, perhaps, for the fact that some ministers preferred much of the advice they got to be unwritten. There were, of course, problems that went with the changes. The decline in anonymity was regretted, in part because it identified the departmental secretaries in public with the programs of the existing government and thus often led to charges of political alignment. But the additional accountability was seen as desirable, even if it created further pressures.

Three comments can provide a general, if world weary, view:

I actually think in many ways the public service is better and more efficient than it used to be. Now I think we have lost some things in that process, but I think we are more generally accountable than we were, and I think we are better managers than we were. I suppose I regret the passing of some of the things that I think have been lost in that process, but generally speaking I think we are better ... The public has a right to a lot of information we used to guard jealously (Blunn).

Certainly there's a lot more accountability around the place in terms of the information that has to be provided ... There's no doubt that it was much more difficult over the period in terms of accountability and I think also in terms of the volume and complexity of activity ... And much more review; another thing old-time secretaries didn't have to deal with was reviews of decisions and Freedom of Information requests (Volker).

A broader view looked at the way that society had changed and saw the new requirements for accountability in terms of the expectations of the public for more transparent and open government:

> Society expects an accountable public service. They expect freedom
> of information, they expect judicial review or administrative review.
> They expect access to people, reasons, so it's not a problem. But
> yes, there are more people holding me to account (Mathews).

Assessing the quality of policy advice

Much of the pressure for accountability has been external, driven by
demands that the APS be seen as responsible to the parliament for its
actions. Yet much of the activity of departmental secretaries is private,
serving the minister by providing policy advice and managing the
department on behalf of the government. How well do they do the
job? It may seem an obvious question to ask, but it is harder to answer
because it raises a number of issues about the nature of the job and
the relationship of the departmental secretaries to their ministers. It
is therefore worth a diversion to ask how policy advice might be
assessed as a useful prerequisite to asking whether it should be done
and by whom.

In the past, there seems to have been an implicit assumption that
good people give good advice. If the system ensures those who reach
the top of the civil service are properly talented, then it follows that
the quality of advice will be based on firm foundations. Where policies
fail, it can be argued, it is because the government failed to listen.
Since ministers take decisions, failures need not indicate the advice
provided by officials was poor. However, such assumptions need to
be tested. Program evaluation is routinely undertaken and used as a
guide for future action, it may show flaws in the planning and the
original policy advice, but is not usually used for that purpose. The
evaluation of policy advice had traditionally been left to more
informal mechanisms. Yet policy advice is a crucial part of the activity
of departmental secretaries and, if asked what their most significant
role is, many will respond it is giving policy advice.

Policy advice is difficult to assess. It is, after all, eventually a matter
of judgment, an art or craft rather than a science (Wildavsky 1979;
Waller 1996:12). It usually requires the reduction of a complex
problem to a set of options, based on assumptions about causation,
and compatible with government policies or directions. There is no
guarantee ministers will accept the advice. Nor should there be.
Hence, in the process of evaluation, the emphasis must be more on
the development of advice than on resultant action. Acceptance
cannot be an absolute criterion for determining that advice is good.
Even when advice is accepted without change, there may be problems

of implementation. Further, since advice from a departmental secretary is usually confidential, there may be some problems in seeking to judge its quality. Ministers have many sources of advice and disentangling them is difficult, so there can be no certainty that the public service's policy, for better or worse, was responsible for the outcome.

None of these caveats is novel. Nor are they restricted to any one country. The literature on policy-making emphasises its contingent nature. Wildavsky's (1973) famous strictures on planning can readily be applied to advice; it needs a theory of causation and clear objectives against which progress can be tested. Even the fact of acceptance is not a sign of its success, as politicians and officials may agree to a proposal for reasons outside the policy itself (Wildavsky 1979:213). Policy is usually negotiated, the outcome of a political process, a combination of values, ideology and pragmatism, rather than being determined by the edicts of experts. The accepted view of policy-making emphasises the ebb and flow of debate, the processes of policy learning, the creation of coalitions. There is an appreciation of the limits to our understanding of causation, particularly in a more complex world with more links and ideas. Any link between the provision of advice, its acceptance or otherwise, and its impact, cannot be seen as linear or simple.

But are these satisfactory reasons for not trying to assess whether the advice is of good quality? In an era which stresses efficiency of service delivery, and where there is an effort to assess the cost of government services, is there not a case for seeking to test the effectiveness of policy advice? There is, as always, a judgment to be made. Recognising the difficulties, will evaluation promise enough benefits to justify the cost of the exercise and is there a methodology that might suggest the promise of advantages to the political system?

In addition to the theoretical desirability, there may be some pressing strategic reasons for departmental secretaries to consider such a process. At a time when there are serious proposals that policy advice should be privatised or contracted out, there is a need to justify its current mode of existence. Indeed, if policy advice is to be contracted out, there is an even greater need to devise procedures for determining whether that advice is of good quality.

The imperative to try is made more urgent by the perceived costs of policy mistakes, sometimes made on a grand scale and costing billions of dollars, and in part generated by poor advice. In his analysis of policy disasters, Dunleavy identifies as a cause the lack of 'appropriate professional expertise to be able to appreciate risk and cost'; he claims that in Britain there was a 'premium on political responsiveness' and a 'de-emphasis on policy work' (Dunleavy

1995:62). He concludes that 'the shrinkage of the central state machine produced by ceaseless reorganization and efficiency "savings" has led to sadly reduced core competencies' (1995:63).

His diagnosis reflects a broader dissatisfaction with the existing processes. Plowden (1994:104) cites a commentator who claims that 'the most obvious sign of ill-health in the machinery of state is poor performance at policy work'. Plowden argues that 'properly thought-out advice from civil servants ought to include alternative types of solution to those in vogue' (1994:105). The British handbook for ministers, *Questions of Procedure for Ministers*, instructs ministers 'to give fair consideration and due weight to informed and impartial advice from civil servants', but clearly there is some feeling that all is not working well. Yet this diagnosis of ill-health in Britain has not led to proposals for assessing when that advice is, or is not, well informed and of good quality.

The New Zealand government has, at least formally, sought to identify more precisely the range and impact of policy advice. It has calculated the cost of policy advice — NZ$245 million in the 1992/93 financial year — thus putting a monetary figure on the service ministers are purchasing (Boston et al. 1996:129). The government has devised a performance management framework for examining quality with seven defining characteristics: purpose, logic, accuracy, options, consultation, practicality and presentation. Ministers are asked every three months to indicate their level of satisfaction, as an input to the review of the performance of departmental secretaries by the State Services Commission (Hunn 1994:31–32). But the authors of the initiative acknowledge that ministers may not always be the best people to judge quality and that they may have a particular problem in those cases when the advice was necessary, but not welcome. In addition, the evaluation of advice was part of the process of assessing official performance; policy advice was not the principal subject of inquiry. Even after this attempt to calculate the best performance, observers can only comment that 'some departments have acquired a well-deserved reputation for producing excellent work, whereas others have been much less successful' (Boston *et al.* 1996:133).

That the problem is a difficult one is not in debate. Central agencies were faced with an additional problem: when parliamentary committees asked what 'value-added' they provided, the response was that, among other things, they provided 'policy advice'. If the question was then asked: 'How well was it provided?' there was little evidence to justify the confidence that it was of a high standard. The central agencies therefore need a means of assessing policy advice in order to conform to the same standards of evaluation imposed on line departments.

It is worth illustrating how Australia responded as a prologue to the more precise question of whether and how the policy advice of departmental secretaries might be assessed. A Working Party made up from officials of the four central agencies (Prime Minister and Cabinet, Treasury, Finance and the Public Service Commission) was established to examine the problem. It first explored the experience of other nations:

> The overseas trip was interesting and useful in teasing out very different cultural and philosophical approaches to whether, and if so, how the business of policy advising should be evaluated. With the French it really was the 'Gallic shrug', as though to say that we really were quite mad in wanting to ask any of these questions. Whitehall was somewhat different. Paraphrasing Dr Johnson, the British saw it as not a question of whether you ought to do policy evaluation well. Instead it was a question of why on earth would you want to evaluate policy advice at all given that, self-evidently, anybody in the Whitehall advising policy game must be doing it well.
>
> The United States was quite different again, and useful. Though structurally and constitutionally distinct from the system that we are accustomed to here, there was a great deal more yeast and openness in terms of questioning the mores, the value and the appropriate application of policies (Waller 1996:70).

The Task Force's report, *Performance Assessment of Policy Work* (PAPW 1992), was judicious and careful. (An abbreviated version has been published in Waller 1992.) It explained the process for developing good advice and acknowledged the contingent nature of evaluating good policy advice which involves:

- taking a difficult and sometimes poorly understood problem or issue and structuring it so that it can be thought about in a systematic way;
- gathering the minimum necessary information and applying the appropriate analytical framework;
- formulating effective options addressing, where necessary, mechanisms for implementation and evaluation; and
- communicating the results of the work to the government in a timely and understandable way (PAPW 1992:8–9).

The object of the evaluation — policy advice — was seen as more than merely consideration of the final paper to the minister; it incorporated the whole process of understanding the problems, coordinating the responses and formulating their advice — in essence, the whole policy cycle from issue identification through to implementation and evaluation.

The report notes the need to consider three aspects: inputs (staff, management practices, information), process and outputs. It acknowledges that the first two are easier to analyse than the utility of the advice. Assessing that utility, the report points out:

> involves assessing the effectiveness of policy advice, firstly in terms of its effect on the recipient of that advice, secondly whether that person adopts the advice and advocates it and thirdly its effect on the decision-making process.

This need to understand causal links between the quality of the advice and the outcome is made harder by the problem of judging impact, and deciding whether short- or long-term perspectives are the more appropriate time horizons.

Good advice is therefore both procedural — getting the content right — and presentational — telling it as it is. As the report says:

> policy advice is an art or a craft, rather than a science. What the policy adviser is required to do is reach a professional judgement about both the underlying situation and the appropriate course for policy. These judgements must be honest, disciplined and rigorous and be transparent to those to whom the advice is directed (PAPW 1992: 9).

Good advice, not necessarily advice that they are comfortable with, is what ministers should hear. The working party emphasised that policy advising must be confidential, to protect the relationship between ministers and their advisers.

The Working Party report (but not the version later published) then canvassed options. It admitted that informal methods of analysis — ministerial advisers, a better informed private sector, interest groups and governmental research institutes — provided some analysis through the process of contesting and debating policy alternatives. The public service no longer had a near monopoly on policy advice. Ministers are, anyway, always able to make informal assessments of policy advisers. Some political assessment has existed, if not in a systematic way, through parliamentary committees. On behalf of parliament, the Australian National Audit Office could assess program performance and report to the Public Accounts Committee. But these methods were informal or tangential to the central issue; none of them provided any formal consideration of the procedures and problems of formulating advice.

The working party proposed that a series of Policy Management Reviews (PMRs) take place to assess the development and delivery of policy in a number of areas in which the central agencies had been active (for details, see Uhr and Mackay 1996; Weller and Stevens 1998). Each of the reviews drew lessons from the experience that might be of value to the sponsoring departments. PMRs had some strengths: they allowed a broad view of policy and an assessment of how all the different actors played their roles; they were able to provide a catalogue of best practice that was useful for training and reflection. But they could not examine precisely what contributions individuals such as departmental secretaries might have added to the process; rather, it is assumed that the departmental secretaries are always responsible for the quality of the major pieces of policy advice, even if they have little personal involvement in their preparation. PMRs were a useful initiative in the evaluation of policy advice and could be developed in an inventory against which departmental secretaries' performance might be evaluated. However, there was still a need for greater refinement of the processes.

The debate on assessing policy advice in broad terms shows the complexity of the exercise. How much harder it is, then, to assess the performance of the departmental secretary in this area when the direct involvement in the policy development may be limited. Instead, they have to be assessed as a policy manager, a facilitator who brings together the threads of policy to present to the minister. At that level, of course, the departmental secretary is responsible for all the significant advice that goes to the minister and may be judged by its quality.

Often, as the discussion on formal performance assessment will show, it is regarded as too hard, but there were some areas where attempts have been made. One departmental secretary has an arrangement with his ministers to give a rating from one to five stars on advice that is provided. As he put it:

> There's no use just saying I am going to produce timely, well-argued policy advice; I need to know what the minister, our client in this regard, actually thinks of it. I know it's very difficult for my staff when they get no more than a 3 on a 5 star rating from him. It's quite painful. Most of them are proud of their work. What is interesting is that I have to keep showing them [his staff] the dictionary definition of 'satisfactory', i.e. 'fulfilling all demands', which is a 3 on the scale, because they all thought they'd get fours and fives ... On occasion the minister gives them 1s and 2s and writes down why he's given them a 1 or a 2. From that point of view it's particularly effective in that it encourages the minister to provide reasons for his dissatisfaction. Assessment is made in terms of timeliness and presentation and the force of argument ... I reckon it's much better to know than not to know (Shergold).

On the whole, the departmental secretary 'tended to agree about the quality, though he might have been slightly more generous'. But the principal point was that, if the minister indicated a proposal had not been thought out enough, it was a reflection as much on the departmental secretary as on the area of the department.

At the end of the first year, there was an analysis of the trends in ministerial responses. Ministers were asked to assess: (1) the timeliness; (2) the presentation, which consisted of the purpose, logic, style, accuracy and evidence of adequate consultation; and (3) the quality of advice. This section was made up of four parts:

- *Robustness:* frank and honest assessment of options;
- *Creativity:* an innovative range of options which meet the directions set by government;
- *Responsiveness:* showing awareness of the government's policy agenda and identify anticipated developments;
- *Practicality and relevance:* consideration of practical issues including implementation, technical feasibility, timing and consistency with related government policies.

Ministers gave ratings on 84 per cent of briefs. For the first three-quarters, around 85 per cent were given a 3, as satisfactory. Less than 1 per cent were less than satisfactory. Around 12 per cent were better than satisfactory. In the last quarter, the last category rose to just under 20 per cent. In ministers' eyes, there was a slight improvement in quality.

Such a scheme required a rare minister, a confident departmental secretary and a robust relationship between them. Clearly it can work. (It would be interesting to see the minister re-rate the advice after the impact of the proposals contained in the briefs has been assessed!) But this scheme is an exception. Often it is hard to get any feedback from ministers; at times, the briefs do not come back at all so there is no indication of what impact it had — or even whether it was read at all.

Performance appraisal of departmental secretaries

Questions of performance appraisal are concerned with three issues:

- *How* can it be done in a way that is both accurate and helpful?
- *Who* should do it?
- Should *pay* be related to performance for departmental secretaries?

All three are matters of dispute. Another way of conflating the three issues is just to ask whether it can be done fairly. If it can, it implies someone is capable of doing it and there will be no problems with the decisions on pay.

The post-1994 system did not introduce a system of contracts or performance targets. Secretaries were not asked to sign anything but a general letter of agreement to the new terms that were standard across all departmental secretaries. For those appointed before the 1994 contracts, their five-year terms started again. But some only found out about the terms from their department's personnel branch when it received a routine memo. Unlike the arrangements in New Zealand and Victoria, there are no generic or particular performance criteria, just a set of general employment conditions that were accepted as a consequence of their decision to give up rights of tenure in the service. The changes were not designed to improve the performance of particular secretaries.

In determining the details of a performance agreement, there are three choices. First, there can be no detail. Second, it can be expressed in general terms. Third, it can be very specific and related to the individual departmental secretaries and their ministers. There is a constant need for trade-offs, for a balance between flexibility and specificity. If it is too detailed, it would require constant variations so that the contractual demands reflected the changing political situation. If it is only very general, it is of no value in assessing the performance of the departmental secretary.

A common point of discussion with the secretaries was whether it was possible to make each position subject to a more specific set of performance agreements. The government's discussion paper foreshadowed the possibility of formal performance agreements for all agency heads that would include criteria for the measurement of performance. The experience in New Zealand was often mentioned as a contrast or as a possible model, even if only for learning what not to do. There the contracts of the heads of departments distinguish between the outputs that the department is required to deliver and the outcomes that are to be achieved by the government's policy. Some contracts are for short periods — even as little as six months. While it was widely accepted that the logic of the debate was moving down the route of performance agreements, there was some scepticism about whether there were real benefits to be achieved.

There were several reasons behind this scepticism. First, there was some doubt about the ability to define what the secretary as an individual might be able to deliver. Surrounded by constraints caused by changes in government policy, by the demands and restrictions of central agencies, and by the difficulties of defining output in departments which primarily deliver policy advice, secretaries do not have discrete jobs with clear individual outputs. There is always a danger it will be driven by negatives — not overshooting the budget, avoiding complaints, minimising parliamentary attacks — rather than a set of positive achievements. The New Zealand experience was not seen as uniformly beneficial; some sets of targets were trivial or too easy to achieve, other relationships had become too legalistic. On the other hand, very broad generic criteria were problematic for the purposes of judging individual performance:

> I certainly believe it is possible to have a contract, a performance-based contract between a secretary and a minister. How you would write that contract depends upon the style ... My preference is not too much detail, but I like to get the outcomes or the objectives very clear and have some flexibility in how to achieve them (Higgins).

There was seen to be a danger that if the secretaries had agreed targets that were no longer consistent with new government policy, that would reduce the degree of flexibility required for good policy development. Some secretaries were concerned about the regimentation involved in specifying performance criteria, and the rigidities such indicators imposed on managers. If the cabinet's priorities changed, did they simply add further criteria, continue to amend the performance agreement, replace criteria or augment the agency's budget to accommodate new priorities? Many performance criteria would also involve considerable lead times before likely achievements would be reported. And the frequent amending of criteria was counterproductive to agreed targets.

Some thought it better to rely on the corporate plans, with six or seven principal targets, which should have been developed in concert with the minister and signed off by both the minister and the secretary as a guide to action. Then the secretary was in effect being judged by the capacity to manage the department within the agreed parameters. Indeed there were likely to be benefits for the coordination of whole-of-government policy if these departmental targets were not only discussed with the minister, but also outside the department, because that process would provide a means of determining the parameters for satisfactory performance for secretaries in terms beyond that of ministerial satisfaction. Again, reliance on corporate plans illustrates the trade-off between government flexibility and the degree of specificity needed for appraisal. If the objectives are too general, they cannot be used to fairly assess performance.

But many of the concerns were less technical than contextual. It was, after all, to be a personal assessment: 'It is about what your particular role is; what you can add to the process; some secretaries tend to be impersonal about what they are trying to achieve for the portfolio' (Sedgwick). For Sedgwick, the major change was that everything was now more explicit, and that was not necessarily a bad thing. Other secretaries often believed that the links between them and the minister could not be reduced to performance indicators; that was based on a misunderstanding of the way in which they perceived the job. This was partly because it would be possible to agree to standards that might be easy to meet, but primarily because, if the chemistry had broken down, no set of indicators could mend that relationship:

> I think it is pretty hard in many ways, but that is not to say it can't be done. It depends how you do it. One of the problems I have always felt for secretaries is it is very hard to distinguish between the performance of ministers and the performance of secretaries. In other words, it is a partnership appointment ... In my view it has to work on a very flexible basis and there is a relationship that can only work on a basis of trust (Stevens).

In evidence to the Senate Committee on Finance and Public Administration (7 July 1997), Michael Keating argued that, for performance contracts to work:

> First of all, it seems to be dependent on the government itself being able to write its portfolio performance plan ...

> Secondly, the relationship with the secretary is very much a partnership if it is to work well. There is a real question whether it is a good idea to commit what is a partnership based on trust and loyalty to a written agreement. There are many examples of partnerships where people think it will destroy the partnership if you try and specify exactly what each party expects of the other. We certainly do not try it in marriage as a general rule. When we do and start writing out whose property is whose, that is usually taken to raise the question about whether we are thinking about breaking up ... There is a role, when you are working in a partnership, for trust and not getting too specific. Beyond that, it will be very difficult to assign responsibility.

He believed a specific contact would change the nature of the relationship.

Besides, a set of indicators might create an expectation that, if the targets were met, then the position of the secretary was safe. But it does not work like that. A discontented minister will still try to move a secretary, even when all the criteria are met — in itself perhaps an indication that ministers do not think the criteria are adequate:

> I know in my heart of hearts that if I was to write out a detailed performance contract on what I hoped to achieve with my minister, that alone would probably not be how he would judge my performance. In a sense my performance is based, I think, on leadership behaviour as much as on specific outcomes — and I hope I know the sort of behaviour that he wants to see ... And therefore the assessment of performance is in my view dependent on how much trust and confidence he places in my ability to manage this department and to offer him advice and to implement the decisions

of the government, and I don't think they will be neatly captured in formal outcomes, still less specific outputs (Shergold).

That was not to suggest that some people did not like the system of contracts; one departmental secretary was not concerned that he was hired at the minister's pleasure:

> I found that enormously satisfying, couldn't work out why. I guess because it's very clear who is responsible for the future. It took away a lot of the ambiguity and it gave me a real sense of focus and a real sense of personal success (Rosalky).

Another felt it was less the detail than the general tone of change that was significant:

> What's changed over the last few years is the implicit nature of the contract that parliament and the government of the day have with the public service; there's now generally less presumption of permanence than there was 20 years ago. The implicit contract that has developed is as critical as the actual terms of the contract (Departmental Secretary 1990s).

It might be possible to go further and argue that the whole system is antipathetic to the idea of contracts:

> Democracy is not a managerial system. Departmental secretaries basically are tasked to carry out the remit of a democratic system. It's not a contractual system; a democratic system is a reflection of the will of the people at a particular point in time, which can be extremely variable (Moore-Wilton).

Its success also depended on the atmosphere, the general level of trust. One departmental secretary thought initially the debate on performance appraisal got nowhere after the 'lemon' hunt because:

> It depends on the environment and the environment was characterised by that whole (what language can I use around here?) ... 'fuck up' is the only word that comes to mind (Rosalky).

Later the atmosphere may have improved, but it had an unfortunate start.

Essentially, therefore, there is no contract because a contract requires both sides to commit and to hold to it. Real contracts can be legally enforced, but there is no guarantee of continued employment subject to satisfactory performance. There is no way in which ministers can be bound by conditions that could restrict their freedom to change policy direction or the demands for support from departmental secretaries. If contracts are two-way commitments, then no set of performance indicators will protect a secretary who falls out with the minister, however well the targets are being met. There is no likelihood of coming up with a list of criteria that ministers would be prepared to abide by and which departmental secretaries would see as a fair estimation of the role they have fulfilled. Certainly no such list exists at the moment. The system is too fluid, too fast moving, too unpredictable to allow a detailed and enforceable set of performance arrangements. Perhaps at some stage it should be recognised that the task of compiling criteria is too hard and a much more subjective set of criteria needs to be accepted.

Who should do the appraisal and by what process?

Nonetheless, since there is a desire to assess the performance of the departmental secretaries, who should do it? There are several choices. In Canada, the Clerk of the Privy Council chairs a committee of review to assess the performance of the deputy ministers (the Canadian departmental secretaries). In New Zealand, the chair of the State Service Commission reviews performance. In both cases, the opinions of the ministers may be sought but the final decision lies elsewhere, with senior officials who have an interest in the health of the public service. There are, in other words, a number of schemes that can be adopted that are consistent with the traditions of non-partisan and professional public services.

The system that has been introduced goes through a number of stages (for some details, see the hearings of the Senate Finance and Public Administration Committee, 22 May 2000). First the departmental secretary provides a self-assessment, based partly on the performance criteria agreed with the minister, and discusses it with the minister. Then the secretary of PM&C and the Public Service Commissioner interview the ministers about the performance of their departmental secretaries and get an indication of what ranking the minister might give. The departmental secretaries are to be classified as Outstanding, Superior and Ordinary. The first group get a bonus of 15 per cent, the second get 10 per cent and the third nothing. Then the secretary of PM&C and the Public Service Commissioner discuss the ministers' proposals with the prime minister, with whom the final decision lies. At one stage there was talk of tabling the results, but that has been shelved, although it may be possible to infer the result from the departmental annual reports in a year's time by considering the bands in which the top salaries appear. Around that formal process there are doubtless a number of informal discussions, particularly between the leading assessors. The system is highly centralised and relies on the judgment of the prime minister and his principal public service advisers.

In Australia, a scheme for evaluating performance has been

anticipated for some time. In itself, this move was not necessarily a concern:

> One thing to remember is we have always been assessed. We just never knew about it ... In some ways, if the life is going to be more precarious, so be it. The thing, I think, is that we all know the rules (Sedgwick).

Another commented that the prime minister and the secretary of PM&C had always reviewed performance, but behind closed doors. Now it would be done up front by the secretary of PM&C in conjunction with ministers. 'Would they prefer he simply did it and told them later?' (Hawke) It was possible to find people who were relaxed, even up-beat about the proposal:

> What is the risk to me? At the moment they can fire me, and they can fire me on their perception of my performance. Why the hell shouldn't I run the risk of getting more money. Being threatened with a reward is not actually a thing I worry about at night. It's not introducing firing; that's been around for years (Departmental Secretary 1990s).

Some had doubts that the secretary of PM&C could actually know what was going on within departments:

> Well, you don't have a [Public Service] Board, somebody has to do it. I mean, the real question is, how can the secretary of PM&C know how each of the permanent heads is performing. Departmental secretaries performing in an area where he has no vision of what's going on from the minister downwards. I mean we operate basically in self-contained departments (Visbord).

One former departmental secretary of PM&C, Michael Keating, agreed; he felt that the departmental secretary of PM&C only knew what was going on when there was a crisis, or with the advent — or potential advent — of bad news. He may know when there is a risk of termination (as in the case of Moore-Wilton and Barratt, see Chapter 9), but is not normally aware of day-to-day activity. He thought that when he was the departmental secretary of Finance, he probably had a better chance to assess their management effectiveness.

Nevertheless, if it was done in an official way, at least it would be seen to be above board. One departmental secretary, at a time of great uncertainty, said:

> I have told a minister of this government, I don't know your rules. I don't know whether I will be reappointed. I said I didn't say I expect not to be, I said I don't have an expectation about whether I will or I won't. I don't have a basis on which to form an expectation because I don't know your rules (Departmental Secretary 1990s).

There was also the question of whether the minister's performance and that of the departmental secretary could be distinguished. If it is indeed a partnership, then the minister would not be the appropriate person and could use the opportunity to try to pass the buck.

One person felt that only the minister could possibly have the range of knowledge required to make a valid assessment, while accepting there might be problems:

> My view is the minister is best placed to do it and should do it, but that's not the system we are going to have ... Well, it does depend on your minister because they know your work — you're producing services for them. [What if you've got a very ordinary Minister?] You have just got to take the rough with the smooth, and that's why I'm in the public sector. For me I think a performance system is important and I have a great desire to achieve things. If the system turns round and then rewards me for that in a financial sense, that's fantastic. If it doesn't, I'm disappointed, but it's not the only thing (Departmental Secretary 1990s).

Others rejected the idea that the minister should be responsible:

> I guess one of the problems is whether or not a minister has got the skills to do a performance assessment where the task being assessed is quite complicated and quite broad. Much of [what] you actually do is beyond the interest of the minister (Departmental Secretary 1990s).

If the minister wanted them out of the job, it would be too easy to give them a bad review. Since some ministers have entered a new job with a determination to remove the incumbent secretary, either because they represent the old order or because they have their own preferred candidate for the job, there is force in their argument. They preferred the secretary of PM&C. Some wanted a panel that also included the Public Service Commissioner. Another possibility was the departmental secretary of Finance. The problem is that there is no consensus about who is best placed to make the judgments:

> It is very hard to appraise performance because a lot of what anyone does is not known to someone else, unless you have a direct relationship. That is not the case between ministers and secretaries. The secretaries do a lot of work which ministers would never know they do, but we are pretty crucial to making the department work. What I am saying is that it is sometimes hard to judge what the secretary has done personally ... There has to be a minister, there has to be some sort of peer assessment, and maybe, if you could do it somehow, some sot of subordinate assessment — difficulty to achieve, but you are asking for a perfect world. Peers, subordinates, ministers at the end of the day (Stevens).

An alternative view suggested that the prime minister might know better what their performance was like:

> I don't think [departmental secretary of PM&C] or [Public Service Commissioner] would really have a clue how I'm performing other than what they may have heard on the grapevine. It is probable the PM knows much more because he's probably heard it from [the minister] (Departmental Secretary 1990s).

That assumes the prime minister is interested in the performance. If problems emerge, he is as likely to rely on the departmental secretary of PM&C to fix the problems as he is to trust the minister, who may have ulterior motives in blaming the departmental secretary. Besides, even more of the departmental secretaries' job is far beyond the prime minister's knowledge than that of the departmental secretary of PM&C.

A third neutral person was advocated by one departmental secretary who liked the New Zealand system:

> They have somebody who's in a sense more responsible for the well-being of the public service. I'm not sure a highly intrusive system or a very detailed system adds value unless it has been managed in terms of career management in the senior public service. You'd want to take into account the minister's view, there's no doubt about that; you'd want to take into account the views of peers and you'd want that view to be put together by someone who had senior public service respect.

He put in a widely expressed caveat:

> There would be a view in Canberra that on balance we could do with more ministers having a better understanding of how the public service works and what its qualities are (Departmental Secretary 1990s).

A person who had fallen foul of the whims of a minister thought that if contracts were to be introduced, 'it's even more important to have a well-understood, well-articulated view of what is good and bad performance. I think having an independent arbiter of that is what is important'. It was not that the departmental secretary wanted the ministers to become de facto public servants or to become too interested in the management of the department; rather, they wanted them to at least understand some of the pressures involved in running a large department.

What then could be done? It remains an essential question because, as part of the package that increased their pay in 1999, the departmental secretaries were required to develop some sort of performance agreement with their ministers. Admittedly, there was a degree of scepticism that such a process would work, but several tried all the same. Some began to set up clear arrangements:

> What I intend to do is write to the minister saying: 'This is what I intend to do, can we have a chat about it?' That would be the written basis. For the performance agreement the criteria won't be well specified. That's deliberate. Has there been a difficulty for cabinet which is the result of mismanagement by the department? Is there evidence of positive management action to enhance the capability of the department? (Departmental Secretary 1990s).

A second departmental secretary went through a process with the minister after the election: 'the most formalised process I have been through and that in a way reflected the personality of the minister. But with every minister there has been some kind of dialogue on a pretty regular basis about the kinds of thing the portfolio does'. Whether that is the best time for such a discussion, perhaps with a new minister, and whether it provides an adequate basis for determining pay differentials, is debatable.

The process went ahead in 2000, although the results are confidential. But it may be possible to make educated guesses about some outcomes. It seems unlikely that the heads of significant agencies that require the trust of external actors (Treasury, Foreign Affairs and Trade, Prime Minister and Cabinet) will not be classed on the top rung; to suggest these are not top people would, if it leaked, undermine confidence in the government's decisions. That should not be taken as a suggestion that they are not worthy of such a ranking, just that there are institutional imperatives that may give added weight to their case. Second, those who get on well with their ministers and whose ministers are senior and weighty, may do well; it is not worth offending a senior minister making a strong case. Longevity may help too; it is easier to put newcomers on a low rank, on the grounds they have not yet proved themselves, than established long-serving performers. Thereafter, decisions may depend as much on the enthusiasm and persuasiveness of the minister as on the objective performance of the departmental secretary. In this process, however measured and proper the interviews and the discussion, the final result is of necessity subjective.

But all the proper procedures cannot remove the personal factors that can detract from the most effective of systems. In all the debate about performance assessment, there is an assumption that departmental secretaries and their ministers are prepared to discuss the performance of the departmental secretary in constructive terms and that ministers can make — and are willing to make — discerning decisions. In practice, ministers are often not good at handing out bad news or facing the secretary with their dissatisfaction. In 1983, a Labor minister attended a council meeting with his departmental secretary all day and discussed what action should be taken, all the time knowing that the departmental secretary would be told that night, by someone else, that he was being shifted. In 1999, the Minister for Defence could travel overseas with his departmental secretary, discuss performance criteria with him and never say that he was working behind the scenes to get him sacked. This comment was perhaps typical:

> Some secretaries have a view of their relationship with their minister that the ministers do not share (Hawke).

And, significantly, are not prepared to share with them. Whether departmental secretaries ought to arrange to meet once or twice a year to discuss their performance is a matter of dispute. Some think it is a good idea:

> There have been some secretaries who thought they were getting on well with the minister and the minister said not one word to them and the next minute, bang, they are gone. I'd have thought there was an obligation to sit down every so often and have a chat on how things are going. But is the minister the right person to do that? (Volker)

Others regard it as superfluous; they ought to know how they are going. But not all do. Besides, meetings would do little good if the ministers were not able or prepared to express their views. Indeed, ministers will resist such a process when they are unhappy but don't want to debate the issues with the departmental secretary. Meetings work best when there is no problem in the first place. As ever in this relationship, the immediate onus is on the departmental secretaries to ensure that they discover what the ministers think of their performance.

How often a review should take place could also be debated — each year, once each parliamentary term, before each election? Timing may be vital both for determining what is discussed and in what climate. Meetings will be regular as policy issues rise and fall, but the satisfaction of the minister with the departmental secretary is a more fraught and difficult topic for both sides. That may explain why it so often avoided.

In practice, assessment of performance is now an accepted part of the scenery. As a minister, David Kemp noted, there was 'a need for a performance element in the contracts of secretaries. Obviously, in terms of reappointments, judgments about performance will be made'. Indeed, there is a need that they be more explicit if decisions are not be entirely arbitrary. This process will become particularly significant as the departmental secretaries reach the end of their contracts and are faced with the question of whether they will be offered a further contract or whether their career in the APS will be allowed to end with a whimper. Some of the potential implications will be discussed in the review of the Barratt case in Chapter 9.

Serving the whole of government?

If, as was suggested in the earlier chapters, departmental secretaries serve a general as well as a particular interest, should this be reflected in their contracts? The departmental secretaries have always been aware that the prime minister is the crucial person for their survival. They may survive the disapproval of their minister for a time because the minister will need the agreement of the prime minister before the departmental secretary is moved or sacked, but none can long survive the opposition of the leader of the government. Two issues arise: do departmental secretaries feel responsible to the prime minister more than their minister; and does this affect their behaviour?

The *Australian Public Service Act* 1999 made the role of the prime minister even more explicit. The prime minister now appoints and terminates without the earlier recourse to the governor-general. At least one former departmental secretary regretted the change:

> There's something symbolic about having the governor-general there. The symbolism, as far as I was concerned, was in respect of you being a servant of the public rather than of the ministry while recognising that is the reality — for you are. There is something that goes beyond just serving the government of the day; it's really serving the community. It's hard to define exactly what the nuances are but there is something of significance unless you really do want to go down a different path (Volker).

The symbolism may be there. But the reality now is that the prime minister appoints and terminates, without the need to go through the motions of an executive council decision. Insofar as there is a contractual relationship for departmental secretaries, it is with the prime minister and not with their individual ministers

The more immediate issue is what happens if there is a clash between a departmental secretary and the prime minister. Prime ministers do not often ring departmental secretaries directly, even in those cases where there was a close relationship because, for instance, the departmental secretary had been a former deputy in PM&C. If he did, it would be normal for the departmental secretary to report as soon as possible the content of his conversation to the minister, a necessary step to preserve trust. The usual practice was either for the prime minister to ring the minister to ask for action, or for the secretary of PM&C to be asked to ring the departmental secretary. Most of the time, such a process works well. Most departmental secretaries will argue there is no clash because they serve their minister. They may keep in touch with the departmental secretary of PM&C, but do not see a clash of accountabilities.

But what if there is a difference of opinion? According to one response:

> If I was given a direction by the prime minister that was counter to my minister, I would respond to the direction of the prime minister. I would see it as my job to convey to my minister that he had to be careful, that there are some tensions with the prime minister. Then if he continues in a direction which I knew was likely to bring him into conflict with the PM, on the whole I would seek to implement it, but I would let [departmental secretary of PM&C] know the direction my minister was going (Departmental Secretary 1990s).

It was a careful response, an acknowledgment of the minefield in which a departmental secretary can become mired if the prime minister is at war with his minister. It is always possible that the departmental secretary will become a sacrifice to expediency, as the politicians look for someone else to blame. There is good reason for their concern. When several ministers were forced to resign over the abuse of their travel allowances, part of the collateral damage was the departmental secretary of Administrative Services, who was fired because the system had not been cleaned up. Forced to sack ministers, a departmental secretary too was put in the sights and blamed, even though he had warned of the problems in advance and been ignored.

In some systems, departmental secretaries have direct links to the leader of the government. In Victoria, all departmental secretaries had contracts with the premier and Jeff Kennett used to meet them on a regular basis as a group and in the absence of the ministers. There was no doubt who called the tune. In Canada, as Osbaldeston's analysis illustrates, deputy ministers appreciate the links:

> The appointment of deputy ministers by the Prime Minister provides a reminder to them of their need for a perspective encompassing the whole range of government ... and emphasizes the collective interest of ministers and the special interest of the Prime Minister in the effectiveness of management in the public service. The Privy Council publication *Office of the Deputy Minister* puts it this way: 'By convention, however, the Prime Minister has

the right to nominate deputy ministers and thereby has the opportunity to discuss their responsibilities with them should he choose to do so. Through the Prime Minister's role in expressing the consensus of Cabinet he may wish to highlight the priorities and objectives of the government and impart his own personal concerns to the deputy' (Osbaldeston 1989:7).

The idea that the prime minister would ring departmental secretaries on a regular basis would not be seen as common in Australia. But the reality remains. The prime minister will receive the report from his departmental secretary on the performance of each secretary. He will determine whether they might be moved, reappointed or released. Whatever the rhetoric, the prime minister's opinion will be a matter of interest to all departmental secretaries.

Performance, retirements and terminations

In the 1960s, most departmental secretaries stayed in office until they retired around the age of 60. The public service was a career. Superannuation encouraged them to stay. There were, besides, comparatively few alternatives for them to consider. A few, like Jim Scully, may have chosen to leave at 55 after 30 or more years:

> I've really enjoyed public service life. I've been very happy ... but if you are a permanent head, you don't have a personal life. After a while I think you get to believe you have above-average abilities or you are an above average important person; I don't think that does you any good (Scully).

But even that was rare and it did allow access to superannuation.

By the end of the 1980s, that had changed as a few chose to leave. One of the first was Vince FitzGerald. He was interested in the development of policy and had been worn down by the demands of managing a large department after the amalgamations of 1987. He decided:

> I didn't think there was much more challenge ahead if I stayed on until retirement and I was anyway interested in the idea of doing something else. It occurred to me that if waiting until retirement was a road only to a fairly sedentary and peripheral involvement in the private sector, getting out when one still had 20 years of vigorous working life ahead was preferable.

He resigned at 45. Another colleague took on overseas posting at 50 and, after some years overseas, had no desire to return to a departmental secretary job. He had had enough: 'How could you go through it again?'

Indeed, there is the problem that more people are making that choice earlier, at the cost of talent within the APS. A departmental secretary reports a recent conversation with a colleague who would probably have become a departmental secretary but who chose to leave:

> He told me: 'It wasn't just that they offered me more money. I would otherwise have liked to become a secretary, but what was the point. If I became a secretary probabilities were I would last five years and then I would be out. Then when I got out I would find it far more difficult to be in the job I've got now. So if the chances are I am going to have to get out, it would be better to get out now when the opportunity arises'. That's a real worrying trend (Departmental Secretary 1990s).

There is a danger that this trend is increasing and, as terms come to an end, may engulf departmental secretaries too. One departmental secretary commented:

> I have been intellectually reconciled to the fact that I will be pursuing a different career, or two maybe, at some point. I guess I am more emotionally reconciled to that now ... I became a secretary in my early forties; I figured then that the likelihood I would still be around at 65 wasn't all that high (Departmental Secretary 1990s).

It illustrates that new calculations are coming into the career planning. Thus one departmental secretary thought:

> I'm going to have to start thinking about [other jobs] before long; and, yes, I guess I'm not going to be waiting around to the last day of the contract to find out whether I have another job or not.

Since there was also a belief that 'the headhunters stop calling once you are over 50', many might be concerned from an early stage. 'One of the impacts of having a reality that tenure is limited is that you begin to think about options outside, yes' (Rosalky). Some feared they might not be good at career planning and besides, as one put it, 'if they [the other departmental secretaries] are like me, they are not very good at any alternative careers'. He was probably too modest, but the impression was clear. Besides, looking elsewhere was not their preference:

> There is no doubt that we secretaries enjoy the work we do and that is why we stay. Many of us say that we are considering other offers but we would really prefer reappointment. Not just because of the security but because it's a great job (Departmental Secretary 1990s).

Under the existing contractual position, departmental secretaries were conscious that they might need to plan a future outside the APS while they still had years of useful work ahead.

That could have an effect on those who might once have aspired to be a departmental secretary:

> I don't think there's anywhere near the same sort of expectation as a career. I think the loyalty that used to exist is not as present as it was and so people lower down, I don't think they are confident about aspiring to the top (Departmental Secretary 1985–95).

> People don't want to work the hours and then risk their heads being blown off for no reason (Ayers).

Whether such a position is desirable is a matter for debate. In a world of multiple careers, it might be seen as normal. When the gurus insist that everyone will change careers several times, the fact that senior public servants are now among that group need not necessarily be a matter for concern. Indeed, there could be benefits if new blood is brought into the service. The idea of a career service that expects everyone to spend a lifetime in the APS and work up from the lower ranks is indeed no longer widespread.

But there are also potential problems. First, as we have seen, the public and private sectors need different skills, most of which are learnt by practice and experience. Second, almost all the traffic is one way, from the public to the (much better paid) private sector. A few return. In 1996, Howard brought back two: Max Moore-Wilton and Paul Barratt from the Stock Exchange and the Business Council of Australia respectively. But both had spent the majority of their career in the public sector; they understood the ways of accountability and could readapt quickly. Third, if many of the departmental secretaries and others from the pool of potential replacements leave, where will the government get the skills and expertise it needs to provide both advice and the communal memory so vital for knowing why things are done the way they are and what had been tried and failed in the past? In one expressive comment:

> If you lobotomise the place thoroughly every three years you are going to end up with a pretty rotten administration. To that extent there is value in the old Westminster system of having something that's relatively apolitical, and certainly so below the top couple of layers (FitzGerald).

The question, then, concerns the extent to which the system of terminations has had an impact on the way that departmental secretaries and their possible replacements see their career prospects. There is no doubt that the way that six departmental secretaries were terminated after the 1996 election had a dramatic impact on the psyche of their colleagues. It was not that no departmental secretary had been terminated before; several had lost their jobs under Labor.

Rather, it was the suddenness, the number and indeed the selection of some people who had been regarded as quintessential public servants that caused the surprise. Said one victim:

> There was no written contract. When we went one of the problems was that nobody could find the bloody terms of appointment or the arrangements. I was the only one who had a copy, just by strange coincidence. I didn't know it was there. I was cleaning out my desk and found the jolly thing ... I was puzzled by what on earth was going on. I'd have to say that I think in respect of the way it was handled at the top of the public service, even allowing for the priorities of a new government and the need for speed, it wasn't handled well at all (Volker).

Perhaps that was how he felt. But there is no easy way to tell a departmental secretary his contract has been terminated and his career in the APS is suddenly over. If the departmental secretaries were in shock, what is their position now? First, the position they are now in should be restated.

The new system has changed the onus of decision. Whereas formerly the government had to make a positive decision to move or rotate a secretary, now a vacancy occurs when the contract expires and there is no commitment to reappoint the incumbent. Of course, only two people have yet got to the end of a five-year contract, and perhaps only a small minority *will ever* complete their five years in the same position. Further, it is in the interests of government to continue the employment of the majority both to ensure continuity, reduce tension and reward performance. Does this make their position all that more unstable? To a degree it does, but it can be overstated. Plenty of people had left under the old system, even if now there was a feeling that ministers could be a bit more capricious. Nevertheless, whereas there may be less loss of face in not being reappointed, rather then left unused in limbo on gardening leave, there are still some areas where the new system has yet to be fully developed.

The primary problem is that there has been little consideration of the impact the process might have as the five-year terms expire, perhaps again because few people have yet got that far, and certainly not a large group together. At what stage can the secretary be provided with feedback on the level of performance and the degree of ministerial satisfaction? And what is the relationship between the outcome of the appraisal and the continuation of the contract? Is satisfactory performance sufficient to secure an additional contract, or is something better needed. Or, quite simply, when the decisions about reappointment are finally made, the earlier calculation, which was linked to pay, may not be regarded as significant. Surely there ought to be a link between performance and extension, but it will not be surprising if the calculations are based on different factors. Perhaps the legislation could be changed to indicate an intention to rotate departmental secretaries at the end of five years if their performance is considered satisfactory. It does not make any easier the issue of determining what is satisfactory, but it may provide some declaration of intent.

This uncertainty may potentially create another problem: a period in the last year of a contract when the authority of the secretary is undermined, making them lame ducks as their potential termination nears, particularly compared with the sustained authority of more permanent heads. Otherwise people can actively undermine a departmental secretary who is trying to change things on the 'perfectly rational response, how long is this guy going to be around?' Reappointment is of course an option, but may not be decided until near the end of a term. Management of a department should not be judged on a day-to-day basis; it takes time to develop personnel and strategy:

> You certainly need a few years in the job; there is a lot to be said about having continuity in how the department operates its people management, succession planning, its re-skilling arrangements; there is value in having consistency in the way the culture evolves, and a balance needs to be struck between having an injection of new blood and new ideas at the top and having sufficient continuity (Sedgwick).

Rotation every five years may be useful before, as one departmental secretary put it, 'I learnt to say no in too many languages; you bring me a problem and I've done that before' (Kingsland). It may keep ideas and people fresh. But many thought five years was about the proper length — 'at that point you can be held accountable'. The problem becomes more pressing with the tendency recently to give departmental secretaries contracts of less than five years. And all that time the possibility of extinction may make anyone too cautious.

A second question is whether there should be a statement of reasons given to a secretary who is not reappointed, or is terminated. There are arguments on both sides. There was a belief that a requirement for reasons might slow down an unfair decision and perhaps make ministers think again if no obvious justification can be provided. There was a feeling that there was a need to protect secretaries against the fickleness of rumour, particularly in new governments where oppositions might be regaled by dissatisfied groups or individuals with untrue stories of the political alignments of officials and have no means of checking their veracity. The occasional existence of hit lists, based on false information, can be devastating. Some thought that the provision of reasons was just natural justice, but should be provided on a personal basis and not be subject to appeal for unfair dismissal or negotiation. The court hearing the appeal against dismissal by Paul Barratt agreed that he should receive procedural justice. He was duly told that the minister had no trust in him and that was not in the interests of good government. It was true but scarcely enlightening. The Court of Appeal found it sufficient. Should more nevertheless be given? Take a comment made before the Barratt case:

> I am not in favour of a more objective report for secretaries. Like most organisations, if you are at the top at some stage and someone says you've got to go, there can be complex reasons why you've got to go. They don't necessarily relate to incompetence; they don't relate to anything; you just don't fit at that time. But it's terribly important if you don't fit you go. It is not in anyone's interest to specify particular reasons in detail. It could be damaging to reputations. It is important to have a transparent approach which establishes loss of ministerial confidence. There must also be an agreed process for termination (Moore-Wilton).

Such a process could be seen as self-defeating. It was always possible to concoct a set of reasons if necessary and their creation might later enter the sphere of partisan politics and do more damage to the terminated secretary than no reasons at all. Whether the risk of a political bucket was balanced by the possible advantages was the subject of differing views. Politicians, it was argued, are professionals at belting people up in debate and in public. In that battle, former departmental secretaries can hardly have a hope of winning and should not enter the fray.

Many secretaries would believe that, at the time when there is a change of minister or a new government is elected, they should be given the opportunity for a fair trial, of perhaps three or six months, during which to show their wares before any decision is made on their future. They argue, with some justification, that too many reputations are undermined by rumour and hearsay and that, given the opportunity, they would be able to prove their capacity to work with a new minister. It is not just at the change of government that departmental secretaries may be vulnerable. One Labor minister got rid of his departmental secretary because he had been too close to his Labor predecessor. In that case (in the early 1990s), the departmental secretary was found an alternative position and the displaced secretary has continued to provide efficient service to both Labor and coalition governments. A similar process followed when Moore became

Defence Minister in 1998; he wanted his own person as departmental secretary and chose to undermine and remove his departmental secretary. In this instance, the departmental secretary was driven right out of the service, although he might have been saved if a transfer or exchange of positions had been arranged; in practice, political pressure prevented it happening. Some continuity is usually desirable, but such a process cannot be guaranteed to provide effective administration; there may be particular problems when both minister and secretary are changed. Nevertheless, the idea of a trial, however advisable and fair, could never be set in stone. As one departmental secretary explained:

> If you have a minister who hates a secretary and is determined to maintain that stance, all three months will do is give that secretary three months of ritual humiliation. In a less prejudiced environment, those three months could be used to show what you can do, how well you can manage. It depends so much on the situation and the personalities. It could be a time of challenge or purgatory (Departmental Secretary 1990s).

It would remain no more than a wise practice that should be followed most of the time.

It is important, where limited terms could end careers, that a process of managing difficult relationships between ministers and secretaries is clearly defined. It is, however, difficult to conduct a fair trial without the cooperation of the minister. At the very least, it could anticipate the deterioration of a relationship before it became unworkable. In the past, the secretary of PM&C has acted as mediator in some difficult cases and that role may need to be widely accepted by all in the field. But the new systems put additional loads on the position, as confidant to the departmental secretaries, as judge of their performance and as adviser to the prime minister on their continuation in office. It will take remarkable skills to balance those demands and it will not be surprising if they make the job as confidant harder to play.

Following the salary loading for the loss of tenure in 1994, secretaries were classified into three levels which received $152,755–$161,360–$174,560 in salary; they had related superannuation benefits and a uniform notional package of $35,436 that included a private vehicle, parking, spouse travel in Australia and (once a year with ministerial approval) overseas, and leave loading. The total packages ranged from around $210,000 to $240,000. Some comparisons may provide a perspective. In 1994, in all the Commonwealth entities, 56 people had packages over $250,000 and a further 54 between $200,000 and $250,000; departmental secretaries were far from the best paid in

Commonwealth employment. The highly paid positions tended to be outside the APS structure, in arm's-length statutory authorities. The BHP group had 138 people with packages over $200,00 and 69 over $250,000 in 1994, and that is just one company, until recently Australia's largest.

There were two subsequent rises, paid on 31 March 1999 and 31 March 2000. After the second rise, the top three departmental secretaries — those for Defence, Treasury and Prime Minister and Cabinet — received a base pay of $222,5000 and a total remuneration package of $305,000. All the other departmental secretaries are now on the one level and receive base salaries of $205,000 and packages worth $285,000. Even with the possibility of performance pay of an additional 10 or 15 per cent, these are not large salaries when contrasted with people who have equivalent responsibility and get paid far more.

Pay is and will remain a continuing problem. Said one departmental secretary:

> Departmental secretaries are related to politicians' [pay]. Their wives particularly would say: 'We can't have them paid more than you, darling'.

So rises were limited. A consequence was that some departmental secretaries liked the prospect of heading statutory authorities where the pay was detached from ministers; there they can 'swan around'. There were great benefits for those departmental secretaries who found such comfortable billets:

> You're not only not going out to pasture; you're not only not going to get the credit card and three overseas trips a year with your wife but you don't have to put up with all the crap here. It's a completely perverse outcome. Bad government (Departmental Secretary 1990s).

Competence was not rewarded.

But even the pay rise and the possibility of performance pay is not in itself enough to keep people. Most are sceptical it will make much difference. The Public Accounts Committee in 1997 (before the 1999/2000 rises) asked a panel of departmental secretaries if any of them felt they 'are not adequately recompensed'. The response:

> *Dr Hawke:* If you look at a secretary's pay against equivalents in other public services, then I think the answer is yes.

> *Mr Sedgwick:* I think that is right. I think there is an obvious question that then follows from that which is: why the hell are we here? I think we would need to give a personal view on all of that. I am here because I like the work. I would prefer more money. I can cope with being underpaid; I cannot cope with being undervalued.

> I think one of the things that really is important for an organisation like the parliament, for example, is to not only set down its expectations of the public service but also to support the public service when it meets them ...

After a discussion, Sedgwick concluded:

> So the answer to your question is that it is adequate because we are here, but as to whether it is appropriate or fair, we probably do not feel that it is.

It was the job, rather than the pay, that kept people. One consequence was that performance pay was not necessarily a big deal: 'Do you think I'm going to change my advice on whether I get 10 or 15 per cent performance pay? It won't make the slightest difference' (Shergold). When compared with private sector levels, to some state governments and to many statutory officers, they are still well behind.

Conclusions

Are there better ways of assessing performance? A MAB report, *Building a Better Public Service* (1993) thought that the existing arrangements for appointment could be broadened by getting two people at departmental secretary level to join the departmental secretary of PM&C in preparing recommendations to the prime minister. That could also provide a model for the examination of the performance, and even the termination, of departmental secretaries. Instead of — or in addition to — the other two departmental secretaries, perhaps two people from outside government who appreciate the problems of managing in the private sector could be included. The assumption should be that if this board finds the performance of the departmental secretaries satisfactory, then the government has an obligation to find them an alternative position when the contract expires or relations with the minister become untenable, either by rotation or by some other means.

One outcome would be a slowing down of the process. That might not be a real problem. It might discourage ministers from seeking to remove departmental secretaries whose performance has been found to be satisfactory by a third body as it is likely to reflect on the minister. It might save for public service capable officers whose public service career might otherwise be lost. Above all, it may appear fairer than a process still shrouded in secrecy, even if it could prove uncomfortable to those under scrutiny. The current uncertainty requires some solution that can deliver better outcomes than those that now exist.

8

Inside out: The departmental secretaries' stories

Collective portraits can only take us so far. They provide an amalgam of views, a majority voice constructed by the author as a representation of the spectrum of opinions expressed in interviews. Behind those collective studies are a number of individuals, each with their own experiences and views, each with their vision of what the APS is and should be and where it is going. So in the sections below they are given the opportunity to speak for themselves. Each portrait interweaves details of their careers with their own opinions on a number of topics as expressed in the interviews with them. Of course, the selection of material is still mine; it is not possible to reproduce all the interviews — they would be too long. In each portrait, too, the emphasis is different, depending on the subject and their experiences. While the images are separate, the hope is that, brought together, they provide insight into the way that the departmental secretaries worked. These mini-biographies are not intended to be critical analyses; I do not ask whether others saw them in this image or whether their views are correct. Instead, this section is intended to let the people behind the names and titles come through. Those selected were among the more remarkable of their generation. Let them use their own words.

Sir Roland Wilson, Labour and National Service 1940–46; Treasury 1951–66

Roland Wilson was secretary of the Treasury from 1951 to 1966. At a time when the mandarins were reputed to hold sway over the decision-making in Canberra, he was the most dominant of the mandarins, the intellectual master of his colleagues and capable of creating trepidation among the ministers he served.

One of six brothers born to an Ulverstone builder in Tasmania, he was educated at the local high school. Small, only 165 centimetres (5ft 5in) tall and weighing less than 57 kilograms (9 stone), he was at first extremely shy. But his intelligence shone through. While a second-year undergraduate at the University of Tasmania, he wrote an essay that attracted the attention of a member of the University Council, L.F. Giblin, an adviser to governments and a legend in the small society. He also received support from two other members of the economics department who were to be significant public figures, Douglas Copland and James Brigden. With their encouragement, he won the 1925 Tasmanian Rhodes Scholarship to Oxford, the first state school and commerce graduate to do so. In quick succession, he then gained doctorates from Oxford and Chicago. To the surprise of his colleagues there, he chose to return to Tasmania to take up a lectureship in economics.

He did not stay for long. Giblin was temporarily acting as government statistician in Canberra and persuaded Wilson to come to Canberra as assistant statistician and economic adviser to the Treasury; he was the first trained economist to be employed in the federal public service. By 1936, Wilson was Commonwealth statistician, a position he held until 1951, although he was for a time from 1940 to 1946 permanent secretary of the Department of Labour and National Service, a department he created and developed. In 1951, he became the secretary of the Treasury and stayed there for fifteen years, longer than any other person has held — or is ever likely to hold — that position.

Secretaries of the Treasury are seldom likely to be popular as they are the keepers of the purse strings and thwarters of the policy ambitions of others. Wilson appreciated the inevitability of the process, even while acknowledging the supportive role that the Treasury played for the government. In the L.F. Giblin lecture (Wilson 1976) from which the following comments are drawn, he said:

> We tend perhaps to see the bad, as well as the good, in schemes that come before the government a little more clearly than their promoters do. It isn't our job to decide, but it is our job to make critical analyses of all that is put up to the government. Hence, perhaps naturally, we tend to be looked on as pullers-apart of other men's pet ideas. What we do is a necessary part of the process of government. God knows, Australia has enough people promoting new schemes — there is no shortage of ideas. It's our business to help cabinet to try to pick the best.

Wilson did regret the fact that his dominance had led to a degree of publicity, even often the blame for decisions made by the government, especially the credit squeezes undertaken to reduce inflation in 1961, when he was cast as an economic Rasputin. He thought that after a time the criticism did not trouble him:

> In my job you can't do much about petty spite — or even well-informed criticism. One of my obligations is not to comment publicly on government policy, and that means, for practical purposes, that I must avoid being drawn into controversies. Visiting British civil servants are astonished at the way I have been dragged into the news and held up to derision and hatred in certain sections of the press, but what's the use of worrying about it? I can't fight the bastards with their own weapons! They'll have the last word — fair or foul.

Nevertheless, he seems to have found public service both fascinating and at times frustrating. He said the attraction of the private sector was not money, but control over your own fate:

> No matter how high you get in the public service you are still working for other people — you are still answerable to others for everything you do.

But it was fascinating:

> It's absorbing, particularly in the Treasury where you are dealing with all the world's business and have a broad canvas to work on ... There's never a dull moment. The business of government throws up new problems every day. One hour you are dealing with the implications of a change in the bank rate in London, the next with some development problems in north-west Australia or Pakistan. You don't fix the timing of these things. Events do that to you.

Wilson did not see economics as a science that was sufficient by itself to determine public policy issues. He was technically very skilled and saw a significant role for technical expertise, but he thought more was needed for good policy:

> In the application of economic theory to public policy the need was greater rather then less for the cultivation of people who could combine a basic mastery of theory with knowledge of the mysteries of a constantly changing society, with intimate experience of business and political realities, with intuitive understanding of the behaviour of individuals and groups within society — and above all with humility.

He argued that giving advice should essentially be the responsibility of a government agency:

> Advice from all quarters can be of help to governments, and in certain areas it is essential. But 'taking five minutes off' or even five days or five months, is not going to produce solutions to the more vital problems of public policy and economic management. We must continue to rely heavily on the full-time advisers who staff the various agencies of government.

There is no problem in getting advice whether from inside or outside the regular channels. It can be good or bad, or it can be like the curate's egg; it can be self-seeking or objective, but it is never in short supply. The real problem is for ministers, not themselves always technically proficient, to select the good from the bad and to relate it to their own broader appreciation of political and economic realities and their own philosophical approach to the task of government. It is to assist in this that the policy units of government departments exist.

He condemned the habit of blaming the officials when things went wrong:

It is sometimes suggested by ministers, and often accepted by the public, that blunders of which they have been guilty are the result of bad advice. Whether this is true or untrue is never too certain nor is it particularly relevant. It would not be correct to assume that decisions of government are always based on the views of official advisers. What goes up from them is not always what comes down as official policy ... If the advice given is in fact bad, it is its acceptance by ministers which constitutes the fault.

Wilson challenged the benefits of systems of alternative advice. (He was speaking in 1976 at the time of the publication of the Coombs Royal Commission.) He suggested that the Treasury was geared to offer alternative courses of action and was well aware that its own policy preferences would not always prevail. (That was a view that not all ministers accepted!) He thought there were already other ministers and departments who would provide alternative suggestions. 'The problem remains: not how to get advice but how to evaluate it. To set up competitive evaluators still leaves the task of evaluating the evaluators. As Harry Truman said: "This is where the buck stops"':

Thus it is foolish and graceless to denigrate the advisers when things do not always go to a government's liking. The Treasury needs the whole-hearted support of the government more than most departments, partly because its formal powers are in reality quite limited. Upon being told many years ago by a former prime minister to perform a miracle, I asked what power I had to execute his commission. 'You are the secretary to the Treasury, aren't you?' he said. My answer was that my legal powers didn't go much beyond the regulations of the *Audit Act*, but if I had the promise of his moral support I thought I could give the powers of darkness a run for their money.

Without such support the Treasury will not be capable of giving its best, no matter how adequately it is staffed and organised. It cannot and would not claim the right to make the final decision.

But in advising on available policy options it should certainly enjoy
the right to be heard with respect

Yet Treasury under Wilson developed a reputation for rigour and
dominance over the scene. Ministers in his period may have been
effective politicians; two went on to become prime minister. But
there is no sign that they seriously challenged the technical advice
that was provided. Nor was the Treasury noted for the options it
provided, particularly in later years when arguments were expected
to be kept within its doors.

Wilson is described as enigmatic, difficult to read at times, keeping
people guessing. One observer described him as 'a man who has
deliberately encased himself in a psychological armour. If he had not
donned a protective outer plating, he would never have risen to be a
senior public servant, much less to be secretary of the Treasury,
because he was born pathologically shy'. He went on: 'He gradually
fought his shyness down and more or less mastered it — more or
less, because the remnant of his early fear, that other people might
be brighter than he, is still inside him, and probably always will be.
He gives no sign of it now, however. He has even become a public
speaker of fluency, lucidity and wit on the rare occasions on which
he addresses a public audience' (Hetherington 1975).

He was quick with the repartee. Met in the 1980s with the
comment 'Roland, the older you get the smaller you get', he retorted,
tapping his forehead, 'Yes, but I am a giant up here' (Castles 1997).
Once he read a 10-page memorandum that ended with the
recommendation that a particular action be taken. It was returned
without any comments, except on the last page Wilson had inserted
the word 'not' before 'taken' and added 'the proposal is approved as
amended'. One of his protégés told in a speech how he imagined
himself plucking up the courage to say to Wilson: 'Roland, you're a
genius'. And he then imagined the withering reply: 'How would
you know?' The stories about Wilson are legendary, but they add up
to the same picture: a dedicated public servant who worked hard
and productively (allowing himself time to retire to his workshop at
home where he was a skilful carpenter); he brought to the Treasury
'an intellectual vigour, concern for the public interest, organisational
ability and combativeness that it had not previously enjoyed'. He
was seen as 'confident, authoritative, resolute, academically gifted,
coldly logical, acerbic and quick-witted'. He recruited good staff to
Treasury, put them into positions where they could best use their
talents and then 'gave them their heads'. Under his leadership,
Treasury became the dominant force in the Canberra bureaucracy
and government decision-making.

To the young turks of the APS in the 1960s, Wilson was the most influential figure among a number of leading figures. But he was a distant one; to one future departmental secretary who worked in the Treasury for the whole of the time that Wilson was secretary, 'Wilson was the most intellectually terrifying person of my time. He made original contributions as an economist, he preferred to be invisible, he played his own game'. In fifteen years, despite rising to the top of the then third division, and despite the smaller size of the Treasury then, he was not in Wilson's office more than a couple of times.

No public servant is again likely to wield the same influence, a fact explained by his intellect, the longevity of the government he served and the circumstances that gave Treasury an ability to develop a centrality in decisions that is unlikely to be recreated.

Tony Ayers: Aboriginal Affairs 1979–81; Social Security 1981–86; Community Services and Health 1987–88; Defence 1988–98

Tony Ayers initially joined the public service because he wanted to work in prisons. He started work as an education officer in Pentridge in Victoria. He did not regard himself as a public servant at all. He became a parole officer, went into prison administration and in 1967 moved to Canberra to become director of welfare in the ACT.

Then Hewitt decided to change the nature of PM&C:

> He was getting people to headhunt people, a few stirrers; I went across to Prime Minister's and that was the sort of the end of me. I got hooked into the crazy game of real public administration.

When McMahon became prime minister and they created a new department for Hewitt, Ayers went with him and started the Office of the Environment. Then he headed up the Children's Commission under Labor. When that was abolished, he returned to Prime Minister's, but as a surplus officer, so he was put in charge of the implementation unit for the Royal Commission on Australian Government Administration. Then there was internal promotion to the head of the welfare division and to deputy secretary and under secretary in the department. He worked closely with Alan Carmody and Geoff Yeend:

> Geoff's health wasn't all that good and so I spent a fair amount as acting secretary there, which was fun. And I guess at that stage of the game I knew I was going to become a secretary. It was only a question of which one.

At times, as acting secretary, he could be put in some tough positions:

> Fraser was out bush and he had this new radio telephone. He loved
> gadgets. He rang late on a Saturday evening and wanted to know
> the opinion of several ministers that he nominated on a paper he
> had with him. I pointed out to him that anyone could listen in on
> a conversation on these phones. But no, 'get me these opinions.
> Over and out'. So I contacted the ministers. The last one I got to
> late in the evening and he was 'Brahms and Liszt'. 'The prime
> minister wants your opinion on this paper'. 'Tell him to get stuffed'.
> 'The prime minister explicitly asked for your opinion'. 'Tell him
> to get stuffed'. So I gave up and rang off. Then I rang Fraser and
> gave him all the other opinions. 'What does X think?' I took a big
> breath and said 'Well, on the one hand he thinks this and on the
> other hand he thinks this, but on balance he prefers this'. 'Thanks,'
> said Fraser and rang off. The next morning I rang the minister and
> said: 'I thought you might like to know what you told the prime
> minister last night'. I received a sheepish thanks.

Protecting ministers from themselves was always a significant
function for senior officials.

In 1980, Ayers was offered the position of departmental secretary
of Aboriginal Affairs. He could have knocked it back. He talked to
Fraser, who wanted him to delay for a couple of months to complete
things he was doing, but Ayers insisted on going at once:

> Once everyone knows you are going, you're a feather duster; it's
> not good for the other department not to have a permanent
> secretary.

There was no training for the position:

> We train everyone from the dogcatcher up but we don't train
> departmental heads. It's assumed you can do the job. When I took
> over in Aboriginal Affairs, Bill Cole, good bloke, was chairman of
> the board. Bill sent me a stack of reading, didn't talk to me, just
> sent this out. Most of it from the UK. And most of it I never
> bothered reading quite frankly; it's irrelevant.

Training may have been required because of the background of the
departmental secretaries:

> By and large they come from policy departments in recent years,
> so the days of telegraph messengers are over for most of them
> because they couldn't ride the bike properly. But most of them
> came from a policy area and suddenly they go from a policy one,
> in my case in Prime Minister's, to running very much a hands on,
> sensitive hands, two sensitive hands on, really, in Aboriginal Affairs
> and Social Security.

Ayers worked with Fred Chaney in Aboriginal Affairs and, after Chaney was shifted to Social Security, followed him there. In 1987 he was seconded for a year to the Efficiency Scrutiny Unit, and then was briefly departmental secretary in Community Services. Then he was approached to be departmental secretary of Defence; the minister had been persuaded that the department did not need a Defence specialist but someone who had a good grasp of management issues:

> I got a phone call the night before from Nick Greiner, wanting me to go up and run Premier's [in New South Wales]. He had just got elected. I wasn't going to do that, but he did say, well, before you knock it back come and talk to me and I said OK, I'll do that. So I rang Mike Codd the following day and said: 'Look, I'm not going to do it but I had better tell you because someone will tell you'. And that night I got the phone call to say, what about Defence? I didn't know what I was going into but I enjoyed it, thoroughly enjoyed it.

His predecessor there, Alan Woods, had been pushed into retirement. In effect, Ayers also became the shop steward for the department heads, the person who could act as adviser and supporter to those in strife and who could sometimes organise support for those who had lost out. It started with Woods: 'My role [as shop steward] was to try to line up two or three things for him to do, which he did very well including the air safety review'. That shop steward role also had him speaking out in public after the sacking of the six departmental secretaries in 1996. He got into trouble, but he was regarded as sufficiently untouchable that he could get away with it. Ayers was to stay in Defence until his retirement in 1988, one of the few to last until the age of 65.

Ayers saw the role as managing people:

> I have learnt over the years that it is no good saying the quality of people is no good unless you do something about it. At every level now I'm a head hunter ... I have the simple theory that good people will attract, retain and train good people and bums do likewise with bums because they don't recognise talent, or if they do, they are threatened by it ... One problem is to get the right people in the right jobs. I put an enormous amount of time into that. I would have a system of rotating senior people around and identifying those who weren't performing and seeing what we could do about those and bringing through the bright ones, those who you feel might need a bit of a break.

His role was to set the priorities. He might brief the minister when there was a crisis, but at other times he would send his officers over. The departmental secretary managed the process; he was not the sole policy adviser.

Ayers supported the advent of administrative law; after his time in Social Security he was all too conscious that public servants could make mistakes that could have detrimental effects on individuals. He wanted the process informal and fast. But administrative law had an impact:

> I take the view that I don't care what people see; I mean, if I'm writing something I would write it on the basis that someone is going to see it, so who cares?

But he wrote less after he became secretary:

> I used to write a hell of a lot in Prime Minister's, but I tended as department head to write very little to ministers. You don't keep a dog and bark. I recruit good people and get them to write the papers down. Even if I disagreed with what they were saying, I would let it go to the minister. I might put a note: 'I don't agree with this and actually we might discuss this', but I would never censor.

Ministers should be told what the departmental secretary thinks:

> I have always been jack blunt. I'll hit someone in the mouth; I will never stab them in the back.

The minister he liked least was the one who never disagreed to his face but:

> You would find out later that he disagreed with everything you wanted to do ... [By contrast] I used to get into brawls with Malcolm [Fraser] and people would really go white, the language would get pretty wild on both sides and on one occasion he said: 'I don't want to hear that'. I said: 'I'm not paid to tell you what you f'ing want to hear; I'm paid to tell you what you f'ing ought to hear'.

Styles differed, but 'you wouldn't say that one model was better or necessarily worse than the other'. The adviser should be able to say to the minister:

> OK, this might not to be great for you in the short term, but it is for Australia in the long term ... there are limits to that. If you're going to lose fifteen seats or something by some bloody policy, few governments are going to run down that path.

Ayers did list the vital qualities for ministers:

> They have got to have ears. I think it's a characteristic of a lot of politicians that they listen with their mouths rather than their ears ... They've got to be able to stand up and get counted in cabinet meeting. Most prime ministers, all the ones I've ever met, are bullies ... and it's obviously nice to have someone who's good up front.

Strong ministers are valuable because with weak ministers nothing will happen. Strong ministers can't be bullied; some of the junior ones can. Even that does not give departmental secretaries scope for independent action: 'The reality of life is there is no future in a situation where you have your own agenda'. Still, he could relate to the experience of a career civil servant in the Pentagon who constantly had political appointees coming in over her head:

> She said: 'Well, Secretary, it's like house training a cat; you just teach one lot where the kitty litter is and what it's for and then another lot come in and crap all over the carpets'.

Ayers was concerned by some recent trends. He thought the pay was inadequate:

> All the old arguments: you got poor pay in exchange for good super and security of employment; now you don't get good pay, you don't have security of employment and you don't have good super. And everyone hates you.

He feared this would have an impact on the ambitions of those coming through the system:

> I had some excellent people and I put enormous effort into supporting the people. They would make it clear, they'd say, we see the hours you work, you get in here at half past seven in the morning and you leave at half past seven at night, and that's on a good day, and then there are weekends here. We don't want to live our life like that ... You get two-thirds of three-fifths extra pay and as a consequence run the risk of having your head blown off for no apparent reason other then the fact that their hair was parted the wrong way. A lot of people have gone out to the private sector; they haven't gone for the money, although they are getting more money, but it's because they don't want to be a department head.

He thought the sacking of departmental secretaries in 1996 was wrong, and said so. But he thinks it illustrates that ministers, especially new ministers, are less positive about the public service. Indeed, too many did not really understand how the system worked. Ayers met a coalition member at a dinner:

> He told me he could not understand how public servants of the calibre of Geoffrey Yeend and Michael Codd, who had served the Fraser government so admirably, could possibly serve those dreadful socialists. My reaction was to point out that he obviously did not understand the fundamental principles of the Westminster system (Ayers 1996:6).

Ayers still believes that those principles will serve Australia much better than some system that pretends to sit midway between Westminster and Washington. There are basic principles worth defending:

> I have no argument if they got the sack for non-performance. My worry at the moment is that people get sacked because someone doesn't like the colour of their hair or whatever. Why would you sack Volker or Hamilton? Very competent public servants, wouldn't know where the political parties were. And even if they did, that wouldn't have been the issue. This business now of half the departmental secretaries under threat because their ministers are not getting political outcomes. Since when has it been the public servants' job to achieve a political outcome? That's bloody nonsense. Quite frankly, if someone's contract is coming up and they are 42 and they've got a mortgage and they have four kids they are trying to put through school, I wonder if you are going to get as frank and fearless advice as you once would. I suppose I'm a nasty outspoken guy, but I suspect I wouldn't have lasted.

But he thought departmental secretaries should have a chance to prove themselves under a new government:

> I think there should be a six months' stand back. If people aren't performing, I have no argument about getting rid of people then.

Ayers is careful not to pretend all was good in the good old days. Nor does he like the American system that grinds to a halt in the lame duck period before an election or in the process of Senate confirmation. He remembers when a senator was knocked back as a nominee for Defense secretary:

> I was in Washington when this was on. Kim [Beazley, his minister] rang me at some ungodly hour of the night and said what's it all about? I said, well, as far as I can see, and it's been on prime time television, he's been accused of womanising and excessive drinking. He said, Jesus Christ, we couldn't get a cabinet from either side of the House on those terms.

How would departmental secretaries go if there was careful Senate scrutiny? Probably fairly well. Still, the Australian system has some advantages that he would like to see retained.

Michael Codd, Industrial Relations 1982; Employment and Industrial Relations 1982–83; Community Services 1985–86; Prime Minister and Cabinet 1986–91

Mike Codd joined the public service because he was interested in public policy, an interest that sprang from his degree in economics. He had played Australian Rules football as a means of paying his way through university. He failed to get into Foreign Affairs, but was offered a valuable cadetship in the Bureau of Statistics. The deputy statistician, Keith Archer, had skill in developing young talent and soon took Codd to a meeting of Commonwealth statisticians in Ottawa where he presented a paper he wrote:

> That international exposure was a terrific experience for me at that age. I enjoyed the intellectual challenge of the work.

After six years, he wanted to broaden out. Offered positions in Treasury and Prime Minister's, he opted for the latter because he felt he would be able to cover a wider range of issues. He was to stay there until 1981. The excitement was immediate:

> On the first day I was given by one of the deputy secretaries, a notorious fellow called Don Munro, three or four cabinet submissions on which he wanted briefs by lunchtime. So you were thrown in at the deep end in those days. Part of the role that I had was advising on Commonwealth–state financial relations. I got sucked into that as a major issue for Australia. And I was involved in studying the Canadian system. In part of 1969 and early 1970, the premiers all got together, they were all coalition, very unusual, they thought, while they had a coalition prime minister as well, they could get a deal along the lines of the Canadian model. They produced a unanimous report. It was an interesting way to go, I thought. Those above me, including Gorton who was something of a centralist, threw the proposal out. But those were the beginnings of a deep-seated interest that I've had ever since in Commonwealth–state financial arrangements.

After Prime Minister's was reunited when McMahon became prime minister, it inherited a bunch of young turks recruited by Hewitt for a more activist style. Bunting took Codd on as executive assistant. Working at the centre of government, 'for one of the most outstanding' secretaries, kindled his ambitions.

But when the Whitlam government came in, it was suspicious of those who had worked for McMahon. There was an attempt to isolate Bunting and those who were close to him. That included Codd:

> I was certainly clearly seen as in this camp of resistance to a Labor government, which was totally untrue. The McMahon period was one which appalled me and I was most enthusiastic about the change of government. But that was not the way it was perceived. So you could say that was potentially a career-stopping move.

He was able to distance himself from the scene with a scholarship to Whitehall for twelve months. When he returned, the new secretary, John Menadue, promoted to him to head the resources division and the message got through to Whitlam's office:

> I ran into Gough in the corridor of his office; he paused, looked at me and said 'I hear you've been reconstructed'. It's an interesting story because it does show that you can, even in those days, perhaps

more so now, if you're intent on just being a good professional adviser, your career can be brought to a very smart halt by some people forming a view that's based on ideology or a misconception, and particularly by assuming some sort of political allegiance, which I've never had, and still don't, to any party. We went through that little episode and I enjoyed Gough's remark and many others that he made to me which I've stored up for when I get around to writing a book, which I won't.

His interest was in what could be achieved:

The opportunity to run something yourself, to influence public policy and public management was what was driving me. You can't really do that unless you are in a position of reasonable power. But you can be put in a position of power and have no particular wish to do anything except sit on top of the mountain. My interest was in actually trying to do something worthwhile. Indeed, most of my colleagues were driven by this desire to improve public policy and to make some contribution to the national interest.

Codd spent six years working in PM&C under Fraser before he was appointed as secretary of the Department of Industrial Relations:

The day I was appointed it was announced that the department was being moved to Canberra from Melbourne. I knew it was in their minds and I said to the prime minister: 'If that's what you want to do, I want that announced before my appointment. If it was seen as being three days later and it was me doing this, it would have made my task awfully difficult.

Codd later had to reintegrate the Employment Department into the portfolio when the two were united under a different minister. Management of large programs was a new experience:

That gave me a portfolio perspective, a non-central portfolio perspective. I was in battle with Finance and the other agencies in a way that I hadn't thought about much before and it was a management challenge of a kind I had never faced before. I actually found that fascinating. I loved it. I thought, gee, this is something that is really worth doing and I learnt a hell of a lot from that experience ...

In 1983 he was shifted soon after the change of government to the exile of the Industry Assistance Commission, a reaction to his closeness to Fraser. In 1985 he was 'rescued back from the IAC' to start a new Department of Community Services:

So later [when establishing a new department] the management challenge of that, of putting together a new department, of getting all the top team, the structure done and getting the whole thing rolling. And most important getting policy reviews underway and major reviews in aged care, for example, where we really, in a period of a few months we got the new policy framework in place which led to enormous improvement in the way we measure success and managed age care in nursing homes and hostels. So getting all that done, and again having a reasonably large staff and management being a major part of the role, that was a great experience.

When Hawke asked him to come back to head PM&C, he gave it some thought, but decided that:

It would send a signal through the service that sometimes the vagaries of political leadership meant that you'd be pushed out into the cold, but if you stuck to the last and just kept being professional that could turn back again. So there was a symbolic significance, I think, after having been sent out to grass by Bob Hawke.

(It should be added that now the 'out to grass' option is not likely to be used. Under the system in 1983, at least Codd's services were still available for the government to use.)

As secretary of PM&C, Codd was not only able to influence the daily decisions of government, he could make distinct and personal contributions in specific areas of interest. Around the 1987 election, he wrote two detailed papers for the prime minister, one on machinery of government, the other on federal–state relations:

What I think was appalling about the system up to 1987 was the frequency of changes and the little bits and pieces being shunted around on a regular basis. Like the arts area. They were being moved in many cases largely on the basis of the interests or capacities of individual ministers as perceived by the prime minister and not for any good public policy purpose. That was extremely disruptive. The driving force throughout the period when these changes were being put into place was to try to get more effective, better policy advice through to government and better management practices in place. And in doing so, to try to learn something from the experience of private sector management, to apply some of those principles in the public sector where thought appropriate, to try to respond to the increasing pressure for forward planning and to adjust to the increased complexity and size of government.

One element of the changes was to broaden the perspectives of the departmental secretaries:

That was much enhanced by the '87 changes. I think it actually led to greater cooperation across departmental boundaries on a day-to-day basis. Department secretaries who used to feel threatened for one reason or another, who felt part of their empire was about to be taken over by somebody else, that went much more quickly than I'd expected. They all saw that they were large outfits with a place in the sun and they began to cooperate across their boundaries where there was a shared policy interest much more effectively than in the past. Also, in my perception and [that of] others I think, the cooperation of Finance and the central agencies increased.

The other major initiative was federal–state relations; that had remained a passion for Codd since his early days in the department. He proposed new initiatives in 1987, but Hawke knocked back his suggestion on the grounds that absorbing the machinery of government changes, together with major election policy initiatives, was as much as the government could deal with in one term. After the 1990 election, Codd tried again, this time more successfully. His detailed proposals led to a prime ministerial statement in July and a special premiers' conference later that year. Codd headed the officials' taskforce that was to lead, after his departure, to the establishment of the Council of Australian Governments. It is rare for two such significant initiatives to be traced to the one official. Both were the outcome of a long interest in better and more effective government.

Codd was clear that departmental secretaries should adjust their style to suit the working habits of their minister, even more so when they were the prime minister. Fraser liked an oral briefing before question time every day. He held regular sessions each day with advisers:

> So I would be up every morning reading every conceivable newspaper and working out what I thought was likely to come from the opposition and then I would get written briefing responses done for him on those questions. I would choose the ones I thought most likely and we'd sit down and I'd fire questions at him. And he had a room full of people, Tony Eggleton would come from the Liberal Party and Petro Georgiou, John Rose, all scattered around. He liked interchange, he liked the oral way of preparing himself, sort of being pushed to think as though he was on the floor of the chamber, that suited him.

> Hawke wanted paper. He had our briefing folder and he would go through it at the beginning of the session and his advisers would pop in updates and, on a particular day, if he had time, he would go through the latest little set of updates and just think it through himself before he went into the chamber.

> The last thing any head of department should do is try and convert a minister to a different style. If the minister prefers to deal with things face to face, you respond to that. If they prefer not to see you unless there's a piece of paper in front of them, you respond to that.

How does he see the future for the service? There are two particular problems that might emerge. The growth of the ministerial offices might reduce the attraction of a public service career. Whereas once the offices included the best people from the departments, now more are political:

> Power has become far more centralised around the private office. That's a really fundamental change. It means departments are having views, robust advice, filtered and the frustrations creep in. It has the potential to damage the quality and fabric of the public service in the end. Because people who are very good and who want to have some chance of influence of the kind I was talking about earlier in relation to myself, those sort of people will not stay, especially given the poor remuneration at senior levels compared to the private sector; they won't stay if their influence is being muddied and their views filtered, by some people who are very able but others who are frankly not.

Codd was uncomfortable with some recent innovations. He did not think that performance pay could be fairly calculated. He supported the principle of rotation after five years 'in the sense that it fits with the idea that perhaps there ought to be a point at which there is a review and people ought to be willing to move and try new challenges if they've given their best, but I think to make it absolutely fixed and say, right, your five years is up, ergo you must go, that's silly. If sensibly applied it's not an unreasonable framework to have in place'.
But he was concerned that the term contracts:

> Had the potential fundamentally to take away from a career professional public service and that's the bottom line. As soon as you have a perception that people will be changed, not because of their professional performance but for other reasons, whether it's political, perceived political allegiance or some ministerial peculiarity or obsession, as soon as people perceive that it's not their merit on which their tenure at the top will be based but some other set of circumstances, then it will discourage the best people from wanting to join and stay in a service like that.

Codd would prefer a more protected process than currently exists:

> I think there are ways of bringing in a contract system that would protect the integrity of the public service. For example, you might have in the provisions a requirement that at the end of the five-year contract the secretary would be reappointed unless there was a report from X, Y and Z, the Public Service Commission chair or somebody that indicated their performance was lacking. That wouldn't necessarily guarantee them the same department but a renewal of contract would be expected, indeed prescribed, unless there was a failure to perform, measured by some independent

person, not the minister. Now I'm perfectly, not perfectly, I'm quite comfortable with a system of that kind, but I don't think it's the system we've got.

He has a real concern about the quality of the senior APS because 'it's a very hard thing to publicly persuade people that there's some value in having a professional career public service, that the memory and quality of work that can come through that system is in the national interest'.

Codd's career finally ended when prime ministers changed. Keating replaced Hawke: same party but new demands. He wanted his own man. Codd offered to resign; the offer was accepted. In the end, political fluctuations ended the distinguished public career of a person who is described by his colleague Michael Keating as 'the outstanding public servant of my generation'.

Tony Blunn, Capital Territory 1981–83; Territories and Local Government 1983; Housing and Construction 1983–87; Arts, Sport, Environment, Tourism and Territories 1987–91; Arts, Sport, Environment and Territories 1991–93; Social Security 1993–98; Attorney-General 1998–99

Tony Blunn joined the public service because the firm of solicitors for whom he worked would not give him time off to attend his law lectures:

> I knew the public service did absolutely no work and paid very handsomely, so I thought, I'll go and join the public service, get my degree and go back to practising law. And somewhere along the line I was seduced.

He joined the Navy Department in Melbourne in 1956 and quickly shifted from Accounts to Navy Intelligence:

> Which I loved. At 21 I was given the keys of what was then a brand new Holden and told to debrief the merchant ships that came in from around the world because Melbourne was still a busy port in those days and they all had intelligence officers on them.

Then he shifted to the Department of Air, where he stayed for eight years, then to the Department of Immigration. Blunn had an in-house legal position there, but he did not enjoy working for the then chairman, Fred Wheeler, and grabbed an opportunity to join the Department of Interior as an assistant secretary. That move he saw as the breakthrough:

> I suppose I have always had an ambition to be a department head. But it wasn't something I actually plotted career moves for and I never did plot career moves. I mean, it happened and it all worked out. Why some people are chosen to be promoted to FAS or deputy secretary I defy anyone to actually work out.

Interior became Capital Territory when the Whitlam government was elected and Blunn spent twelve months overseas in Canada. On his return he became city manager, an FAS position. He shifted to Finance as an FAS but was only there for fifteen months before being promoted to the Department of Business and Consumer Affairs as a deputy secretary. After abut a year, he was appointed departmental secretary of Capital Territory. His minister was Michael Hodgman. After Labor returned to office, he worked briefly for Tom Uren as departmental secretary of Territories and Local Government, but he found him too mercurial for comfort:

> You did not know if he was going to hit you or hug you, and I mean that's hard. I'm too old and traditional and conventional to accommodate all that. So when Chris Hurford offered me his new Department of Housing and Construction, I must say it was like an emissary from the gods.

Blunn stayed in Housing until the 1987 reshuffle and then he was appointed to one of the new amalgamated departments, Arts, Sport, Tourism and Territories. 'It was a bit of a rag, tag and donkey sort of thing but of course what it had was the fascinating thing of the environment and Graham Richardson'. Soon he lost his senior minister, John Brown, who resigned after allegations that he had misled the parliament. Richardson became the portfolio minister, but over the next six years Blunn had to deal with a plethora of senior and junior ministers in a sprawling portfolio. By the end of the period, his initially good relationship with the then senior minister, Ros Kelly, had effectively broken down. She later resigned over the 'sports rorts' affair, when sports grants were determined on the white board in her office. As Blunn recalls:

> The trouble was she did not tell me. I firmly believe we could have properly achieved what she wanted without breaking any rules and in a way that could have had no repercussions for her and which would have achieved a good result for everyone concerned. Because what she tried to do was not silly, but the way it was done was. But our relationship had soured to the point where we were not talking effectively ... in the end we weren't really communicating and I had reported that fact to Mike Codd who was then the PM&C departmental secretary and also to Mike Keating when he came in.

After the 1993 election, Blunn shifted to Social Security. He expected that the five years there would be his final post, but in 1998 he was offered Attorney-General's. He was then the only departmental secretary with legal qualifications. He could not resist the challenge and shifted there for the last two years of his career. He retired, at a time of his own choosing, in 1999.

Blunn was the head of five departments (given that some changed their names and functions) over eighteen years and across three governments. He was one of only two people who served the Fraser, Hawke–Keating and Howard governments. Apart from a short stint in Finance, he was never in one of the coordinating departments. His perspective may therefore be unique. What in his view has changed over that long period?

> The seeds of change, I guess started with the Whitlam government, particularly the creation of the ministerial offices. Funnily enough the new Parliament House has been a factor in that because it provided room for the development of offices that just wasn't there in the old Parliament House ... partly the department and departmental secretary were as powerful as they were because there wasn't very much alternative in those days ... alternative sources of advice became more and more significant and you had very professional organisations developing very professional techniques for advising government.

> The whole concept of the public service as the partner of the government rather than the servant of the government changed ... those reforms said, no, no, the minister is responsible. You didn't hear that the minister being responsible for the management of the department before the Dawkins reform; technically and legally it was always the case but no one ever mouthed it. Dawkins really placed the responsibility for managing the department with the minister, with the secretary as his principal agent. That was a big shift.

Blunn thought he was fortunate in the quality of some of the ministers he served. He noted the qualities of a good minister:

> One that can actually deliver so that they can get cabinet to agree to things that are important to them. That they can articulate what is important to them; they give you a clear message about what's important. That they will listen to you, that they will tell you why they disagree with you; and where they disagree with you. And at the end of the day that loyalty is a two-way street.

> I don't think a lot of politicians believe they owe much loyalty to the public service. If you go back to where we started, there was a high dependency relationship at that stage and dependency's a great

thing for encouraging loyalty. But it varies hugely from minister to minister and departmental secretary to departmental secretary.

Blunn does not dispute for a moment the right of the elected to make the policy choice: 'Indeed most of us would say that is one of the pluses of all these changes'. The problem is different:

> The elected representatives themselves don't have a view about the public service or don't have a view of the public service as a continuing entity. So it's there to serve them and the devil take them after they go. That's one of the friction points. Because a lot of us believe that our role is to ensure a reasonable mechanism for transferring power from government to government. Not a lot of governments show much sympathy for that and I understand.

After 1987, Blunn was faced with an additional problem: junior ministers. He accepted it could be hugely complicated, particularly if the junior minister had been senior or if they wanted to make a mark. Whether the senior minister gets all the briefings and takes the running for the portfolio in cabinet:

> depends on the senior minister and on the junior minister and on the subject matter. There are some junior ministers through prior arrangement who would have total carriage of matters. Now they would be co-opted for a cabinet meeting and they would present their own arguments. It's done with the agreement with the prime minister, but it's the relationship between the senior and junior minister which would be crucial. Clearly you work primarily for the senior minister, but you have to be a bit careful that you don't offend the junior minister, and that can be quite difficult, particularly when they are in different chambers as they often are because in my experience the Reps ministers have little respect for the Senate and its traditions and its mode of operations. In my general experience, they say they have, but they really don't. They think the Senate is a nuisance. In fact, a number of Reps ministers have said, oh, just don't worry about Estimates Committees, oh, tell them to mind their own business. It's not that easy if you are in the firing line. There is very little understanding.

But faced with minister with no experience, a departmental secretary like Blunn is sometimes required, explicitly, by the prime minister to break them in, or at least to look after them in their early days. That requires the skill to put ideas in the minds, even words in the mouths, of ministers:

> to have the minister accept your advice or the direction without making them feel that you are telling them what to do and how to do it.

On the more general question of the provision of frank and fearless advice, Blunn feels:

It was once a luxury. The public service had the capacity to be right almost for the sake of being right. Partly because of the changes that have happened in the structure we don't now; we are very much risk managers. So when you are into risk management, you are less confident of the position, so you are more inclined to compromise on some issues because that's all risk management is, it's compromising on some issues.

Contracts have made a difference. In the past:

if you had done a reasonably good job, then an incoming government would respect your professionalism and not punish you for having worked for a minister. Now, in at least one case [among the 1966 sackings], I think the popular view would be that one department head was sacked because of his closeness to a particular minister. Some of the others were quite mysterious and have never been explained ... there is a suggestion that there will be a review of departmental secretaries early in the new year [1999] and that one should not assume those positions are safe. It just keeps people off balance ... the sort of attitudes that are reflected in Max Moore-Wilton's appointment and in some respects in the way he has managed the job are very different to the traditional public service. And that puts people off balance too. You are not quite sure where things are coming from, so you are less inclined to perhaps be as frank and fearless as you previously may have been unless it is a major issue.

On the other hand, some ministers were intent on reminding Blunn to keep giving frank advice. After a disagreement:

We had a robust discussion, but at the end of the day, he said I disagree with you entirely and am not going to accept your advice, but don't you ever stop giving it to me.

Management was a significant function for many of the departments Blunn ran:

To run any department it's desirable to understand the elements of public service, the professional ones. That ranges from things like the constitutional basis for what you do through to the way the finance system operates, through to the way parliamentary committees work and question time.

Then there were the technical areas:

I was very heavily involved in the network when I got into Social Security, almost from day one. There are three things that were dominant in Social Security. There was computing, because it's very big, it's the partner to the people in a way I have never seen in any other department ... neither could work without the other; it was a totally symbiotic relationship and critical ... Then there was the policy development role, but what had happened was that the policy in a sense was fragmented over a lot of departments. That in itself is not a problem if those departments work together, but they weren't working together so there were chasms into which people were falling. Then there was a need to develop a much more focused service delivery ethic.

In addition, the devolution of responsibilities adds to the departmental secretary's responsibilities:

We've devolved things like being able to establish different pay structures between the departments, different terms and conditions of service; we're outsourcing. We have built in huge problems when you want to change the administrative arrangements. Most people don't realise quite how significant it's been. But the problems that that's creating haven't been worked through yet.

He feared, too, the consequence of the Department of Finance becoming involved in performance and outcome audits:

That is fairly ominous because what it means is that the portfolio minister is no longer responsible for the policy; the Minister for Finance will become a partner in responsibility for the policy. An effective mechanism to achieve that will be running costs. If you are not doing what Finance likes, then you will pay a penalty; that's been a developing trend over some time ... the common cry now is, well, absorb it, you want to do it, absorb it.

The departmental secretary's role is not getting any easier.

Blunn doubts that the departmental secretaries act much as a team and appreciated the regular meetings of departmental secretaries that Codd and Keating convened. But they were not always conducive to discussion of the most crucial topics. Blunn did support regular meetings with departmental secretaries in contingent areas when he was in Social Security:

We established regular, semi-formal meetings, often over lunch. We would meet every month or couple of months, to make sure the policy or delivery plates were not bumping too hard against one another. This was particularly Vets Affairs, Socials, Health and DEETYA. For a variety of reasons, we used to sometimes invite Tax because we has an issue that related to it. And for personality reasons and no other we made Alan Hawke [departmental secretary of Transport] part of them all because he was interesting ... Now the lunches worked; we could certainly talk much better with each other as a result. Each one of us had an informal agenda, and sometimes there was a more formal sharing of the agenda, very often not, but sometimes.

The meetings were unofficial. They never got round to telling the central agencies.

In general, Blunn thinks:

> The traditions of the public service that we like to think are there have been significantly shifted. If the prime minister and the head of the Prime Minister's Department are going to assess performance and, more importantly, award salary, or even maintain employment and tenure, on the basis of performance and perceptions of performance you are going to shift it. You wonder where it is going to end up. It will end up with something very different perhaps to what it is, but that's not to say it won't be effective to meet the needs and conditions of the government.

The final mix will depend on the balance of principles and motives. But for him there was always a consolation:

> Believe it or not there are still people who believe that working in the public service is a good and noble thing to do. They may be becoming fewer, but there are still people who believe. Allied to that, maybe indistinguishable from it, is that the work we do in the public sector is pretty bloody interesting work actually. I mean it's real adrenalin stuff. If you are a professional and you are interested in the Constitution, here [Attorney General's] is where you should work. You don't work anywhere else and get that experience.

Michael Keating, Employment and Industrial Relations 1983–86; Finance 1986–91; Prime Minister and Cabinet 1991–96

Michael Keating joined the public service after he lost his job on a golf course. While raking out a bunker, a member hit a ball right up to him. He threw it into the bushes. One of his lecturers at Melbourne University knew the deputy statistician, Keith Archer, and organised a holiday job there. He was then offered a cadetship at the Bureau of Statistics, along with Mike Codd, in the first year of the scheme. It was a great opportunity, not because he saw the public service as a career but because it provided him with the money he needed to get married while still at university. His professors were surprised; they told him 'you could have been one of us'. In their view, only those who could not make it as an academic would join the public service.

In the Bureau, Archer put time into the nurturing of the potential high flyers. He encouraged Keating and gave him time off to enrol for a PhD in economic history at the ANU. Although he only did a year full time, he continued to do research while back at the Bureau. But once his bond was paid off, he left Australia for the OECD:

I was conscious that I had no overseas experience and I was dead keen to go overseas. Now for someone with my level of experience who had three kids, it was very hard to go overseas unless I could go to the IMF or the OECD. No university could pay my travel expenses and I didn't have the funds myself. I was offered a job by the IMF as well but there were a lot of riots in Washington in 1968; there were a lot of riots in Paris too in 1968, but those in Washington were more devastating.

There he headed the forecasting division and dealt with the first oil shock, the shift from the gold standard and the international energy agency.

He was not impressed by the APS he had left. He was remote from many of the key figures, aware mostly of the intimidating Roland Wilson:

If you look for the high point of the politics of expertise around the world, he took it to a high point in Australia in his career. That sort of idea that the experts have to be listened to. People don't see the key issues of policy these days as being terribly amenable to expertise, but you had a view in the 1950s and into the 1960s that experts could design a solution that would be the right solution. And you should listen to experts. The standard excuse those days was they [the politicians] acted on expert advice. Occasionally you hear it now, but it would usually only be reserved for legal advice and it sounds fairly lame ... The vast array of policy issues, the notions that there is a rational way of developing policy to be done by experts is in disrepute now. But here is the high point. [Wilson] added to the stature of that sort of view of the world.

It lived on among his Treasury successors.

In 1974, Keating returned to work in the Department of Urban and Regional Development (DURD) as head of the economic division. Almost immediately, he was in conflict with the Treasury when his advice to his minister helped to derail the Treasury's preferred strategy for the 1974 budget. After the government fell, he went back to Paris and the OECD. He had planned to resign, but the commissioner suggested he take leave without pay. Keating asked for four years, thinking it was impossible, but it was granted. Perhaps it was fortunate because this time he found the self-censorship of the OECD stifling. He had changed as a consequence of his job in DURD, but the OECD had not.

He was persuaded to return to PM&C, primarily by Ian Castles. When Fraser was told whom the department was proposing to appoint, in anticipation of possible opposition to a high-profile ex-DURD official, he asked only if he was any good. (Keating comments that when he headed PM&C he would not normally have discussed FAS appointments with his minister.) After three weeks in the welfare division, Keating became head of the economic division and thereby one of Fraser's key advisers.

In 1982, Keating accepted a position as deputy secretary at Finance; he had earlier turned down offers in departments he did not wish to work in, but he felt the promotion was due. Further, Ian Castles was now the departmental secretary in Finance. 'I liked Ian; that was certainly a factor because you don't want to be a deputy to someone you don't respect and like. And I think in those days I didn't want to join a department that might not be there in six or twelve months' time'. Castles left much of the management of Finance to his deputies, but apart from the budget time, it was one of the easiest jobs Keating had in the last 25 years.

Three months after Labor was elected, Keating was asked to be departmental secretary of Employment and Industrial Relations. He said he would think about it, only to find that action was proceeding as everyone else had assumed he would take it. 'I appreciated that the culture for everyone but me was that you just took departmental secretary jobs'. Why that job? In a sabbatical at Melbourne University in 1981, Keating had written two articles suggesting that an incomes policy was feasible. Almost everyone else in Canberra was strongly in favour of a deregulated system. He speculates that he got the job because he was the exception at a time when the new government wanted an incomes policy and when the Accord was largely run out of the industrial relations portfolio.

He stayed at Employment and Industrial Relations until February 1986. He had made it clear that at some stage he wanted to go to Finance, but:

> I was furious when I was shifted from Employment and Industrial relations to Finance. I remonstrated with [Wilenski, chairman of the board]. He said, but I thought you wanted to go, I said, yeah, I had, it didn't mean I wanted to go now. I knew they had a five-year policy, I was still in my forties, I thought I would go in the future. I couldn't say anything to anyone of course; the last thing you want is your new department to think that you don't want to be there.

He stayed for six years, being extended beyond the nominal five-year term for rotation. Then, when Paul Keating became prime minister, he asked Mike Keating to head up PM&C, where he remained until his retirement in mid-1996. Only three departmental secretaries served longer in the 1980s and 1990s, none in the central agencies.

For much of the period, he was at the centre of economic decision-making. He held firm views of the way in which senior departmental secretaries should interact with ministers. For much of the time, an inner troika, consisting of the prime minister, Treasurer and Finance Minister, would meet accompanied by their advisers. Because they met regularly, were largely in agreement about the strategy, and the meeting was small, there was a free exchange of views between officials and ministers. On a couple of occasions, Keating had 'a monumental row' with the Treasurer. 'Once, we went hammer and tongs for over an hour, with Hawke just loving it'. On another, Paul Keating 'stormed into my office [in Finance]; I was sitting at the desk and he was standing over me on the other side of the desk and he told me he was going to rip me apart limb by limb and take Finance apart brick by brick'. Such debates were possible as the combatants knew each other well. Notably, the rows did not prevent Paul Keating appointing Mike as head of his department when he became prime minister.

But the larger the meeting, the less public servants should become involved. With larger meetings, Mike Keating didn't:

> think public servants should debate the issues. You can debate the issues at a very small meeting when they don't feel exposed to colleagues; that's why the troika can debate the issues and it won't be like a briefing, but I don't think you should start debating with ministers who don't know you well, especially if you make them look fools. Expenditure Review Committee is a bigger committee; you've got five to seven ministers on ERC plus the responding minister and perhaps the responding minister's junior ministers, plus the raft of officials. You shouldn't be in there debating policy. You should supply factual information. If you're sitting next to the minister you can whisper in his ear if you think there's a point that's been missed or misrepresented; if the minister calls on you, you might say it. But even then it should be put as a clarification, rather than 'my judgment is better than yours'.

Cabinet typically, or vary rarely, has public servants there; if a public servant was called into a cabinet meeting, the decision wouldn't be taken while the public servant was there. The public servant would be called in, invited to say his piece, asked questions and then out. Then they would discuss amongst themselves what they should do. There were clear distinctions in role that should be maintained. In providing advice, you need to remember the context:

> A new government comes in with a fair set of ideas. But even there you don't want to press too far. To a large extent, oppositions run by offering a set of values, rather than a set of policies. The Howard government had explicit and tough policies on industrial relations,

but not much else, mostly values. There is a role for the public service in identifying where policy action is needed, options and so on ... the essence is to tell ministers what they really need to know in terms of making a decision and that clearly includes warning them when things could go wrong. I never felt that terribly difficult; it somewhat puzzles me that people feel they could be under threat. My experience is that ministers are mostly rational and they would prefer to be forewarned about what could go wrong before the event than after the event, and forewarned by somebody they can essentially trust. You wouldn't be in the job if they can't trust you. So you are trusted and they expect a degree of loyalty from you and that by the way is a traditional public service value.

I personally think you have an obligation to have regard for the objectives and values of the government of the day, rather than, if you like, impose your own objectives and values. I have a sense that in times gone by there was a tendency by some public servants at least to impose their own values and objectives with very little sensitivity to those of the elected government.

Public servants could put their view, but should not belabor the point, particularly if it was off the political agenda:

I certainly didn't think it part of my responsibility to go down to the Press Club every Friday night and tell those bloody monkeys that the government was hopeless because it hadn't taken my advice and I do know a senior public servant who did that every bloody week. I don't regard that as being independent; I regard that as unacceptable behaviour.

He thought that the old days were just as 'political' as more modern times. He used the examples of comment being requested on opposition policy proposals and question time briefs:

The briefs that we wrote for Fraser under Sir Geoffrey Yeend, I think, tended to be more strident than the briefs that were written by my department under me. I don't mean that in any sense as a criticism of Geoff; it's just an observation.

And on briefing on opposition policies:

It was an issue as long as I can remember. And I can remember 40 years now. From my point of view that's not political as long as it's done professionally. I think it's quite legitimate for a government to ask for advice on a policy; you shouldn't be concerned about who was the originator of the policy if the government asks for advice. But if, in providing the advice, you make a series of party political scoring points then you cross the yard.

He did not think that contracts would make a difference to the advice given. Rather, ministers were more sceptical about the role of experts and, anyway, had greater sources to which they could look for solutions. The decline in respect for the public service's advice put it under pressure. Competition, rather than tenure, could be a threat. The greatest danger was being ignored, cut off from access because they had nothing to contribute. If the public service were marginalised, then there might be a temptation to make the advice more palatable or acceptable so that it was accepted. The great strength of the APS, its principal comparative advantage over outside experts, was in the provision of advice; maintaining that asset would be significant.

Keating was pleased that the departmental secretaries now both had incentives and the capacity to manage properly. That was one of the benefits of the changes over which he had presided when departmental secretary of Finance. Very quickly, the slogan of 'let the manager manage' had been accompanied by 'make the managers manage'. Now the departmental secretaries:

> Have got to have a focus on output, not just process; beyond outputs they have got to really account for cost effectiveness and make decisions in terms of cost effectiveness. Prioritise and so on. In the past (and I'm not blaming them, I think the blame is as much with central agencies), they didn't feel any obligation to manage because they were being managed by somebody else. If you start doing somebody's job for them, don't be surprised if they don't do it.

All the signals were perverse, like:

> 'Make sure you spend', it didn't matter how you spent it, spend like mad in the last month. What they should do is more important than who should do it. But I don't think you could have changed what they managed unless you clarified the lines of responsibility and accountability. Essentially we had a system where no one was responsible and no one was accountable.

Now departmental secretaries have the authority and responsibility to use resources more effectively.

Keating also believes that departmental secretaries now have a better corporate view:

> I used to go to the old secretaries' meetings and there were very few who experienced both new and old. In the old ones you had over 30 people in the room, there was no dialogue, we were read lectures by the Public Service Board. It gave everyone a sense of importance, but it was actually totally useless ... When it was kept down to fifteen or sixteen representatives, there was a chance for genuine dialogue and discussion. It wasn't the only change. The clear indication that people were going to get rotated, that they weren't typically appointed from within their own department,

meant that their loyalty became much less to defend their territory, and much more to the service as a whole … you recognise that what one part of government does may have more or less significant implications for another part of government. There is nothing new about that, but the implications would become more significant with time.

Can the APS be sustained? Keating feels that there is a distinct difference between the public and private sectors. Public servants have a set of skills that private managers rarely have to develop, an explanation in part for why so few transfer successfully to the APS:

> The public service is an independent source of advice which unlike most others is usually disinterested. Typically it has the capacity to contribute a depth of analysis, sustained over a long period of time, with an understanding of the realities of implementation to assist in policy design. Most importantly, the department secretary will only survive if he is trusted by the minister, and the close working relationship provides the opportunity to iterate and bounce views off each other, which is not available to other sources of external advice.

Keating cannot think of any other way of providing advice which will maintain all these advantages, so he believes the APS will survive in some form not too different from the existing one.

9

Sacking a departmental secretary: The Barratt case

'Paul, it's Max. You're sacked'. So *The Australian* (24 July 1999) reported the sudden firing of the departmental secretary of Defence in July 1999. Barratt immediately sought an injunction in court and over the next months there were three hearings in which the rights of the government to sack departmental secretaries were debated in law. At the end of the day, the rights of the departmental secretaries were seen to be few. Many of the issues discussed in this book were given a public hearing. The case thus provides a good opportunity to see the explanations and defence of the existing rules and thereafter to consider the possible implications for the APS.[1]

The story

Paul Barratt had been a career public servant, joining the Defence Intelligence Organisation in the late 1960s and moving up the ranks until he became a deputy secretary in the Department of Trade. In 1992 he left the APS to become the chief executive of the Chamber of Commerce in Melbourne. There he was involved in a number of forward scanning exercises with the Chamber's leading figures.

A few days after the 1996 election, the new prime minister rang him and asked if he would return to the APS to head the Department of Primary Industries and Energy. When the prime minister calls and asks for help in changing the way things are done, most people respond. Barratt spent almost two years at that department, reorganising it and establishing a strategic direction with the minister, John Anderson. In February 1998 he was asked to shift to the Defence Department. Until the October election, his relations with the minister, Ian McLachlan, were good.

Then a new minister was appointed. John Moore had been the Member for Ryan in Queensland since 1975 when he had knocked off a long-serving (and undistinguished) sitting member. Moore had been a sole-trader stockbroker before entering politics and was already wealthy. He was promoted to the ministry in 1980 but was sacked in

1982 in the 'colour TV' affair after he failed to inquire adequately into a fellow minister's importation of a television without paying the appropriate duty. The episode was a series of oversights and blunders. In the long period in opposition, Moore had been a leading figure in the 1989 coup that removed John Howard and replaced him with Andrew Peacock. In 1996, Howard appointed him Minister for Industry. Ten months later, his departmental secretary, Greg Taylor, was peremptorily removed and posted to the IMF. Taylor had been a departmental secretary since 1989. Moore was not regarded as an easy minister to work for.

Within three months of Moore's arrival in Defence, it was clear that he and Barratt were not working closely together. On 21 January, Moore told Barratt he was concerned about a proposed overseas visit as he wanted to push ahead with some important issues. He gave Barratt a letter:

> Since becoming Minister for Defence we have had a number of discussions on issues I believe to be of importance for the Department and on the most appropriate way of dealing with those issues. I thought it might be useful for me to summarise those issues and my expectations in relation to them.
>
> Before doing so there is an important general point I would like to make. It is the strong view of the Government that two important fundamentals of the Government/Defence relationship in a democratic society are firstly the responsibility of the Government to Parliament for the actions of the department and secondly, in the ultimate, the importance of civilian control of the military.

He went on to specify some issues of concern, including 'the need for the Department to adopt a much more contemporary and professional approach to public affairs and to develop a public affairs strategy'.

The same day, Moore met the secretary of PM&C, Max Moore-Wilton, and told him:

> I have substantial reservations about the Secretary's commitment to actively manage the department in pursuing the Government's reform agenda. He does not appear to want to drive issues to a conclusion. I asked for comprehensive reports on the Collins Class submarine project and they have still not arrived. Moreover he appears to be prepared to 'reign' over Defence rather than actively manage. I am also concerned that the CDF's [Chief of Defence Forces] spouse is Mr Barratt's personal assistant.

On 22 January, and concerned by the letter he had been handed the day before, Barratt flew to Brisbane to try to sort through any problems. He emphasised that, as minister, Moore was the 'highest expression of civilian control of the military'. He commented that in his view he should work closely with the CDF to bring the minister 'a common view. We could always relapse to the bad old days of dumping unresolved issues on your desk for arbitration but I would not recommend that'. The following exchange took place:

> *Barratt:* I also want to be sure that our discussion yesterday did not indicate a lack of confidence on your part in me.
>
> *Moore:* Well, I have been disappointed. There are some things I have asked for that have not happened as quickly as I would have liked. I have asked you to arrange to get me economic advice on a continuing basis. This is very important to me. I am being very blunt with you but that's the way I am.

Barratt promised to take rapid action on the issues raised. He told Moore:

> that they needed to work hand in glove and that if ever Mr Moore was dissatisfied with the advice or service he was receiving he should just pick up the phone. Moore replied that Barratt might get a lot of phone calls. Barratt said that that was what he was paid for. At the conclusion of the meeting, he told Moore that he was sorry to have jumped his diary, but he thought it was important to resolve those issues quickly. Moore said words to the effect of 'Not at all. Glad you came'.

Throughout the meeting, Barratt was concerned that, whenever he asked detailed questions, they were answered by Moore's ministerial staffer, who seemed to be the key person in making policy decisions.

Barratt was sufficiently concerned to see Moore-Wilton on 27 January. Barratt thought he had convened the meeting because he wanted to warn the secretary of PM&C of a situation where the staffer seemed to be making all the running and hence a possible problem for the future. In a later affidavit, Barratt said he told Moore-Wilton that, at the meeting with Moore, the staffer:

> did most of the talking. I would ask a question of the minister and get an answer from Loughnane [the ministerial staffer]. Frequently Loughnane would talk across the minister. An outside observer would have difficulty discerning who was the minister and who was the adviser. This is an unhealthy relationship, particularly in a portfolio as sensitive as Defence, and is potentially a problem for the government.

He alleged that Moore-Wilton replied that the staffer was a senior Liberal Party adviser who had been 'rusted' on to Moore. 'You will never get rid of him'. Moore-Wilton wanted to warn him of the potential difficulties he had with his minister. He said: 'In my view the situation is unsatisfactory and you should discuss with your minister an improved basis for carrying out your duties'. Perhaps because of the misunderstanding about the origin of the meeting, the alarm bells did not ring for Barratt as much as they might have done.

Nor did anything else warn him things were still bad. Moore-Wilton told the prime minister in February that the Minister of Defence had negative feelings towards his departmental secretary but advised that, as the minister had not been there long, there were not sufficient grounds to recommend action; he suggested Barratt's performance be reviewed in a year's time. In February, Moore was told by Howard that he should work harder at making the relationship with Barratt work as he was stuck with him. In March, Moore-Wilton told a meeting of departmental secretaries that, after the review of performances, the prime minister 'determined that there would be no changes at the present time and no minister is seeking the replacement of his current secretary'.

Perhaps there were some signs that all was still not well. On 11 March, in an expletive-laden discussion, Moore accused the department of snowing him. Then, not satisfied with the advice from the department, Moore had established a review of the Collins Class submarine, headed by Malcolm McIntosh, the head of CSIRO and a former deputy of Defence at the time the Collins project was initiated. Moore had worked with McIntosh in Industry and Science and was reputed to want him as the new head of Defence, a job that McIntosh too desired.

But in May, Moore and Barratt travelled overseas together to China and Korea. On the plane they discussed the proposed goals that Barratt was required to set for the performance agreements which the government was introducing at the time. Barratt went through a draft document, 'Draft Key Goals for Secretaries'. He explained the details. Moore wanted something on Indonesia added, but otherwise did not demur. He did not indicate any great dissatisfaction with Barratt's performance.

Moore had grumbled on and off to Moore-Wilton about Barratt's ability to manage the government's reform program. On 28 July, as the National Security Committee of Cabinet discussed the Collins report, Moore told Moore-Wilton he was considering the need for a new departmental secretary.

On 2 July, Moore-Wilton and Barratt had an off-the-record discussion. The two affidavits that recount the conversation provide different emphases and words. Moore-Wilton told Barratt:

> Your relationship with Moore was 'just about terminal'. I'm not supposed to be telling you all of this, so this conversation never took place. But I can't let it go on behind your back and the prime

minister will probably want to talk to me on the plane and I want
to get a feel for where you stand ... John Moore said to me he
wants you moved and [CSIRO chief Malcolm] McIntosh put in
your place.

Moore had suggested Barratt might be interested in the High
Commissionership in New Zealand; Moore-Wilton, according to
Barratt, responded: 'Jesus Christ, the trouble with you blokes is you
have got no corporate memory. Barratt put up with years of this
from the Labor Party. He has already been an ambassador and hates
Foreign'. McIntosh had proposed he be sent to a university in the
United States 'to learn about defence' so he could be appointed
temporarily to clean the place up. Moore-Wilton recollects that he
asked:

> Are there any other positions within government that interest you,
> although it must be recognised that it would be difficult to make a
> clean transition within the government in Canberra after your
> relatively short period at the Defence Department?' He said: 'I
> have no interest in an alternative position as Secretary of another
> department'. I said: 'What about a senior overseas posting?'

He suggested the High Commissioner in New Zealand. Barratt
(whose affidavit does not include the comments about his
unwillingness to serve in another department) responded that he was
not interested in New Zealand, but 'I might be tempted by Paris'.
When told it was unavailable, Barratt said:

> Well, Max, people have to make choices. If I am to be put out to
> grass then the grass will have to be lush. As far as I am concerned,
> they will have to sack me. If there is one thing I have demonstrated
> in the past it is that I can be quite stubborn and I have staying
> power.

Moore-Wilton replied, according to Barratt's affidavit, that he could
probably hold the line until Christmas but:

> I am not sure how much longer. There are too many vultures
> circling and you don't have too many friends around that table at
> present ...

He added that 'termination would send a very bad signal. The prime
minister would want to look at all the other options'. Moore-Wilton
said, on his own memory, 'that Moore has said that if he was not
able to reform Defence he would go home to the bush'. According
to Barratt's account, Moore-Wilton said: 'The prime minister realises
it's not too good, but he's not going to stand in Moore's way because
that is what Moore wants ... so you have a senior minister putting
himself on a limb'. Moore-Wilton denied he said those words. He

concluded: 'The PM and I are going overseas on Monday and nothing further will be done while he is away but I want you to be aware that you are facing potentially a very serious situation'. He acknowledged: 'It's a rough game'.

Barratt recalled that they discussed the performance of Moore and McIntosh; Barratt could not understand why the latter was being supported when Moore-Wilton said the he 'was playing a very pernicious role' and was seen as a possible source of the leaks to the press (after Moore's office had denied to the prime minister that it had done it).

On 7 July, Moore and Barratt met at a lunch. Unable to reveal the content of the discussion with Moore-Wilton because it was off the record, Barratt asked Moore if there was anything he wished to discuss. Moore replied in the negative, saying everything was fine.

The knife fell on 21 July while Barratt was waiting for a flight at Sydney airport. Moore-Wilton told Barratt that the minister was meeting him and the prime minister to discuss the management of the department. Barratt asked: 'Can you give me something specific that I have done?' Moore-Wilton said: 'No, just things in general'. Barratt said he was not interested in any overseas appointment or in alternative Commonwealth employment. He wanted to remain in his job. Moore-Wilton concluded that the position was pretty hopeless. On 22 July, Moore-Wilton met the prime minister and Minister of Defence.

When Barratt arrived in Manila later that day, he was told he was needed on the phone, and everyone else had to keep their mobiles turned off. The CDF was warning Barratt that the press had got hold of the story that Moore was meeting with the prime minister to demand the appointment of McIntosh as secretary of Defence. The CDF told Barratt that 'my sources say that the leak is designed to force the PM's hand'. Barratt rang Moore-Wilton and caught him on a mobile while he was having his hair cut. Moore-Wilton said the prime minister had instructed him to ask whether Barratt would be prepared to accept appointment as High Commissioner in New Zealand. Moore-Wilton told him it would not be tenable for him to continue as departmental secretary of Defence 'if you and Moore were unreconciled'. He said the prime minister wanted him to see Moore before 27 July. Barratt does not recall the last rider on reconciliation; he saw the termination as already decided. Barratt refused the offer of an appointment and said he wanted to stay in Defence. So Moore-Wilton said, in that case, the only alternative seemed to be to initiate the process to terminate the appointment and cabinet would consider it on 27 July in view of the press speculation (itself fuelled by careful leaks, allegedly from the minister's office).

As departmental secretary of PM&C, Moore-Wilton was required to write a report for the prime minister. On 23 July, he duly wrote a draft that recommended the termination on the grounds of the irreconcilable relations between minister and secretary. He signed it and put it in a drawer to give himself some time for reflection, 'just in case I have second thoughts'; that was a normal practice, he told the court later.

When Barratt returned to Australia he met the CDF who reported a conversation with Moore. Both sides agreed there was little point in them meeting. Moore said, recalled the CDF, that 'he sought your removal back in February this year but Moore-Wilton and the PM were too weak kneed to go through with it'.

On 28 July, Barratt filed an application in the Federal Court to restrain Moore-Wilton from writing a report recommending termination until he had been afforded procedural fairness, including a reasonable opportunity to be heard. There were hearings in early August at which he argued that he should receive natural justice, that he had reasonable expectations that he should be allowed to serve the contracted five years and that he should only be terminated for due cause, for something that he had done or failed to do. The government argued that the termination could be made for any reason, that the departmental secretaries in effect served at the governor-general's pleasure and that good relations with the minister were crucial. The government's counsel argued:

> I was going to give the analogy of a judge and an associate but that perhaps might in some sense be an inappropriate analogy but in some senses it is an appropriate one. The relationship is necessarily a personal one. There must be an ability of the judge to say, we don't get on but it doesn't have to prove misconduct to a tribunal in that sort of situation. This is a different relationship to that because the secretary of course is closer to an equal level but the secretary nevertheless is a person who does have to work closely with the minister.

The judge concluded that Barratt indeed was entitled to procedural fairness before his appointment was terminated:

> That means that the applicant is entitled to be told why termination of his appointment is proposed before the expiration of its five-year term, and he is entitled to a reasonable opportunity to put his case as to why a recommendation to that effect should not be made by the prime minister.
>
> It means no more than that. The application fails in his additional claim that the power of termination can only be exercised for cause

consisting of some fault or incapacity that goes to his fitness to continue to occupy the office for the remainder of the fixed term.

He had no right of audience to press his case with either the departmental secretary of PM&C or the prime minister.

The day after the judgment, Moore-Wilton wrote to Barratt saying that he intended to report to the prime minister recommending his termination on the grounds:

(a) that the Minister for Defence has lost trust and confidence in your ability to perform the duties of Secretary to the Department of Defence; and

(b) that this lack of trust and confidence is detrimental to the public interest because it is prejudicial to the effective and efficient administration of the Department of Defence.

He noted the material on which the recommendation had been made and said he would disregard his earlier views and reconsider the whole matter.

Barratt asked for more detail; he said the terms 'trust and confidence' were so broad that he was precluded from answering in any adequate fashion. He pointed out that the reasons for termination had changed, from 'irreconcilable conflict' to the new terms. In reply, Moore-Wilton stated that:

My conversation with Mr Moore took place after the Federal Court decision had been handed down and I was considering whether or not I should make a report to the prime minister ... in relation to your appointment as secretary to the Department of Defence. For that purpose, I said to Mr Moore words to the effect: 'What is your current view of your relationship with Mr Barratt in relation to the management of the Department of Defence?'

Mr Moore replied to the following effect: 'I have no confidence in Mr Barratt'.

Barratt then filed a second application arguing that he was entitled to a statement of the grounds for the view that the minister had no trust and confidence. The seven words said by Moore were, it was argued, not sufficient to end a career without further evidence. The appeal was not accepted. If there was a cause given that related to his performance, Barratt was entitled to know it, but if the recommendation were to be based solely on the fact that the minister 'rightly or wrongly and for whatever reason' had lost confidence in Barratt's ability to perform his duties, then he was not entitled to know why that had occurred. As the judge said, it was for the departmental secretary of PM&C to decide whether the lack of trust was a sufficient basis to make a report to the prime minister, without inquiry as to the reasons or justification for that lack of confidence. It was up to the prime minister to decide if he would act on the advice. Barratt's position was terminated.

In March 2000, an appeal was heard. It began with common ground: 'that the termination of Mr Barratt's appointment as Secretary to the Department of Defence was not related to his competence nor to any misconduct on his part'. The judges argued that a fixed-tem appointment was not held 'at pleasure' and that some reason had to be given for its termination. They concluded that, as long as the reason was related to the principal objective of the act (in this case, section 6: 'the efficient, equitable and proper conduct ... of the public administration of the Australian Government'), then the reasons were adequate. They did not have to be based on the conduct of the departmental secretary:

> Why there is a lack of trust and confidence is a matter that is relevant to the exercise of the discretion to make a recommendation but is not, of itself, determinative of whether the ground is made out or whether the recommendation should be made. It is open to the secretary, in preparing his report, to enquire into why the minister's trust and confidence were lacking, but he is not required to determine whether, on an objective basis, the reason has been established to be well founded. It is because the reason relied upon is the minister's loss of trust and confidence, and not that the loss of trust and confidence is well founded.

The appeal was dismissed.

Lessons from the Barratt case

We need to start with a caveat. The Barratt case is an example of things being really bad. That is not the normal state of affairs. The problems are starker, the denouement more dramatic. But they also illustrate what can happen and why these issues need to be considered carefully.

Ministerial–departmental secretary relations

A determination to make the relationship between minister and secretary work must be two-way. It is not enough for the departmental secretary to be professional and responsive if the ministers decide they do not like the person they must work with or if, as in this case, they seem determined to install their own chosen candidate. Moore had only been in Defence for two months when he declared he wanted a change — scarcely an adequate time to allow working styles to adjust. He was told by the prime minister to work it out, but seemed determined that it would fail. By several accounts, the final report of the submarine contract, which was written by his chosen candidate and which he used as an excuse to demand change again, adopted many of the solutions presented by the department. Trust and partnership can never work in these circumstances.

Barratt had been brought back into the APS by the prime minister, had been promoted by the prime minister to a senior department and had worked smoothly with two ministers as a departmental secretary before Moore arrived in Defence. His record was good.

But the comparison — even if eventually oblique — of the departmental secretary to the judge's associate was telling. To some ministers, it seems that a departmental secretary is no more than another chief of staff to be employed and disposed of when cordial relations disappear. In fact, that is an entirely inappropriate analogy; the departmental secretary has far more personal responsibilities and is closer to being an equal. The associate is an executive assistant, no more.

One problem is that many ministers are, on the whole, not good at providing feedback on their level of satisfaction. They insist to the departmental secretary that all is going fine, even when they are dissatisfied. Barratt argued that he had no idea that he was in trouble until July; he may have been slow to read the signs for it seems the grumbling was continuous. But by the time he was told that much was wrong, the minister had long regarded the relationship as terminal. Certainly departmental secretaries may — and some do — sit down on a regular basis once or twice a year to ask how things are going, but even that may not be as informative as they would wish. The Barratt case suggests that there is a need for that process to become even more formal, if only for the protection of both sides.

The question, then, is the degree to which this type of situation may become more common. It might not, for many ministers are reasonable people who understand the benefits of working smoothly with their departments. But there is a model, however dangerous, to follow. In this case, careful leaks to the media forced the prime minister into backing his minister. What else could he do in the circumstances? He could have tried to pull the minister into line, but that would bring little political gain. As it was allegedly put, the prime minister was not going to stand in the way of a senior minister who wanted a change. A departmental secretary is easier to remove than a minister because it can be done with less fuss — usually anyway, even if not in this case. To remove a senior minister is harder and threatens the prime minister's own judgment. Will a stage be reached where the ministers can remove departmental secretaries simply by saying they have no confidence and giving no reasons? In theory, clearly that is a legally adequate reason. In terms of public administration, it is a dire (and fortunately unlikely) result as it may remove far too much of the onus on the minister to develop a good relationship with a professional public servant.

Ministerial staff

The dangers of advice contested by a political but not necessarily technically competent staff were made explicit. A newly appointed minister with no background in the portfolio relies heavily on a trusted staff member who has shifted with him from one job to the other. The minister gives his advice precedence over that from professional advisers. From one angle, the staffer might be seen as the strong man standing up to the department on behalf of his minister and preventing it snowing him. From the other, it is a person intervening between the departmental secretary and the minister and preventing the advice being properly explained. Whichever the perspective, the potential to influence decisions is clear and the favourable position at the side of the minister is emphasised. The staffers are as important as the ministers choose to make them.

Performance appraisal

Barratt was promoted in October 1997 from Primary Industries to Defence. The decision was made by the prime minister and is presumably evidence that he had done a good job in his former portfolio and was seen as the best person to tackle Defence. In March 1999, Moore-Wilton reported to a meeting of departmental secretaries that the prime minister planned to make no immediate changes. At that time, he was aware of the tension in Defence and had told Moore to work it out. In May, Barratt started to develop the criteria for assessment of his performance and had discussed them with his minister. He reported to a meeting of departmental secretaries on 2 June that he had 'completed the necessary consultation on my performance objectives with my minister'. All these factors suggested that, in the minds of the central players, Barratt was still in a workable, if fraught, position. He might have expected a positive appraisal and a substantial financial bonus.

But this case shows how essentially irrelevant such a process might be for the survival of the departmental secretary. A good appraisal will be of little value at the moment if the ministers decide they have no trust in their departmental secretary and are prepared to push the prime minister into action to remove them. There was initially talk that, under the requirements of the *Remuneration Act*, the findings would have to tabled. It is unlikely that it will now occur if it can be avoided. First, a satisfactory performance, and certainly any better result, *ought* to protect a departmental secretary; if the departmental secretary is said to be performing well, what justification is there for dismissal, especially if there is a possibility that the report may become public? After Barratt, it may be harder for a government to say that a departmental secretary is performing well and then, a few months later, to sack the same person. Where is the consistency and credibility of the process and what would the damage be if such an event were to happen again and again? Second, ministers now have an interest in the success of their departmental secretary. If a departmental secretary falls short, what does this say about the minister's performance (unless, that is, they are seeking to blame the departmental secretary for policies that the minister has devised but which are not working; blame shedding is not unknown and could be most unfair). Third, if the assessments were to be public, they are likely to be given even greater scrutiny as analysts look for hints to see who may be in danger; consequently they will need to be carefully argued and presented and based on greater evidence and a more careful case than they might otherwise have done. Even if they are not tabled, they may have to be written in the expectation that they could become public. At the very least, the Barratt case will ask questions about the terms of employment and performance appraisal that are likely to lead to a careful assessment of whether they are designed to do much more than provide salary bonuses.

The mediation process

Traditionally, the secretary of PM&C has been the safety valve when tensions rise. Departmental secretaries who have problems with the minister can discuss their situation and seek help; the secretary can then, if appropriate, discuss the case with the prime minister. We do not know how often these discussions occur, as they work well only when the discussions are kept secret and when neither side is seen as a loser; otherwise, a continuing relationship may be hard to sustain. In the Barratt case, there were at least two meetings between Barratt and the Secretary of PM&C, and the prime minister asked the minister to keep trying to make the relationship work. But by July, Barratt was told that a split was a matter of time and that the secretary of PM&C thought it could be only put off until perhaps Christmas. Barratt was offered an alternative position — Wellington — but chose not to accept. The saga illustrates the pivotal role of the secretary of PM&C as adviser to the prime minister, confidant to those departmental secretaries in trouble, protector of the departmental secretaries to an extent and then the critical link required to provide a report to the prime minister setting out the reasons for the termination.

There was a clear appreciation in this case, on both sides, of the difficulties in Barratt's recollection of the 22 July conversation from Manila:

Moore-Wilton: I feel bad about this. I feel I played a role in getting you into this predicament because it was my idea that you should move to Defence.

Barratt: You shouldn't reproach yourself on that score, Max. I am a grown-up person and I made an eyes-open decision to accept. It's a great job and I'm glad I did so. I am just sorry it has turned out this way.

Moore-Wilton: I feel I have been as straight with you as I could in the circumstances.

Barratt: I do too, Max, and I really appreciate it.

There is no doubt that, in the past, secretaries of PM&C have managed this system, but precisely because it was done in private, there is no evidence of how often similar situations were resolved. Although there were reports before each termination, they have usually been kept confidential. Nevertheless, the attempts to mediate were not always successful; there had been a number of occasions when a departmental secretary was eased out or retired early when relations with the minister became terminally bad.

Appraisals also were not formalised. But now part of the process will inevitably become more public. The question, now that the several stages have become public or have the potential to do so, is whether others should now be involved. The secretary of PM&C is pivotal because he advises the prime minister for whom the appointment of departmental secretaries is, and will remain, a key prerogative; the Public Service Commissioner has not had similar clout or standing. Perhaps some of the responsibility for appraisal could be shared. It might provide better feedback on performance from ministers and others and be less tense if not done exclusively by the person who also advises on terminations. In addition, if the secretary of PM&C is seen — whether fairly or not — as closer to the prime minister than to their departmental secretary colleagues, then there may be greater freedom of expression if talking to those who are not directly involved in determining their future.

Moore-Wilton did what he could to protect his departmental secretary, but there were clear limitations on what he could do once the dispute had become public. The usual solution is to arrange a shuffle of departmental secretaries. Given time, he might have managed to do that, perhaps swapping Barratt to Transport, headed by his former minister, John Anderson. Transport departmental secretary Alan Hawke, who was eventually sent to Defence, could have gone earlier. That is the type of arrangement that has earlier saved departmental secretaries' jobs and would doubtless been the preferred arrangement. In that way, the services of departmental secretaries could be maintained and one breakdown of relations between a departmental secretary and minister might not have had such terminal consequences. But in Moore-Wilton's affidavit, it is noted that Barratt had declared he did not want another departmental secretary position, so it was perhaps not a realistic option. anyway.

Once the brawl was in the public arena, however, such careful planning was not possible. Unless the prime minister was prepared to distance himself from the minister, he had to support the change, and in a time frame that made it hard to come up with a softer solution. Ministers will usually win when the fights become public; they are more used to that form of communication. The process of mediation becomes almost impossible to manage.

Justice and reasons
Were the reasons given adequate? Legally, clearly so. As long as the reason had an impact on the efficient administration of the government, the departmental secretary had to commit no fault or make no mistake. It was enough that the minister — whether justifiably or not — felt that he had no trust in the departmental secretary. In one sense, that might be a bonus. The government did not have to invent a reason to sack a departmental secretary by arguing that there was some deficiency on their part; it was always possible to find an excuse and doubtless one that would rebound on the reputation of the departmental secretary. It is hard enough being terminated without reasons; it would be that much harder knowing that public reasons were a sham.

Now there is little point challenging such a termination. Departmental secretaries might be owed natural justice and a statement of reasons, but they have no right of audience and no capacity to argue the case. Besides, the Moore-Wilton exchange with the minister has now provided a form of words that has been legally tested and which cannot be challenged. Who would know why a minister has lost trust or whether it is justified? It is enough that they have said they have. Departmental secretaries under threat know what awaits them.

Whether that is adequate or desirable in terms of good public administration is a different question. A mantra that 'I have no trust in ...' seems barely adequate as a means of ending what was presumably a distinguished public service career. How it might be dealt with is a matter for the next chapter.

Some implications for recruitment
Barratt had been a long-serving public servant before he spent some years in the private sector. There is still only one case of a person without senior APS experience being appointed as a departmental

secretary in a senior position and making a success of it (that was John Menadue). After Barratt, it may be that hiring one will be even more difficult. It was always hard as a departmental secretary is far more at the beck and call of the minister than any private sector CEO is to a chair of the board. And who will come now to still-mediocre pay, requiring accountability to parliament and liable to be terminated, not because of any error, but because the minister does not like their style. It seems likely that recruitment of good talent from the private sector will be harder, while at the same time career prospects within the service are perceived to be more limited and many more good people are being lost at all levels. The APS needs all the talent it can get. The Barratt case was probably a disincentive to achieving that aim.

Conclusion

Crises may teach bad lessons. In this case, they have provided some salutary warnings. Departmental secretaries can, through no fault or action of their own, be terminated because their minister has no trust in them. What they do elsewhere in the portfolio does not matter if their relationship with their minister is poor. These cases will erupt only when the traditional means of mediation have failed; indeed, those processes can work only when the tensions are private. Leaks, the currency of politics but not so often of administration, make the issue a matter of public concern. Because such actions are likely to occur in crisis terms, reshuffles become harder to arrange. As a consequence, the APS may lose the services of a talented individual. That is the problem that really needs to be addressed.

Fortunately, such incidents do not occur often. Most ministers and most departmental secretaries manage to work together; it is in the interest of both to have a good working relationship, even if not always a smooth one. But the Barratt case shows what can happen and provides in stark relief the need to consider where the position of departmental secretary might be headed, and with what implications for the shape of our future governance.

Note

1. The following account is taken from the press coverage of the affair, from the affidavits of Paul Barratt (29 July and 5 August) and Max Moore-Wilton (2 August and 8 August), from the transcripts of the hearings on 6, 9, 12 and 25 August in the Federal Court and from the judgments of Mr Justice Hely on 19 August 1999 and from the Appeal hearing on 10 March 2000.

10

Whither departmental secretaries?

It was inevitable that the roles and positions of departmental secretaries would change over the last five decades. The different activities of government, the new ideas on how government should run, the expectations of citizens and the employment conditions outside the APS have all affected their position. But the particular choices and decisions that had an impact on the world of the departmental secretaries were not inevitable. They were made because of the intersection of people and ideas at a given time. If we ask how a public service can best be organised, and what are the optimal circumstances for getting the best out of a person in a departmental secretary position, there is no single answer. Parliamentary democracies across the world have made different choices — about the availability of expertise, about competitiveness of advice, about tenure, and about political affiliation of senior officials. It would be hubris to argue that somehow Australia has got the balance right and by implication others have not. Rather, each country develops its own patterns of behaviour. What is important is what we can learn from this analysis of our experience and what can be usefully extracted from experience elsewhere.

Several of the factors that influenced the position of the departmental secretaries in this country have been analysed. Change was determined in part by social developments, by modern technology with its capacity to deliver services and organise data more effectively, by the rapid dissemination of news and information through the media, and by the spread of education to a much wider proportion of the electorate. As society changes, so the APS and its leaders must change too.

The public service was affected by the rhythm of politics, too. Australia changes its governments rarely. With the exception of the Whitlam government, every government in the last five decades have survived for at least seven years and three elections. Ministerial experience is not often transferred from one government to another because political turnover is high when a government loses. Most incoming ministers have some residual suspicion of those who have long served their predecessors — a suspicion sometimes, but not always, alleviated by the good service they receive. Recently, even new ministers in incumbent governments have been dissatisfied with the advice and support they received from their departmental secretaries and sought to shake up the official ranks as a consequence.

So senior officials are constantly under review, more so at some times than others. Since 1972 — perhaps even since Gorton — there has been no long period of stability. There is no given target for reform, no agreement on what is an ideal situation, little thought for where their counterparts might be in ten years' time. Rather, there is constant evaluation of how the APS might be organised and where the departmental secretaries should stand in that new world. As the marketplace for ideas has grown, and faith in any one 'correct' solution declined, so the supremacy of expertise over values has also declined. Competition for the ear of the minister can be fierce, solutions are uncertain, the battle for good ideas continuous and the traditional grounds for dispute constantly shifting. Even if the departmental secretaries have the advantage of being ever-present, with the resources of their department to back them, they have to fight for attention. They have to make their case and deliver the programs in a way that satisfies the government.

What can be seen as an acceptable situation? Perhaps, instead of arguing about institutions, we should start a review with some of the values that are needed to underpin the working of the APS. Those values were spelt out on the *Public Service Act* 1999, an Act that had been gradually developed over the previous decade. As such, they represent not just the existing government but a wider range of opinion. Some of the values in the Act (section 10) are particularly relevant to this discussion:

(a) the APS is apolitical, performing its functions in an impartial and professional manner;

...

(b) the APS is a public service in which employment decisions are based on merit;

...

(e) the APS is openly accountable for its actions, within the framework of Ministerial responsibility to the Government, the Parliament and the Australian public;

(f) the APS is responsive to the Government in providing frank, honest, comprehensive, accurate and timely advice and in implementing the Government's policies and programs;

(g) the APS delivers services fairly, effectively, impartially and courteously to the Australian public and is sensitive to the diversity of the Australian public;

(h) the APS has leadership of the highest quality

...

(k) the APS focuses on achieving results and managing performance;

...

(n) the APS is a career-based service to enhance the effectiveness and cohesion of Australia's democratic system of government.

Laudable objectives all. However, the existence of them in the Act is no guarantee of their practice. The crucial question is not whether they are listed but how they are applied. Each of them may also be open to abuse if pushed too far. To be too non-partisan may be to be too unconcerned, too distant to care, too conservative and uncommitted. To be too responsive can lead to charges of politicisation, or cravenness, bowing to every wish of the dominant political class. Professionalism can be narrow, refusing to do what does not fit that image, or to recognise ideas and solutions that do not fit the predetermined criteria of what is proper or 'professional'. An emphasis exclusively on results may ignore the impact on people or areas not directly connected with those performance criteria. A career service can become an inbred élite, self-referencing, protective and immune to the introduction of new talent. I am not suggesting that any of these outcomes is necessarily occurring, but rather that in the application of values there is a need for balance, for the sensible examination of what is being done and why.

The old system of departmental secretaries appointed for life and long surviving their ministers had its problems. Coupled with an élitist attitude to decision-making and a virtual monopoly on advice that gave them distinct advantages over other participants in the process, the most effective mandarins could be dominant figures when paired with all but the most effective ministers. At times, their advice had a take-it-or-leave-it quality, with few options and little support if the ministers did not like what they were given. Besides, we should not assume that every departmental secretary is necessarily effective. Some may have been promoted beyond their competence and need to be gently moved aside. It was what a minister described as an 'imperial bureaucracy'.

Recently, the bureaucracy has sought to be more responsive to the elected government — or, putting it in terms that the politicians would appreciate, it has become more amenable to political control.

There can be few objections in principle to the notion that the direction of government activities is determined by the politicians who are elected. But there is a question about the extent to which the APS ought to be the instrument only of the incumbent government. For some, the Barratt case is an indication that the pendulum had swung too far, and that elements of the career service need to be protected against a situation in which, even if only occasionally, a departmental secretary's employment can be terminated so suddenly and so absolutely. If former departmental secretaries were too hard to remove, the new secretaries are too easy to shift.

So what is required is a system that has a degree of balance, a system that ensures that the departmental secretaries can give the best service to the government and the people, and that can adopt those laudable values to best result. We should not assume that the Australian way is the best. It is worth seeing how other countries and states deal with a number of the issues raised in this book.

To whom should departmental secretaries be responsible? In Victoria, the departmental secretaries had contracts directly with the premier and, when Kennett was premier, sometimes used to meet with him as a group, but without their ministers, to discuss the future directions. There was no doubt that they had a direct responsibility to the premier, emphasised by the fact that he controlled their contracts. In Canada, as was mentioned earlier, a line of responsibility to the prime minister was seen as part of the duties of deputy ministers; the occasional deputy minister had the task of monitoring a minister whom the prime minister did not trust. Both examples provide different lines of accountability and conceptions of where the main game is played: at the level of the individual portfolio or as part of the government team. The latter may be more significant in the workings of the APS now than it was 30 years ago, but it still plays second fiddle to the support that a departmental secretary would give to the individual minister.

In New Zealand, contracts are designed for each departmental secretary, at times with detailed performance criteria that may include a distinction between outputs, to be provided by the department, and outcomes that should be the consequence of government policy. At other times, key performance indicators are noted, with targets set and bonuses determined on the basis of the degree of success in meeting the targets. There has been extensive debate about whether these contracts have actually assisted in determining the quality of management because most ministers still have only a marginal interest in such detail; they are concerned, quite properly, with the political impact of their programs, however defined, and less with the way they were achieved. Nevertheless, the New Zealand experience provides an example of — or perhaps a cautionary tale about — the application and benefits of detailed contracts signed by minister and departmental secretary. Not everyone is yet convinced of their value.

Performance appraisal of departmental secretaries has become institutionalised in some places, and these provide examples of the different ways that the process is undertaken. In Canada, it is the responsibility of a peer group of deputy ministers who hear the evidence from number of sources, including the minister, and then make a recommendation to cabinet which has the final authority to approve. It is rare for cabinet to disagree with a process that has been so measured and careful. In New Zealand, the State Service Commissioner will discuss the performance of the departmental secretary with the minister and with peers and then make a determination about the level of satisfaction. Both processes are undertaken by officials, in consultation with the relevant players. It is still not clear that they have overcome the basic problem: the fact that, battered by the uncertainty of politics, ministers may be both unable and unwilling to define the tasks that their departmental secretaries are required to fulfil and thereafter to stick to that agreement. Ministers should not be required to be managers; they have different skills.

The proposed Australian system, which relies on the departmental secretary of PM&C advising the prime minister, is much more centralised than the other officially driven models. That may have the advantage that it is easier to make tough decisions if fewer people have to agree, but it might also suffer from the potential problem that the fairness of the process will be more open to challenge as it will depend in the final resort on the judgment of the two people at the centre of government. That is why there are some desires expressed to establish a board of review that may include other departmental secretaries and possibly people from outside the APS who are skilled enough to understand the conditions under which the departmental secretaries must work.

Not every country is as concerned as Australia with the dangers of political affiliation of senior officials. In Canada, it is true, there is almost a tradition of senior officials being found seats and being parachuted into ministerial office. Two prime ministers of Canada had previously been deputy ministers. In 1953 the clerk of the Privy Council Office began one cabinet meeting as an official and ended the meeting as a newly sworn-in minister. In the Chrétian government, a former head of the PCO became the minister responsible for the public service. That is not true of other Westminster systems where the careers of politics and public service are much more distinct. But it illustrates that the separation is a matter of convention, rather than constitutional necessity. It is a convention that, on the whole, should be retained if the non-partisan public service is to be retained.

In continental systems, many senior officials have a well-known affiliation of officials with political parties. Often it helps a career if the official's party is in office but it need not mean that no progress is made under other parties. In France, the system is enclosed and looks after its own. The graduates of the *grand écoles* might be shifted out of sensitive positions when the governments change but they are found other positions within the governmental system. Of course, such a practice may be seen as the élite looking after itself, and it makes it harder for outsiders to break into the chosen few. It also assumes a much larger state presence which can be found in a large unitary state such as France that can provide a wide range of alternative employment. But the system takes account of the desires for the ministers to have someone with whom they are comfortable working with them: technical competence combined with political affiliation is perhaps the French way. There is one distinct advantage: those who are out of favour with the government are not lost to public service. They are placed in less politically sensitive positions and available when the political fortunes change.

Nor have all countries found it necessary to limit the tenure of officials or to introduce contracts. In Britain, the patterns of promotion have remained similar over the last decades. Recruitment is still largely internal, with the permanent secretaries serving until retirement at around 60. In Denmark, those who are promoted come from within, products of what is called 'the Island Culture' after the island that houses most of the principal offices in the middle of Copenhagen. The heads of departments argue that they have changed their roles to meet the new demands on ministers and, by so doing, have largely retained their monopoly on advice to ministers. Adaptation has served them well.

So which system is right? None of course. All countries have adapted, and are adapting, their systems to overcome perceived problems and to meet the challenges that come from outside. All of them reflect the institutional culture and historical norms that have been established over time (see Rhodes and Weller 2001). We should not expect that practices can be transposed from one environment to another without some adaptation. None of them, of itself, provides a model to be adopted uncritically. On the other hand, the experiences of other countries provide questions: how well would that procedure work here, what are the benefits and potential problems? They also provide a useful lesson: there is nothing necessarily given, ideal or superior about the way that Australia organises its staff at the moment and it requires constant debate about possible changes.

In many places, indeed, there has been fairly little change of the basic elements of the system. There is a higher premium on tradition and established practice. Those in operation now are recognisably similar to those around a few years ago — or at least more similar than would be true of the local conditions in Australia. That is not surprising. Australian governments have often been far more cavalier about adapting and adjusting the structures of government than their counterparts. Machinery of government has been changed far more often than in other Westminster democracies, whether it is the tinkering with the odd function or the extensive shuffles that affect large sections of the departmental structure (Davis et al. 1999). As the departments change, so do the positions of departmental secretaries. Little is regarded as being beyond discussion. That may be acceptable if there is careful analysis of the potential outcomes. Too often it is a matter of immediate convenience.

What are the essential requirements for a departmental secretary that need to be developed? There would be little debate about the following:

- to be responsive to the wishes and policies of the government of the day;
- to be a professional in terms of technical competence in giving advice;
- to be an effective manager of resources and people;
- to be a skilful negotiator and diplomat, able to manage networks and contracts; and
- to be a person of talent and high ethical standards.

Most of these ideas can be extracted from the list of APS values. But they need to be kept in some balance. Not everyone will be as good at everything, although there is a need for each skill to a degree. The balance of skills may vary according to the nature and demands of the portfolio. The question, then, is how best these people, who have risen from the ruck to the top level, and who may be performing well, can be developed and retained in government service.

Two points need to be made initially. First, departmental secretaries are not — and should not be — ministers. Nor, in reverse, should ministers seek to become departmental secretaries. They have different skills, and inhabit different worlds. The worlds intersect where policy must be developed and programs delivered, when political accountability is demanded and problems arise. But the worlds are far from identical. Much of what drives the political system is beyond the influence, if not the interest, of the departmental secretary. Much of what the departmental secretaries must do is of no interest to the minister — and indeed in some cases is legally beyond their influence. The skills that make a good departmental secretary are less important for a minister; the instinct and calculations of a minister might be anathema to many a departmental secretary. That is why their roles always have been, and must continue to be seen as, complementary. If they may not be equal partners, they must be partners nonetheless, if the two sides of the executive are to operate at their best.

The second point is to ask whether it is even reasonable to expect that the departmental secretaries can satisfactorily meet all the demands that are now being placed on them. The task is now more diverse and includes multiple relationships:

- greater management responsibility that was once the remit of the treasury or the Public Service Board;
- more frequent and searching appearances before the various parliamentary committees, sometimes to be faced by an MP who wants to develop a reputation for toughness;
- more extensive relations with review bodies;
- greater delegation and devolution, and often the need to develop and monitor contracts for the delivery of services;
- the requirement to put together, both across the national government and often with state governments, packages of proposals for change; many of the initiatives that emerged from the Council of Australian Governments fit this category;
- public relations demands to explain and deliver programs to an increasingly educated and demanding electorate; indeed, they must consult, negotiate and persuade in a way that was not often required before with and among the public;
- the likelihood that they will be rotated to new positions after five years. Their generic skills may be transferable, but the language and culture of the new department must be learnt afresh.

In practice, they do all these things — and often do them well. And yet, amidst all these demands, lies the truth that the one relationship that really matters is that with the minister. All the functions listed above may be fulfilled with aplomb and skill, but to no avail if relations with the minister fail to gel. Certainly, departmental secretaries have much greater flexibility than their predecessors, but also more demands for accountability. They have more freedom to adjust the use of resources, but less hierarchical clout. They are likely to be as much diplomats as feudal lords, even within their own agencies.

So the departmental secretaries are faced with extensive demands and will be judged primarily by a person who understands few of the pressures, and indeed has no reason or desire to do so. How can we get the best out of the skills that departmental secretaries bring and still provide the service that ministers require? It is possible to make some suggestions that might help to achieve the balance, although of course it is far easier to identify problems than workable solutions.[1]

The Barratt case suggests that there is a *capacity* for capriciousness in the existing arrangements that cannot assist in good policy-making. If ministers and departmental secretaries should still be partners, it no longer always appears to operate that way. Sometimes they seem like landlords, with departmental secretaries their tenants at will. Given that ministers are usually poor at giving feedback to the departmental secretaries and that they neither understand nor wish to know about many of the functions that a good departmental secretary must fulfil, that can only breed insecurity. And insecurity is not good for the quality of advice.

That capacity for capriciousness, however rarely it may be exercised, might be alleviated by a board that would look at the case when a departmental secretary is to be terminated, to see if or where the blame for failure might be apportioned. At the moment, the government can readily ignore a report from the departmental secretary of Prime Minister and Cabinet. It is likely to be confidential and it remains the opinion of one person. It might be harder to ignore the report of a group of four or five eminent people, some of whom come from outside the service. If, as was accepted by both sides in the court case in the Barratt case, it is agreed that the breakdown has occurred through no act or fault of the departmental secretary, then there might be a couple of options: to make the minister try harder to make the system work or to provide an obligation to keep the departmental secretary in employment in an equivalent position. In the last resort, the key point should *not* be whether the departmental secretary should be moved. If a minister is determined not to trust a departmental secretary, then the minister can make sure that the relationship does not work, however amenable the departmental secretary is. In those circumstances, the departmental secretary will go unless the prime minister is prepared to move the minister. The crucial issue is whether that departmental secretary is lost to the public service. There is a need to develop and protect talent, but without the potential humiliation of gardening leave. That may not be easy, but it is worth considering. It may well have become harder because (by contrast to state governments) there are not many jobs of equivalent standing to a departmental secretary within the Commonwealth government's gift. Many changes would be seen as a come-down.

After the 'lemon hunt' that followed the 1998 election, all departmental secretaries were eventually confirmed in their positions. One interpretation of that decision was that the government had looked at the potential replacements and found nothing that persuaded it that they would be better than the incumbents. That should be a matter of concern. The APS can attract the cream of graduates, but it may not be able to keep them. If there is a belief that at the top of the service a career can be terminated at the whim of an idle or vindictive minister, then they may lose the ambition to rise, or head for the better financial rewards of the private sector. We need to be careful not to interpret the process of popular election into a transformation of the mediocre into heroic ministers; there is some need to accept the occasional shortcoming there and to protect the other side of the minister–departmental secretary partnership. For a distinguished departmental secretary to advise his children not to enter the APS may say a lot about the changing concept of a career there.

Some form of appraisal might be essential, even if there is continuing scepticism that a suitable set of criteria can be developed or applied in anything but a subjective way. The continuation of a contract or rotation to another departmental secretary position would be assisted by a transparent process that is seen to be fair and to take account of all the activities of the departmental secretaries, not just those that the ministers understand. There needs to be some connection between the assessed performance and career prospects. It is strange, indeed, that a departmental secretary who is classified as superior or outstanding might be terminated a few months later because of a change of minister or of political fortune. That is not to say that they should be granted continuing tenure and guaranteed a lifetime payment, even if they are on gardening leave. Many agree — even some from the old days of tenure — that the present system of agreed compensation when a contract is terminated is better than leaving a proud person stranded with nothing meaningful to do. But there is a case for saying that a contact for five years should mean just that and that there should be an expectation of another contract, perhaps after a rotation to another department, after five years (rather than any expectation of dismissal). That might mean planning some reshuffles or rotations, and perhaps in advance of the completion of the five years, but it is better than the termination of 'superior' departmental secretaries because of a passing whim or treating them as tenants at will.

Most of these discussions relate to the cases where ministers and departmental secretaries have failed to develop a good relationship. That has never been the majority; most of the time, in a wide variety of ways, they work together. Because of the range of personalities involved, there can be no blueprint to explain how that should be done. Each pair must work out their own balance. In 1979, a departmental secretary described the relationship as like a horse and rabbit stew: one horse, one rabbit; the challenge is telling which is the horse and which the rabbit. That remains true: there is no rule that determines the minister will be dominant, but it seems more likely that they may call the tune now for institutional reasons, though there is no reason to assume they will be intellectually superior. Whatever the circumstance, the partnership must be made to work adequately.

We need to ensure that remains so, for cases like the Barratt termination only add to the suspicion that it could happen to anyone. The McLeod report in 1994 began with the words: 'the APS is a national asset'. One lesson clearly comes out of this study: the skills necessary to perform effectively as a departmental secretary have been honed exclusively in the public sector. Departmental secretaries require an appreciation of the regimes of accountability, of the political environment in which they work, of the sensitivity to the use of public money, of the demands for equity in delivering services to the people, of what is appropriate for them to do. Many of the techniques of management may be common to private and public sectors, but the public sector brings demands for particular skills and talents. That is one reason why there is a dearth of people who have successfully moved straight into senior public positions. The public sector is different. There is therefore a particular requirement that the career service be maintained and nurtured.

Nor should we take it for granted. Many countries seek to build a service that has the basic Australian characteristics: integrity, professionalism, non-partisanship, career-based, accountable and responsive. Capability-building is often a priority for United Nations and World Bank programs that seek to design institutions like the APS, on the assumption that an honest and effective bureaucracy is essential for national good governance. We have it and must keep it. But that maintenance needs political and official leadership and national awareness.

Most people are well aware of that need. Twenty years ago, Sir Arthur Tange wrote:

> As to the public service, systems enforcing accountability do not guarantee a good one. It is arguable that if the public service sees in attitudes among politicians, including the ministers they serve, that it lacks respect, and if it knows itself to be overloaded with often unproductive second guessing and inspection in the name of

efficiency, and is subject to symbols of government distrust ...
shortcomings will grow that escape any system of inspection. I
refer to the loss of the spirit of initiative and sense of national
purpose and the courage that are the mark of a good public servant.
There are never enough people with such strengths and with vision
in the national Service, which needs to attract and retain them.

It is not for me to say the Service is presently at risk in these matters.
I do say that at all times the Prime Minister of the day has a duty to
concern himself with the general state of the Service. The Service
needs leadership (which is one of the 'old values') in its own ranks,
by peer consent ... The Service needs political leadership. Every
Prime Minister has a trust to hand over to his successor a Service
in good condition (Tange 1982:14).

The circumstances may have changed and the particular areas of
complaint may have shifted, but the essential message remains true.

The point is accepted at the political level. The prime minister
has declared:

Let me state at the outset my firm belief that an accountable, non-
partisan and professional public service which responds creatively
to the changing roles and demands of the government is a great
national asset. Preserving its value and nurturing its innovation is
a priority for this government ...

No government 'owns' the public service. It must remain a national
asset that services the national interest, adding value to the directions
set by the government of the day. The responsibility of any
government must be to pass on to its successors a public service
which is better able to meet the challenges of its time than the one
it inherited. My government clearly accepts that responsibility
(Howard 1998:4, 11).

There is a need for a professional advisory service to ministers and
for an efficient deliverer of services, directly or through the oversight
of contracts, to the Australian people. It needs to be maintained as a
professional service, a career that can attract and keep the best who
are interested in national service. It needs to be supported and
constantly developed; it requires leadership. In that sense, as Howard
states, the government holds the APS in leasehold, with the
assumption that one day it will be required to serve other
governments. Those future rulers too will need good advice. In the
meantime, there is a need to maintain the values of a good public
service and to ensure that the talent remains there. There are fears
that the pool is being depleted, that the attractiveness as a career has
declined. Nothing dramatic perhaps, but enough indications in the
air to make careful debate and analysis important.

The existing group of departmental secretaries may not loom so large as the mandarins of the 1950s. Times have changed. But as a group they still retain a high degree of skill and commitment and a preparedness in most cases to serve any elected government. We should not undervalue those skills nor underestimate the fact that it takes effort to retain that type of service. National assets should be depleted with caution, and only after proper debate. The position of the departmental secretaries, not necessarily as individuals but as symbols of an effective public service, is of sufficient importance to our system of government to deserve that attention and debate. Who should care? We all should, for the quality and effectiveness of the public service affects us all.

Note

1. I was once sent a cutting from the *Age* of its Notable Quote: 'Nothing is impossible for the person who does not have to do it (Weller's Law).' I was not the Weller (unfortunately) who devised such a pithy epigram, but the sentiment is all too applicable at this point of a book!

References

Ayers, A.J. 1996 'Not Like the Good Old Days', *Australian Journal of Public Administration* 55(2):3–11.

Barberis, P. 1996 *The Elite of the Elite: Permanent Secretaries in the British Higher Civil Service*, Dartmouth, Aldershot.

Boston, J., J. Martin J. Pallot & P. Walsh 1996 *Public Management: The New Zealand Experience*, Oxford University Press, Auckland.

Bourgault, J. & S. Dion 1991 *The Changing Profile of Federal Deputy Ministers 1867–1988*, Canadian Centre for Management Development, Ottawa.

Bunting, J. 1988 *R.G. Menzies*, Allen & Unwin, Sydney.

Castles, I. 1997 *Obituary: Sir Roland Wilson*, 1997 Annual Report: Academy of the Social Sciences of Australia, Canberra, 84–88.

Codd, M. 1990 'The Role of Secretaries in Departments in the APS', *PSC Occasional Papers No. 8*, Canberra.

Codd, M. 1991 'Federal Public Sector Management Reform: Recent History and Current Priorities', *PSC Occasional Papers No. 11*, Canberra.

Cole, R.W. 1979 'The Role of the Public Service in a Changing Environment', *Australian Journal of Public Administration* 38(2):151–56.

Cole, R.W. 1980 'Responsible Government and the Public Service' in P. Weller & D. Jaensch eds *Responsible Government in Australia*, Drummond, Melbourne.

Cooley, A.S. 1974 'The Permanent Head', *Public Administration* (Sydney) 33(3):193–205.

Crawford, Sir John 1954 'The Role of the Permanent Head', *Public Administration* (Sydney) 13(3):153–64.

Crawford, Sir John, 1960 'Relations between Civil Servants and Ministers in Policy Making', *Public Administration* (Sydney) 19(2):99–112.

Crisp, L.F. 1963 *Ben Chifley*, Longman, Melbourne.

Davis, G., P. Weller, E. Craswell & S. Eggins 1999 'What Drives Machinery of Government Changes? Australia, Britain, Canada 1950–1997', *Public Administration* 77(1):7–51.

Dunleavy, P. 1995 'Policy Disasters: Explaining the UK's Record', *Public Policy and Administration* 10(2).

Emy, H.V. & O. Hughes 1991 *Australian Politics: Realities in Conflict*, 2nd edn, Macmillan, Melbourne.

Granatstein, J.L. 1998 (1982) *The Ottawa Men: The Civil Service Mandarins, 1935-1957*, University of Toronto Press, Toronto.

Gregory, P. 1996, 'Policy Management Reviews' in J. Uhr & K. Mackay eds *Evaluating Policy Advice: Learning from Commonwealth Experiences*, Federalism Research Centre & Department of Finance, Canberra.

Gyngell, A. & M. Wesley 2000 'Interweaving of Foreign and Domestic Policy: International Policy' in G. Davis & M. Keating eds *The Future of Governance: Policy Options*, Allen & Unwin, Sydney.

Hasluck, P. 1995 [1968], 'The Public Service and Politics', *Canberra Bulletin of Public Administration* 78:91-101.

Hasluck, P. 1997 *The Chance of Politics*, Text Publishing, Melbourne.

Hawke, A. 1997 'Frank and Fearless Advice Under Contract', *Australian Journal of Public Administration* 56(4):151-52.

Hawke, A. 2000 'What's the Matter — A Due Diligence Report', address to Defence Watch Seminar, National Press Club, 17 February.

Hawker, G. 1981 *Who's Master, Who's Servant?*, Hale & Iremonger, Sydney.

Hawker, G., R.F.I. Smith & P. Weller 1979 *Politics and Policy in Australia*, University of Queensland Press, St Lucia.

Hetherington, J. 1975 'Roland Wilson' in R.N. Spann & G.R. Curnow eds *Public Policy and Administration in Australia: A Reader*, John Wiley, Sydney.

Howard, J. 1998 'A Healthy Public Service is a Vital Part of Australia's Democratic System of Government', *Australian Journal of Public Administration* 57(1):3-11.

Hunn, D.K. 1994 'Measuring Performance in Policy Advice: A New Zealand Perspective' in *Performance Measurement in Government*, OECD Public Management Occasional Papers, No. 5, OECD, Paris.

Hyslop, R. 1993 *Australian Mandarins: Perceptions of the Role of Departmental Secretaries*, AGPS (with PSC and RIPAA), Canberra.

Keating, M. 1989 '*Quo Vadis?* Challenges of Public Administration', *Australian Journal of Public Administration* 48(2):123-31.

Keating, M. 1990 'Managing for Results in the Public Interest', *Australian Journal of Public Administration* 49(4):387-98.

Keating, M. 1995a 'Public Service Values', *Australian Quarterly* 67(4):15-25.

Keating, M. 1995b 'The Evolving Role of Central Agencies Change and Continuity', *Australian Journal of Public Administration* 54(4):579–84.

Keating, M. 1996 'Defining the Policy Advising Function' in J. Uhr & K. Mackay eds *Evaluating Policy Advice: Learning from Commonwealth*, Federalism Centre, Canberra.

Keating, M. 1999 'The Public Service: Independence, Responsibility and Responsiveness', *Australian Journal of Public Administration* 58(1):39–47.

Keating, M. 2000 'The Pressures for Change' in G. Davis & M. Keating eds *The Future of Governance: Policy Options*, Allen & Unwin, Sydney.

Keating, P. 1993 'Performance and Accountability in the Public Service: A Statement by the Prime Minister', 1 July, Canberra

Kelleher, S. 1988 'The Apotheosis of the Department of the Prime Minister and Cabinet: Further Reflections on Administrative Change, 1987', *Canberra Bulletin of Public Administration* 54:9–12

Kemp D. 2000 'Politicisation Barbs Based in Ignorance', 29 June, *Canberra Times.*

MAB/MIAC, 1991 *Accountability in the Commonwealth Public Sector: An Exposure Draft*, AGPS, Canberra.

MAC/MIAC, 1993 *Accountability in the Commonwealth Public Sector*, AGPS, Canberra.

McLeod, 1994 *Report on the Public Service Act*, AGPS, Canberra.

Martin, A.W. 1999 *Robert Menzies: A Life, Volume 2, 1944–1978*, Melbourne University Press, Melbourne.

Menadue, J. 1999 *Things You Learn Along the Way*, David Lovell Publishing, Melbourne.

Mulgan, R. 1998 'Politicisation of Senior Appointments in the Australian Public Service', *Australian Journal of Public Administration* 57(3):3–15.

Nethercote, J. 1990 Submission to the Senate Standing Committee on Finance and Public Administration, 3 September.

Nicholson, J. 1996 'Measures for Monitoring Policy Advice' in J. Uhr & K. Mackay eds *Evaluating Policy Advice: Learning from Commonwealth Experiences*, Federalism Research Centre & Department of Finance, Canberra.

Osbaldeston, G.F. 1988 *Keeping Deputy Ministers Accountable*, National Centre for Management Research, University of Western Ontario.

PAPW 1992 *Performance Assessment of Policy Work*, Report of Working Party, Canberra.

Public Service Board 1973 *49th Annual Report 1973*, AGPS, Canberra.

Parker, R.S. 1960 'Policy and Administration', *Public Administration* (Sydney) 19(2):113–20.

Plowden, W. 1994 *Ministers and Mandarins*, Institute for Public Policy Research, London.

Podger, A. 1997 'Departmental Secretaries: Introductory Notes', *Australian Journal of Public Administration* 56(4):11–12.

PSB, 1974 'The Permanent Head: A Background Paper', Canberra.

Pusey, M. 1991 *Economic Rationalism in Canberra: A Nation-building State Changes its Mind*, Cambridge University Press, Melbourne.

Reid, J. 1983 *Report, Review of Commonwealth Administration* (John Reid chair), AGPS, Canberra.

Rhodes, R.A.W. & P. Weller 2001 *The Changing World of Top Officials: Mandarin or Servant?*, Open University Press, London.

Sedgwick, S. 1996a 'Lessons from Finance' in J. Uhr & K. Mackay eds *Evaluating Policy Advice: Learning from Commonwealth Experiences*, Federalism Research Centre & Department of Finance, Canberra.

Sedgwick, S. 1996b 'Discussion' in J. Uhr & K. Mackay eds *Evaluating Policy Advice: Learning from Commonwealth Experiences*, Federalism Research Centre & Department of Finance, Canberra.

Spann, R.N. 1975 *Permanent Heads*, Report to the Royal Commission on Australian Government Administration, Canberra.

Stowe, K. 1996 'Different Problems, Same Solutions?' in P. Weller & G. Davis eds *New Ideas, Better Government*, Allen & Unwin, Sydney.

Tange, Sir Arthur 1982 'The Focus of Reform in Commonwealth Government Administration', *Australian Journal of Public Administration* 41(1):1–14.

tbp 1996 *towards best practice in the australian public service: discussion paper*, Canberra.

Theakston, K. 1997 'Comparative Biography and Leadership in Whitehall', *Public Administration* 75(4):651–67.

Uhr, J. 1996a 'Lessons from an External Reviewer' in J. Uhr & K. Mackay eds *Evaluating Policy Advice: Learning from Commonwealth Experiences*, Federalism Research Centre & Department of Finance, Canberra.

Uhr, J. 1996b 'Testing the Policy Capacities of Budgetary Agencies: Lessons from Finance', *Australian Journal of Public Administration* 55(4):124–34.

Uhr, J. & K. Mackay 1996 *Evaluating Policy Advice: Learning from Commonwealth Experiences*, Federalism Research Centre & Department of Finance, Canberra.

Waller, M. 1992 'Evaluating Policy Advice', *Australian Journal of Public Administration* 51(4):440–46.

Waller, M. 1996 'The Changing Environment of Policy Making' in J. Uhr & K. Mackay eds *Evaluating Policy Advice: Learning from Commonwealth Experiences*, Federalism Research Centre & Department of Finance, Canberra.

Walter, J. 1986 *The Ministers' Minders: Personal Advisers in National Government*, Oxford University Press, Melbourne.

Waterford, J. 1997 'PS Integrity Must be Retained', *Canberra Times*, 11 February.

Weller, P. 1989a 'Politicisation and the Australian Public Service', *Australian Journal of Public Administration* 48(4):369–81.

Weller, P. 1989b *Malcolm Fraser PM*, Penguin, Ringwood.

Weller, P. 1996 'Commonwealth–State Reform Processes: A Policy Management Review', *Australian Journal of Public Administration* 55(1):95–110.

Weller, P. & S. Fraser 1987 'The Younging of Australian Politics or Politics as a First Career', *Politics* 22(2):76–83.

Weller, P. & M. Grattan 1981 *Can Ministers Cope? Australian Ministers at Work*, Hutchinson, Melbourne.

Weller, P. & B. Stevens 1998 'Evaluating Policy Advice: the Australian Experience', *Public Administration* 76(3):578–89.

Weller, P. & J. Wanna 1997 'Departmental Secretaries: Appointment, Termination and their Impact', *Australian Journal of Public Administration* 56(4):13–25.

Weller, P & T. Wood 1999 'The Department Secretaries: A Profile of a Changing Profession', *Australian Journal of Public Administration* 58(2):21–32.

Wheeler, Sir Frederick 1980 'The Professional Public Servant: Some Reflections of a Practitioner', *Australian Journal of Public Administration* 39(2):162–79

Wildavsky, A. 1973 'If Planning is Everything, Maybe It's Nothing', *Policy Sciences* 4:127–53.

Wildavsky, A. 1979 *Speaking Truth to Power*, Little, Brown, Boston.

Wilson, Sir Roland 1976 'L.F. Giblin: A Man for all Seasons — the Giblin Memorial Lecture', *Search* 7(7).

Woodard, G. 2000 'Ministers and Mandarins: The Relationships between Ministers and Secretaries of External Affairs 1935–1970', *Australian Journal of International Affairs* 54(1):79–95.

Yeend, G.J. 1979 'The Department of the Prime Minister and Cabinet in Perspective', *Australian Journal of Public Administration* 38(2):133–50.

Appendix

List of interviews: Departmental Secretaries and other senior officers 1978–1999

1979–80: 29 interviewed for Patrick Weller and Michelle Grattan, *Can Ministers Cope? Australian Ministers at Work* (Hutchinson 1981):
Tony Ayers, Peter Bailey, Tim Besley, Ian Castles, Mike Codd, Bill Cole, Neil Currie, Laurie Daniels, Barry Dexter, Lou Engledow, John Farrands, Norm Fisher, Charles Halton, Clarrie Harders, Peter Henderson, Gwyn Howells, Ken Jones, Richard Kingsland, Pat Lanigan, Robert Lansdown, Peter Lawler, Doug McKay, Don McMichael, James Scully, Mick Shann, Arthur Tange, George Warwick Smith, Alan Woods, Geoff Yeend

1985–87: 15 interviewed for *Malcolm Fraser PM : A Study in Prime Ministerial Power in Australia* (Penguin 1989):
Tony Ayers, Ian Castles, David Charles, Mike Codd, Bill Cole, John Enfield, Bernie Fraser, Alan Griffith, Mike Keating, George Nicholls, Alan Rose, Mick Shann, Ed Visbord, Fred Wheeler, Geoff Yeend

1996: 21 Interviewed for a report, written with John Wanna to the IPAA(ACT Branch) on the Appointment and Termination of Departmental Secretaries and later published in the *Australian Journal of Public Administration*, 56 (4), December 1997:
Tony Ayers, Bill Blick, Tony Blunn, Ian Castles, Mike Codd, Chris Conybeare, Peter Core, Ted Evans, Stewart Hamilton, Stuart Harris, Sandy Holloway, Max More-Wilton, Andrew Podger, David Rosalky, Steve Sedgwick, Peter Shergold, Stephen Skehill, Neville Stevens, Greg Taylor, Derek Volker, Lionel Woodward. We also had the benefit of a discussion of a draft of the paper in an IPAA seminar with a number of departmental secretaries in February 1997.

1998–2000: The 44 interviewed for the purposes of this book are listed below with the departments they headed and the years in which they held their positions.

Tony Ayers, Aboriginal Affairs 1979–81, Social Security 1981–86, Community Services and Health, 1987–88, Defence 1988–98.

Paul Barratt, Primary Industries and Energy, 1996–68, Defence 1988–99.

Roger Beale, Environment, Sport and Territories, 1996–97, Environment, 1997+

Tony Blunn, Capital Territory, 1981–83; Territories and Local Government 1983; Housing and Construction 19883–87; Arts, Sport, Tourism and territories 1987–91; Arts, Sport, Environment and Territories 1991–93; Social Security 1993–98; Attorney – General 1998–99.

Peter Boxall, Finance 1997; Finance and Administration 1997+.

Pat Brazil, Attorney-General 1983–89.

Ian Castles, Finance 1979–85.

David Charles, Industry, Technology and Commerce 1985–90.

Mike Codd, Industrial Relations 1982; Employment and Industrial Relations 1982–83; Community Services 1985–86; Prime Minister and Cabinet 1986–91.

Sir William Cole, Finance 1976–78; Public Service Board 1978–83; Defence 1984–86.

Michael Costello, Industrial Relations 192–93; Foreign Affairs and Trade 1993–96.

Graeme Evans, Resources and Energy 1986–87; Primary Industries and Energy 1987–88; Transport and Communications 1988–94; Transport 1994–94.

Ted Evans, Treasury 1993+.

Vince Fitzgerald, Trade 1986–87; Employment, Education and Training 1987–89.

Bernie Fraser, Treasury 1984–89.

Graham Glenn, Local Government and Administrative Services 1986–87; Administrative Services 1987–89; Industrial Relations 1989–92.

Bill Gray, Aboriginal Affairs 1989–90.

Charles Halton, Transport 1973–82; Defence Support 1982–84; Communications 1986–87.

Stewart Hamilton, Community Services and Health 1988–91; Health, Housing and Community Services 1991–93; Environment, Sport and Territories 1993–96.

Stuart Harris, Foreign Affairs 1984–87; Foreign Affairs and Trade 1987–88.

Allan Hawke, Veterans'Affairs 1994–96; Transport and Regional Development 1996–99; Defence 1999 +.

Sir Lennox Hewitt, Prime Minister 1968–71; Environment, Aborigines and the Arts 1971–72; Minerals and Energy 1972–75.

Russell Higgins, Inustry, Science and Tourism 1997 +.

Neil Johnson, Veterans' Affairs 1996 +.

Michael Keating, Employment and Industrial Relations 1983–86; Finance 1996–91; Prime Minister and Cabinet 1991–96.

Sir Richard Kingsland, Interior 1963–70; Repatriation and Compensation 1970–75; Repatriation 1975–76; Veterans' Affairs 1976–81.

Robert Lansdown, Urban and Regional Development 1872–75; Environment, Housing and Community Development 1975–78; Post and Communications 1979–80; Communications 1980–86.

Ken Mathews, Primary Industries and Energy 1998–99; Transport and Regional development 1999 +.

Max More-Wilton, Prime Minister and Cabinet 1996 +.

Andrew Podger, Arts and Administrative Services 1993–93; Administrative Services 1994; Housing and Regional Development 1994–96; Health and Family Services 1996 +.

David Rosalky, Industrial Relations 1995–97; Workplace Relations and Small Business 1997–89; Social Security, then Family and Community Services1998 +.

Alan Rose, Community Services 1986–87; Attorney–General 1989–94.

James Scully, Minerals and Energy 1975; National Resources 1975–77; Trade and Resources 1977–83; Trade 1983.

Steven Sedgwick, Finance 1992–97; Employment, Education, Training and Youth Affairs, 1997–98; Education, Training and Youth Affairs 1998 +.

Peter Shergold, Public Service and Merit Protection Commission 1995–98; Workplace Relations and Small Business 1998 +.

Stephen Skehill, Attorney–General 1994–97.

Neville Stevens, Industry, Technology and Commerce 1991–93; Industry, technology and Regional Development 1993; Communications1993–94; Communications and the Arts 1994 +.

Sir Arthur Tange, External Affairs 1954–65; Defence 1970–79.

Noel Tanzer, Veterans' Affairs 1986–89; Administrative Services 1989–93; Arts and Administrative Services 1993.

John Taylor, Aboriginal Affairs 1981–84.

Rae Taylor, Employment and Youth Affairs 1978–82; Transport and Construction 1982–83; Transport 1983–86; Aviation 1986–87; Industrial Relations 1987–89.

Ed Visbord, Employment and Industrial Relations 1986–87.

Derek Volker, Veterans' Afffairs 1981–86; Social Security 1986–93; Social Security 1993–96.

Helen Williams, Education 1985–87; Tourism 1993–96; Immigration and Multicultural Affairs 1996–98; Public Service and Merit Protection Commission 1998+.

Name Index

Subject Index